AMERICA'S ASCENT

The United States
Becomes a Great Power, 1880-1914

John M. Dobson

Northern Illinois University Press   DeKalb

Library of Congress Cataloging in Publication Data

Dobson, John M.
    America's ascent.

    Bibliography: p.
    Includes index.
    1. United States—Foreign relations—1865–1921.
I. Title.
E661.7.D62   327.73   77-90754
ISBN 0-87580-070-X
ISBN 0-87580-523-X pbk.

Copyright © 1978 by Northern Illinois University Press
Published by the Northern Illinois University Press,
DeKalb, Illinois 60115
Manufactured in the United States of America

For my father and mother, whose service abroad
reflected the highest ideals of the American Mission.

Contents

Acknowledgments

I am pleased to acknowledge Iowa State University's generous support for this project. I did the bulk of the research while on a university faculty improvement leave, and supplementary research funds helped defray the expenses of visits to distant archives. Far more important than these tangible evidences of support, the university has also provided me with able and amiable colleagues and inspiring and inquisitive students. Richard N. Kottman provided useful advice on all facets of foreign relations as well as specific encouragement on this project. David M. Wilcox must stand as the representative for all of the undergraduate and graduate students who cheerfully and enthusiastically helped me test the theoretical framework which ties this work together. A similar contribution was made by my friends in the Foreign Service whom I observed dealing every day with the constraints and benefits of a foreign policy based upon precedents and tradition.

A number of individuals read various versions and parts of the manuscript but, because of the anonymity associated with the review process, I am able to thank only three by name: Milton Plesur, Robert A. Divine, and Walter LaFeber. Although the present text bears the mark of all of these reviewers, I am, of course, responsible for its conclusions and failings. Susie Ulrichsen unflinchingly and efficiently typed several versions of the manuscript. Finally, I must mention my great debt to my wife Cindy, who patiently saw me through the elation and despair and the excitement and tedium that accompanied the writing of this book.

1

The Parameters of Policy

With flags flying, an armada of American battleships steamed along in the South China Sea off Indochina. Even though it was early December, the sailors who ventured topside during the day enjoyed balmy breezes as they sought vantage points for observing the fleet. Strewn about helter-skelter, sixteen battleships knifed through the waves, blackening the sky as acrid billows of smoke poured from their tall funnels. Now and then one could spot, wallowing lower in the water, one of the fleet's dumpy auxiliaries or, racing along primly, a long, lean, torpedo-armed destroyer.

Most of the officers and men attached to this impressive war fleet were more than a little bored and homesick. They had left their home port of Hampton Roads, Virginia, a full year earlier, and they knew they would not be back again for at least another three months. The sailors and marines had been monotonously drilled, the railings incessantly polished, the decks repeatedly scraped and sanded. Yet throughout the seemingly endless voyage, the awesome thirteen-inch guns had never been fired in anger. The paint that the sailors had dutifully chipped off and reapplied to the great ships' hulls was pure white, a color symbolic of their pacific intentions. The year was 1908, and the ostensible purpose of this costly, elaborate 42,000-mile cruise, which would eventually take the battleship fleet clear around the world, was the encouragement of world peace.

So unbelligerent was the United States in 1908, in fact, that none of the sixteen battleships of the Great White Fleet had ever served in combat. Indeed, all of them had been commissioned after 1898, the year in which the United States had charged off to fight perfidious Spain in Cuba and the Philippines. Furthermore, no one in the

United States anticipated a conflict in the near future. This, the second most powerful navy in the world, outclassed only by Great Britain's Royal Navy, had been constructed, armed, and sent touring at a time when the United States was utterly free of any threat to its security.

Why, then, had it built such an awesome navy and sent it to the opposite side of the globe? A welter of official rationalizations concerning the necessity for fleet maneuvers and the practice or the wisdom of renewing and strengthening international friendships fooled no one. The fundamental motivation for the cruise was clear to all the world: the United States Navy was dramatically and unequivocally displaying its nation's strength and discipline. The fleet's mission was to win prestige for the United States, to force other nations to recognize explicitly that a great world power existed in North America.

The world cruise was successful in its status-seeking objective only because the United States as a whole had passed through a major transition around the turn of the twentieth century. In the last two decades of the nineteenth century, as the nation commenced the building of its modern navy, the United States began to emerge as one of the world's few great powers. Generally neglected or underrated before 1880, the United States gradually cast off its adolescent image to become a significant element in the world balance of power; so much so that, by 1914, both the Allies and the entente powers in World War I treated the United States with great deference. The creation of a powerful, modern American navy was actually only a symptom of the fundamental change that had occurred in international relations during the three decades prior to the outbreak of the war. The United States had truly become a great power by 1914, and its attitudes and behavior crucially affected world affairs.

To a certain extent, the emergence of the United States as a great world power was preordained—or to use a popular phrase of the period, it was the nation's "manifest destiny" to become great. A growing, developing nation blessed with America's great resources was bound to have an ever-increasing impact upon world politics. The United States had begun its independent existence as a loose coalition of thirteen highly differentiated, fairly primitive, colonial settlements clinging to the coastline of a huge continental wilderness. Through good fortune, hard work, and moral fervor, the American people had expanded their country into a unified, wealthy, progressive nation that rivaled or outstripped its European forebears in population growth, industrial capacity, and agricultural productivity. The continued expansion of the United States in the late nineteenth century made its rise to international prominence inevitable.

Psychological and emotional considerations weigh heavily, however, in the ranking and reputations of members of the international community. Recognition of the United States as a great power depended upon others taking American competition and self-assertiveness seriously. Those nations already recognized as great powers behaved like members of an exclusive club, reluctant to admit newcomers, careful to scrutinize hopeful members' credentials. The succeeding pages describe exactly how the United States, its government, and its leaders developed the credentials essential to the winning of recognition as a great power.

Several dramatic events punctuate the story of the rise of American economic, political, and moral influence in the late nineteenth and early twentieth centuries. These incidents helped focus worldwide attention upon the blossoming adolescent nation in North America. Many Americans have denied that the United States became a great power overnight simply because it won an imperialistic war with Spain in 1898.[1] The American nation obviously had to possess many of the material attributes associated with great powers before 1898 in order to defeat Spain in just three months and to seize her Caribbean and Pacific colonies. Because military victories tended to impress European statesmen, however, the United States' effortless dispatch of Spain immediately boosted the American ranking among the powers. The war and the subsequent seizure of colonies thus had important psychological effects, jarring others into admitting that a major power existed in the Western Hemisphere.

But neither a victorious war nor an experiment in imperialism was really sufficient in itself to create a great international reputation. Minor nations had won wars; tiny Belgium had become colonial overlord of the huge African Congo region. Thus, although the 1898 war and colonialism served as catalytic events in the process of winning great-power status for the United States, other necessary ingredients had to be there in full measure as well. Writing in 1961, historian Thomas A. Bailey took issue with those who claimed the United States had suddenly become a great power after the turn of the twentieth century. The United States had been the Western Hemisphere's greatest power, Bailey insisted, ever since it

---

[1]See Thomas A. Bailey, "America's Emergence as a World Power: The Myth and the Verity," *Pacific Historical Review* 30 (February 1961): 6, and William Graham Sumner, *The Conquest of the United States by Spain and Other Essays* (Chicago: Henry Regnery, 1965), p. 173.

had declared its independence. By the end of the Civil War, with its industrial and agricultural plenty, its modern transportation system, its ever-increasing population, and its trained army and navy of battle-scarred veterans, the United States had definitely acquired all of the material trappings of a great world power.[2] The reason many claim that the United States did not become a great power until after 1900, however, is that it took years of dedicated effort on the part of American statesmen and diplomats to persuade the haughty and reluctant leaders of other nations to acknowledge America's greatness.

The United States thus did not aimlessly wander into world-power status; the American people deliberately chose to seek it. Indeed, the emergence of the United States as a great power represented the full flowering of the themes which had been shaping American diplomacy for some time. The war with Spain seems to tower over all other events in this period, but it, too, fit comfortably into the pattern of the nation's policies both before and after 1898. The emotionalism and fireworks associated with the Spanish-American War tend to obscure the fact that it caused the nation's foreign policy to deviate only slightly from its traditional channels. In fact, the war offered American statesmen an ideal opportunity to promulgate programs based upon the three expansionist themes which underlay and shaped all foreign policy during the nation's emergence as a great power.

This study, then, examines the three major internal driving forces or themes that characterized the United States' rise to international prominence from 1880 to 1914. Economic expansion, political aggrandizement, and moral assertiveness each assisted the nation in its drive to increase its prestige abroad. A desire to expand American commerce, the first major theme motivating and defining American foreign policy in this period, led to the seeking of overseas markets for American surplus production. Successful economic expansion encouraged a second type of expansion, that of increasing American political influence abroad. Through its acquisition of distant colonies in the 1890s, its assumption of informal protectorates in Latin America, and its intrusion into great-power politics in the Far East, the United States was carrying forward a political expansionism that had prevailed throughout American history. The nation's political influence included an ideological component based upon America's own political and social system. Thus, the third major foreign policy theme

[2]Bailey, "America's Emergence": 3, 11, 14.

involved an attempt to spread an American-style moral influence abroad. The United States and its citizens took up the mission of encouraging democratic and republican ideals around the world.

The economic, political, and democratic mission themes had developed over the years in conjunction with the growth of the nation as a whole. They had thus become familiar traditions, each possessing a continuing appeal for Americans. But, although these traditional themes had been influencing policy formulation long before 1880, only in the last quarter of the nineteenth century did they reach their full maturity and effectiveness. From the end of Reconstruction to the collapse of the European peace in 1914, the United States enjoyed an independence from international political alliances, a great abundance of resources, and a blissful freedom from fear. Consequently, the United States government could tailor its foreign policies to suit the basic desires of the American people. A search for markets, an extension of political influence, a desire to spread democracy—all represented parameters of foreign policy which the American people favored. As these themes had complex backgrounds and underwent interesting permutations in the period from 1880 to 1914, each must be examined thoroughly before one can begin a detailed study of how they shaped American foreign policy around the turn of the century and enabled the United States to become an internationally-recognized great power.

Commercial considerations had always characterized American foreign policy. Even before the Revolution, Americans had recognized the necessity of seeking and maintaining overseas markets. As dependent members of the British mercantile empire whom no one expected to be self-sufficient, the colonies had developed lopsided economies. Their role within the empire was to produce raw materials and to trade them for British manufactured and refined goods. The 1776 Declaration of Independence from the empire was primarily a political act; it in no way assured the American people's economic independence. The members of the Continental Congress obviously recognized this, because they charged the diplomats they dispatched to Europe with finding markets to replace those they had cut themselves off from in Britain. This market search intensified after the war had ended, and an energetic and over-productive nation of Americans came into being, a nation whose prosperity depended upon expanded foreign trade. Congress engaged in a never-ending debate over the merits of international trade agreements and tariffs. Successful commercial involvement overseas appeared critical to the development of the preindustrial United States economy well into the nineteenth century.

Economic expansion was already a well-established, traditional theme in American diplomacy when the Jeffersonians became so exasperated with British limitations on American trade that they declared war on England in 1812. The United States' desire to expand into Louisiana, Oregon, Texas, and beyond sprang in part from economic motivations. The predominant economic theories of the day sanctioned and encouraged economic expansion. The classical economists, beginning with Adam Smith, taught that only a nation that possessed a constantly expanding market for its goods could count on sustaining its prosperity.

In recent years a group of revisionist diplomatic historians has rated the desire for economic expansion as the preeminent motivation underlying American foreign policy prior to 1900. William Appleman Williams and his colleagues have assembled an impressive body of evidence which attempts to demonstrate that explicit or implicit economic considerations influenced almost every diplomatic decision. In so doing, the revisionists have uncovered much material essential to the understanding of American foreign policy, while simultaneously underrating other important motivations. Despite this limitation, their analysis of the economic expansion theme reveals a great deal about America's internal and external relationships at the close of the nineteenth century.[3]

The Civil War had induced inflation and economic overheating, but the war's economic impact soon dissipated. A business panic in 1873 sent the American economy reeling; then a long-term depression knocked it flat. Nearly everyone—businessmen, farmers, politicians, and common laborers—developed conflicting theories about how to end this depression. The possible cure-alls included changing the monetary standards, revising tariffs, regulating railroads, and restricting immigration. Although each of these proposals had its devoted sponsors, the revisionist historians have focused their attention upon another widely-applauded suggestion for restoring prosperity: the finding of more markets to absorb the surplus production of American agriculture and industry. The "glut" theory came into vogue, a belief that America had become too productive and had cre-

[3]See William Appleman Williams, *The Roots of the Modern American Empire* (New York: Random House, 1969); William Appleman Williams, *The Tragedy of American Diplomacy* (New York: Dell, 1962); Thomas J. McCormick, *China Market* (Chicago: Quadrangle, 1967); Charles Vevier, "American Continentalism: An Idea of Expansion, 1845–1910," *American Historical Review* 65 (January 1960): 323–35.

ated a glut of goods that could only be disposed of in foreign markets. Williams notes that farmers had been wrestling with the problem of an agricultural glut for years. Their farms produced much more than even the rapidly expanding domestic market could consume. Consequently, politicians representing agricultural interests had persistently called upon the nation's diplomats to search out foreign marketing opportunities. Midwestern farmers gave the dominant Republican party solid support in the post–Civil War years, but the party also depended upon northeastern industrial interests to keep it in power. Fortunately, the party discovered that foreign policies suitable for a surplus-producing farmer were equally acceptable to a manufacturer whose warehouses were filled with unsold goods. Industrialists naturally joined the farmers in viewing the capture of foreign markets as a panacea for the nation's ills. This is how historian Charles Beard described it: "Here, then, is the 'new' *Realpolitick.* A free opportunity for expansion in foreign markets is indispensable to the prosperity of American business. Modern diplomacy is commercial."[4]

The American economy generally remained locked in depression throughout the rest of the decade, but it did exhibit one hopeful sign in 1877. In that year the United States exported more than it had imported after a long string of unfavorable trade balances. Only rarely in the succeeding forty years did the value of exports fail to exceed that of imports. This continuing favorable trade balance enabled the nation to pay off the indebtedness it had accumulated in its earlier, dependent, investment-hungry years. Just after World War I began, the United States became a creditor nation—owed more by others than it itself owed. The favorable trade balance of 1877 came at a psychologically crucial moment, however, as it was associated with an export boom that helped relieve the worst miseries of the depression. According to the revisionists, the coincidence of a slight upward economic turn and an export boom confirmed the nation's faith in the export strategy as the best way to beat the depression. Both the Democratic and Republican parties began voicing support for the market expansion concept in the 1870s, and certainly by 1900, if not before, almost everyone seemed convinced that America would prosper if it could find and control overseas markets for its surplus production.

The Americans were hardly unique in this belief. The glut theory had its passionate advocates in the other industrialized nations, and Europeans, too, were earnestly seeking out international markets. The world's first industrialized nation, Great Britain, had long been

[4]Charles A. Beard, *The Idea of National Interest* (c. 1934; reprint ed., Chicago: Quadrangle, 1966), p. 107.

engaged in a broad-scale effort to capture or create customers abroad. Americans had traditionally found numerous reasons for disliking the British, and the discovery of the Empire's merchants and ship captains ensconced in every port did little to allay this Anglophobia. At the same time, a healthy American respect for the successful English mercantile strategy and a reciprocal British recognition of the growing utility of American friendship led to frequent consultation and occasional cooperation. Nevertheless, Americans remained distrustful and alert to the intrusive commercial endeavors of the world's great powers.

Many American businessmen who encountered stiff foreign competition for markets carefully examined their commercial rivals and then tried to adopt the techniques they used. One such technique was the export of finance capital. Although the level of American investment abroad remained well below what its enthusiastic advocates called for, it did become a tool in the economic expansion drive. The expectation was that nations benefiting from American investments would be more likely to purchase American goods. In addition, the more realistic trade expansionists realized how poor the citizens of subsistence agricultural societies usually were. Foreign investment could help to increase underdeveloped nations' productivity which would hopefully provide their peoples with the wherewithal to become paying customers.[5] Export of American capital might also assist American efforts to expand politically. This motivation underlay the Taft administration's so-called Dollar Diplomacy between 1909 and 1913.

Economic expansion in all its forms did much to enhance the United States' international prestige. Lest anyone doubt the seriousness of the American intention to achieve economic eminence, the nation's diplomats and statesmen repeatedly proclaimed it fundamental to future prosperity. The United States sent overseas a large number of consular representatives whose major functions were to scout trade opportunities and to prevent foreign governments from mistreating those American businessmen who ventured abroad in search of market and investment opportunities. The sheer magnitude of the nation's financial, industrial, and agricultural plenty gave it a significance in the world's economy that could not be ignored. By 1914, American exports had become essential to the very survival of the European nations locked in combat with Germany and Austria.

[5]Charles A. Conant, "The Struggle for Commercial Empire," *Forum* 17 (June 1899): 427; David Healy, *US Expansionism* (Madison: University of Wisconsin Press, 1970), pp. 196–97.

One might well conclude that the United States' primary foreign policy goal in this period was the advancement of the United States economic position in the world.

Any search for explanations of all of the nation's responses to international opportunities and crises, however, requires a much broader perspective than one can find by looking only among economic factors. Several of the most outspoken advocates of American expansion during this period, including Henry Cabot Lodge and Theodore Roosevelt, exhibited only marginal interest in economic expansion per se. They might emphasize hoped-for economic advantages when discussing expansionist proposals, but they never appeared to consider merchants' profits as anything more than a secondary benefit of the policies they proposed. Furthermore, although tariffs were one of the most heatedly debated economic topics in American politics from the Civil War to World War I, they seldom seemed designed to encourage American trade. David A. Wells, a sometime government economist and an outspoken advocate of free trade, favored knocking down all international tariffs and allowing free international competition to determine world trade patterns.[6] The congressmen who set tariff rates blithely ignored such expert advice, heeding instead the requests of American manufacturers who persistently lobbied for protection from foreign competition. Consequently, the United States maintained ridiculously high tariff rates right into the 1930s. Now and then a prominent statesman like Secretary of State James G. Blaine could buck the trend and drive through a reciprocal trade agreements program in order to encourage international trade, but American tariff policy generally reflected domestic pressures, not international trade considerations.

Historians dedicated to proving that economic motivations determined the direction of American foreign policy sometimes use evidence more applicable to a second major theme: the expansion of American political influence abroad. As the United States spread its political influence further afield, the American position on international issues became more respected, strengthening the hands of American statesmen in international conferences, councils, and collective ventures. During the period under study, American policymakers used three distinct methods to broaden the political influence of the United States. First, they issued an increasingly petulant series of unilateral decrees or assertions, most of which were variations on

[6]David A. Wells, *Recent Economic Changes* (New York: Appleton, 1890), pp. 287, 466.

the theme that the United States was predominant in the Western Hemisphere. The second, and much more effective, method involved the direct extension of American control over other peoples through colonization. Finally, after the Spanish-American War had greatly enlarged the United States' area of international responsibilities and interests, American statesmen moved in the direction of creating explicit or implicit protectorates over other peoples. The employment of these three methods merged and overlapped as the United States experimented, hoping to find an acceptable and successful formula through which to increase its influence. By 1914, the experimentation had produced these conclusions: unilateral assertions seldom succeeded without the backing of force; colonialism turned out to be incompatible with American ideals; but the forceful yet scrupulous establishment of protectorates seemed both politically satisfactory and acceptable at home.

When the process of attempting to expand American political influence and prestige abroad began, those in charge of the nation's destiny could do little more than issue their pretentious challenges and assertions. Lacking a historical reputation as a great, influential world power and, at first, the sort of military and naval hardware commonly associated with such status, the United States had to rely upon rhetoric to make its points. It was essentially a public relations campaign aimed at changing the world's image of the United States so that others would respect its foreign policy initiatives. As the following chapter will show, the campaign basically failed to affect attitudes outside of the United States until the nation had developed the requisite strength and had proven its determination through success in war. Nevertheless, these cocky, brash, unilateral assertions represented a fundamental, habitual part of American foreign policy. The habit proved hard to shake. Even after the physical expansion of the nation's political system into that of a major imperial power in 1898 and 1899, American statesmen continued to issue proclamations about the United States' special interests and responsibilities overseas. The most famous of these proclamations became known as the Open Door policy—a policy that consisted essentially of assertions of American political influence in the Far East not always accepted or recognized by other nations.

The Far East was a long way away; declarations of American omnipotence and superiority were much more effective closer to home. Both before and after America's Caribbean adventures in the late 1890s, the United States put forth one declaration after another, referring to or associated with the Monroe Doctrine. This had long served as a primary foundation stone for United States foreign policy. Over the years American policymakers had stretched, twisted and warped this doctrine so much that the intent of President James Monroe's famous message of 2 December 1823 had long since become inoperative. At the urging of his secretary of state, John Quincy Adams, President Monroe had drafted the original statement to cope with two problems: a Russian attempt to extend its control of the northwest Pacific coast southward from Alaska, and a fear that France or some other European power would try to conquer one of Spain's former colonies in Latin America. To stop Russia, Monroe declared that the American continents were no longer open to further colonization. He also brashly warned the European powers not to try to alter the political status quo in Latin America through recolonization of the newly independent nations. In return the United States promised not to meddle in purely European affairs. Far too weak in 1823 to impose its will unilaterally, the United States had fallen back on rhetoric, hoping its pronouncements would somehow discourage European encroachments into its own territories or into areas it might wish to annex in the future. Fortunately, no nation challenged the Monroe Doctrine. Russia withdrew, and the European balance of power as well as the strength of the British navy prevented any colonial changes in the Western Hemisphere. The people of Latin America derived certain obvious benefits from this lack of European interference, but, at the time, the United States considered them of far less importance than its own security.[7]

Over the years, the United States grew powerful enough to ignore any European threat to itself, and the nation's statesmen took a much greater interest in maintaining Latin America's insulation from the Old World. In the 1840s, President James K. Polk expanded the Monroe Doctrine into an assertion of United States supremacy in North America. Twenty years later, although he never mentioned Monroe's now legendary message specifically, Secretary of State William H. Seward put teeth into the doctrine by encouraging France to hasten its withdrawal from Mexico. By the 1880s, Americans had generally come to believe that the Monroe Doctrine had somehow assigned to the United States a responsibility for defending the whole Western Hemisphere from external threats. Skillful policymakers found ways to link it to almost any action they proposed involving Latin America. The Monroe Doctrine had long since lost its original,

[7]John Holladay Latané, *From Isolation to Leadership* (Garden City, N.Y.: Doubleday, 1918), p. 147; John Bassett Moore, "The Monroe Doctrine," *Political Science Quarterly* 11 (March 1896): 22–23.

narrowly-defined purpose; it had become an instantly recognized and, at least in the United States, a highly respected uniform with which to cloak any policy relating to Latin America.

References to the Monroe Doctrine served as convenient rationalizations for policies fundamentally designed to increase the United States' political influence in Latin America and the world. The most blatant statement of this goal came in 1895 when Secretary of State Richard Olney promulgated his famous corollary stating that the United States could dictate whatever solutions it chose to problems in its continent. In 1904 Theodore Roosevelt amended the Monroe Doctrine still further, reserving to the United States rather than European nations the right and responsibility to intervene in Latin American countries guilty of financial mismanagement. The Roosevelt Corollary, in effect, justified the extension of United States political influence anywhere it chose. Stretched so far as to be almost unrecognizable, the Monroe Doctrine had become a useful rationale for any change the United States wished to make in its Latin American policy.

Such extravagant use and abuse of the Monroe Doctrine underlined the widespread American view that the United States had a special relationship to the peoples sharing its hemisphere. As the nineteenth century drew to a close, American humanitarians and idealists became outraged at Spain's ruthless, yet inconclusive, attempts to put down a rebellion in Cuba. An irresistible tide of public opinion urged the United States to implement its frequently reiterated assertions of political supremacy in the New World. The ensuing Spanish-American War helped stimulate the acceptance of imperialistic schemes in the United States. Many Americans became convinced that the United States should abandon rhetoric in favor of the fulfillment of its political expansionist drives through the taking of colonies. In acquiescing to the imperialistic urge, the United States was simply following the pattern of almost every European country and Japan, each of which became swept up in the new age of imperialism.

The revisionists choose to explain this imperialist upsurge as a response to economic factors. Until 1870 British industrial output greatly exceeded that of other nations, allowing British traders to dominate the world's markets for manufactured goods. As long as Britain remained the only major industrial power, there was no need for colonization. Consequently, England favored a continuance of the free trade and open door policies that had brought the empire great riches. After 1870, however, several nations rapidly achieved sufficient industrial maturity to threaten Britain's economic dominance. First, each industrial nation imposed high tariffs to preserve its home markets for its own domestic producers. Then an intensive search for colonies began, colonies which would provide protected overseas markets for producers in the mother country. Worldwide economic depression and an equally widespread adoption of the glut theory spurred imperialism on. By 1880, the race to capture or create colonies in Africa and southern Asia had become fierce. Regions lacking great market potential in themselves were sought to serve as entrepôts for economic penetration into the remaining free-trade areas. Latin America, with its weak and underdeveloped republics, and East Asia, where the Chinese Empire tottered on the brink of collapse, continued to offer markets to all comers. An economic explanation for American colonization in the 1890s would suggest that the United States took over Cuba, Hawaii, and the Philippines in order to provide itself with bases for gaining greater access to these markets in the Orient and South America.[8]

A strictly economic interpretation of the American drive to acquire colonies overlooks the fact that an American desire for territorial expansion was as old as the Union itself. American firebrands were planning an invasion of Canada even before the Declaration of Independence had been drafted; while negotiating his treaty to end the Revolutionary War in 1782, Benjamin Franklin beseeched the British government to turn over all of its North American possessions; Thomas Jefferson violated his own strict constructionist view of the Constitution in order to annex Louisiana in 1803. Historian Thomas A. Bailey points out that in the century before it took overseas colonies the United States consistently engaged in what amounted to the colonization of sparsely populated lands to the west.[9] Territorial aggrandizement must be considered a dominant tradition in American history. The record of the nation's early diplomatic efforts is rife with plans for infiltrating, conquering, purchasing, and delineating the boundaries of additional territory. The United States may have come late to the feast of colonization in Asia and Africa, but it was no stranger to the experience of gorging an expansionist appetite for additional land. Virtually every one of the arguments over

---

[8]Wells, *Recent Economic Changes*, p. 270; J. A. Hobson, *Imperialism: A Study* (c. 1938; reprint ed., Ann Arbor: University of Michigan Press, 1965), pp. 22, 72; David M. Pletcher, *The Awkward Years* (Columbia, University of Missouri Press, 1962), pp. xii–xiii; Charles Callan Tansill, *The Foreign Policy of Thomas F. Bayard 1885–1897* (New York: Fordham University Press, 1940), p. 18.

[9]Bailey, "America's Emergence," pp. 1–16.

territorial aggrandizement brought forward in the colonization debates of the late 1890s had been considered, discussed, and rationalized long before.

The colonies acquired in 1898 and 1899 did of course differ from
their pre-Civil War precedents in that earlier expansion had involved contiguous areas on the North American continent. Defense,
communication, and population assimilation had made continental
expansion seem the most desirable. During the two decades after
President James K. Polk had rounded the nation off at the Pacific,
America's expansionist drive became just one of the countless victims
of the masochistic, destructive national conflict over slavery and economic development. Immediately after the Civil War only a few men
looked outward, beyond the pressing problems of domestic reconstruction. Radical Republican Senator Charles Sumner's appetite for
northern expansion did frighten the British government so much that
it created the Dominion of Canada in 1867. The "dominion" gave
the Canadians a nationalistic focus that helped weaken any desire they
might have had to join the United States but did little to extinguish
the American desires for territories to the north. Another Republican
visionary, William H. Seward, Lincoln's brilliant secretary of state,
considered territorial expansion a fine American tradition. Seconded
by Sumner, Seward persuaded Congress in 1867 to agree to the purchase of Alaska, the nation's first major, noncontiguous territorial
acquisition.

Seward closed the Alaskan deal several years before the revival of
European interest in colonies arose and began influencing American
thinking. Even then, internal, not external, forces continued to play
the predominant role in guiding the United States along the path to
imperialism. Until the 1890s the United States had plenty of war
damage to repair, ample empty land to settle, and a multitude of new
industries to create. As long as Americans lacked any substantial
commercial interest in Africa or southern Asia, they expressed little
concern over European colonization in those areas. The independent,
republican governments characteristic of the United States' southern
neighbors appeared to protect them from European imperialism
(particularly after Seward had disapproved of French designs on
Mexico), so the United States never developed any great desire to
colonize in the New World either.

Colonialism began to gain some appeal in the United States as
acceptance of the glut theory became widespread. Patriotism contributed to the growing popularity of expansionism because imperialists
played up the excitement and prestige associated with the planting of

the Stars and Stripes throughout the world. Many Americans firmly believed that the frontier experience had kept the nation true to its course, and they felt new colonies might provide an approximation for the rapidly dwindling western frontier. Simultaneously, strategic arguments for colonization developed. The devastation of the nation's merchant marine by a few Confederate raiders during the Civil War had illustrated the importance of naval power as a commercial weapon. By the 1890s, Afred Thayer Mahan was evoking popular support for his theories on the benefits of sea power and the need for an isthmian canal. Such a canal would, in turn, need protection, possibly in the form of naval bases in the Caribbean and Hawaii. The articulation and popularization of this sort of strategic thinking encouraged naval and military planners to devise justifications for a worldwide string of bases to defend the United States and its commercial interests.[10] Most important of all, however, was the fact that the United States was used to expanding. Americans loved to redraw their maps to show the ever-increasing size of the Union.

All of these impulses for colonialism peaked in 1898 and 1899, with the acquisition of the insular colonies of Hawaii, the Philippines, Puerto Rico, Guam, and Samoa. If the desire to expand the nation's political influence was truly characteristic of American diplomacy, one might expect to see further additions to America's colonial empire. Nevertheless, the United States took only one major colony after 1899: the Virgin Islands, purchased in 1917 from Denmark. Historian Ernest R. May suggests that a lapse of interest over time as well as the disturbing complexities Americans encountered in dealing with the new colonies explains the dissipation of interest in colonization after 1900.[11] The Philippine insurrection was costly, bloody, and unpopular, and even after the rebellion had been put down, American administrators faced countless intractable problems and resentments. The imperialist urge died quickly.

The United States then moved on to an alternative that achieved the advantages of colonialism without the attendant drudgery and danger. The political expansion impulse thus moved into its third phase: the creation of formal or informal protectorates in its spheres of interest. The Platt Amendment exemplified the new method because it obviated the need for the United States to make a colony out of Cuba while simultaneously guaranteeing that American political

[10]Richard D. Challener, *Admirals, Generals, and American Foreign Policy 1898–1914* (Princeton: Princeton University Press, 1973), p. 410; John A. Logan, Jr., *No Transfer* (New Haven, Conn.: Yale University Press, 1961), p. 259.

[11]Ernest R. May, *American Imperialism* (New York: Harcourt, Brace, 1968), p. 215.

influence would prevail in the island republic. When the Panamanians revolted in 1903, the United States immediately extended its protective umbrella over them and made plans to dig a canal. Protection of the canal required further extensions of the American political influence in the Caribbean. It is hardly coincidental that in 1904 President Theodore Roosevelt designed a financial protectorate for Santo Domingo. The Dominican customs agreement that Congress finally approved in 1907 served as a model for future United States efforts to encourage the development of stable and responsible governments in the vicinity of the canal. By the beginning of World War I, American naval vessels and marines had become all too common sights in the Caribbean. The United States had abandoned colonialism in favor of an equally effective means of maintaining its expanded political influence in Latin America. The nation had apparently found a method of implementing the Monroe Doctrine in a way that appeared to be philosophically and morally acceptable to its citizens.

The United States could not unilaterally control the Far Eastern situation. All the major powers maintained naval forces in or near Chinese ports. Having obtained its own nearby base in the Philippines, the United States resorted to petulant criticism of any suspected attempts to dismember the Chinese Empire. The American Open Door policy was primarily an effort to preserve free trade in all of China. The Chinese government encouraged this American initiative because the United States was the great power least interested in taking physical control of some region of China. The American presidents used different techniques to maintain political influence in the Far East. Roosevelt skillfully brought Japanese and Russian diplomats together to work out a treaty to end the Russo-Japanese War in 1905. The Taft administration decided to compete with other great powers for concessions and investment opportunities in order to limit or neutralize the foreign influences in China. Although Taft's Dollar Diplomacy failed, at no time after 1900 were United States attitudes ignored in Far Eastern affairs.

Advocates of the expansion of United States political influence on the American continents or abroad marshaled a whole army of justifications for their views. Among the most emotionally satisfying were those that claimed that God had preordained that the United States would expand. This so-called manifest destiny doctrine had been defined first in the 1840s; it was extensively and imaginatively applied in the 1890s. The basic premise was essentially that God had selected the United States over all other nations to be the exemplar of His works on earth. Consequently, Americans presumed they had a divine right and responsibility to expand their system worldwide.

This justification for political expansionism serves to introduce the third major traditional foreign policy theme: America's sense that it had a mission to democratize the world. The prevalent view held that American-style democratic self-government was an absolute good, superior to all other systems. Because of this innate superiority, many Americans concluded that they had a God-given mission to share the benefits of their system with all peoples. They could share it directly by annexing territory and later admitting it to the Union as a state or states; less directly by benevolently controlling colonies; or less directly still by serving as an ideal model, advertising the benefits of their system so that others would emulate it.

Like both the economic and political expansion themes, the sense of mission had deep roots in American history. An important philosophical foundation for the impulse came over in 1630 with the self-righteous Puritans who intended to carve out of the American wilderness an ideal Christian community to serve as an example for others. The American people's image of themselves as both noble and superior gained clarity and vibrancy through their Revolutionary War struggles and, later, when they established a novel, democratic form of government in 1789. At first the mission remained a passive one, in which the United States served as a model for others. The American people were quite willing to express sympathy for Greeks, Hungarians, or others fighting against autocratic governments, but they never actively assisted them.

This commitment to passivity gradually began to wane. Christian missionaries are not content simply to be one with God; they can achieve true spiritual fulfillment only in attempting to convert heathens. A similar sort of missionary spirit took hold in the United States on a secular level; Americans felt an irresistible urge to take positive steps to spread the benefits of their system. Europe as well as less-developed areas could benefit from America's secular mission. An article published in the *Atlantic Monthly* in 1898 eloquently described the American democratic mission sentiment:

> For centuries we have practiced the art of self-government, until to govern has become an instinct, and to be self-governed a habit. To us power means opportunity to help others; it also means responsibility not to man only, but to God, for the wise use of the power thus given us. And for this reason we are especially fitted to act as trustees and guar-

dians of inferior races, and peculiarly qualified to fit them eventually to govern themselves.[12]

Historian Frederick Merk's definitive work on expansion in the 1840s deals with the first rash of activity associated with the democratic mission theme. The great, emotional outpouring of Manifest Destiny sentiment began with the annexation of the Republic of Texas which had modeled its institutions after American examples. The Americans then sought a philosophical justification for a move into Mexico, which was an independent nation, not a colony as Florida and Louisiana had been. They rationalized their expansive actions by insisting that America's benevolent institutions should be spread over as broad an area as possible. The conquest of New Mexico and California furthered the divine plan to expand the benefits of American-style democracy. Then, as one military triumph followed another, the thought of simply annexing all of Mexico sprang up. For the first time, Americans grappled with the disturbing question of whether to admit a large, settled, alien population into their nation. The enthusiasts in the All-Mexico movement confidently argued that American example and Yankee organizing ability would "regenerate" the Mexican people into law-abiding democrats. Fortunately, President Polk ruled out the taking of southern Mexico, and the United States was able to avoid testing the dubious regeneration proposition. Merk does note the crudeness of one attempt to fulfill the idealized mission. John C. Fremont's presumptuous and futile effort to force republican forms on California with his Bear Flag revolt created much ill will among the native population.[13] Some of the later attempts to translate the ideal into action also had disturbing consequences. A notable example was the vicious guerrilla war that ravaged the Philippine Islands for two years after the United States had determined to bring the glories of its system to the benighted islanders.

Having resolved their own differences of opinion and doubts about their political system through the mechanism of a savage civil war, the American people in the 1880s and 1890s once again rekindled a burning desire to spread their benevolent system abroad. The sponsors of this revived missionary attitude insisted that the extension of American democratic ideals would help "civilize" the world. Civilization, in turn, would mean peace. Theodore Roosevelt firmly believed in this civilizing function of the democratic mission. He disliked

[12]Horace N. Fisher, "The Development of Our Foreign Policy," *Atlantic Monthly* 82 (October 1898): 559.

[13]Frederick Merk, *Manifest Destiny and Mission in American History* (New York: Random House, 1963), chaps. 1–3.

backward peoples, and he felt his nation should take up the task of educating those he considered inferior. Thus, racism, paternalism, and condescension all infected and corrupted the purity of the mission sentiment. Rudyard Kipling's apt definition of imperialism as the "white man's burden" struck home with Roosevelt, William Howard Taft, Elihu Root, and other Americans who eventually had to deal on a practical basis with colonial administration. But vigorous Anglo-Saxons responded to the call to duty. With a determination that any dedicated religious missionary would envy, they intended to impose their beliefs and practices on others, regardless of the resistance or disappointments they would encounter along the way.[14]

In a striking article published in 1891, Admiral Stephen B. Luce, the founder of the Naval War College, described what he considered one among several benefits of war: "But for war the civilization we now enjoy would have been impossible. The swath cut by the reaper's sickle through fields of ripened grain is not more marked than the way cut by the sword for the path of human progress."[15] The concept that human progress might result from war reassured those who felt they must take extreme measures in their attempts to spread American institutions. Although they claimed to favor independence and self-government, they frequently found the only effective methods they could employ involved military conquest, martial law, or the imposition of external controls on economies. As America's recent experiences in Southeast Asia have proven, any attempt to force democracy upon other peoples almost inevitably necessitates some form of antidemocratic coercion. Yet compulsion seemed essential to the Americans in the 1890s who had become impatient with the slowness of others to copy their model system. On the other hand, too much progress might be unacceptable. The overall goal was to enable all peoples to become self-governing, but the fulfillment of that goal would necessarily limit the extent of American political influence. In this way, two traditional themes, expansion of political influence and commitment to the democratic mission, sometimes worked at cross-purposes. Similar conflicts arose among all three major themes at one time or another.

Practically speaking, spreading democracy often worked best on a personal level. Religious missionaries frequently performed the incidental function of advertising the American way of life and value

[14]Healy, *US Expansionism*, p. 235; Howard K. Beale, *Theodore Roosevelt and the Rise of America to World Power* (New York: Collier Books, 1962), p. 47.
[15]Stephen B. Luce, "The Benefits of War," *North American Review* 153 (December 1891): 673.

system. American missionary schools were established in China and
the Middle East. Because education seemed crucial to the spreading
of civilization and to the functioning of democracy, Americans gave a
high priority to the building of school systems in occupied Cuba and
in colonial areas like Puerto Rico and the Philippine Islands. Those
convinced of Anglo-Saxon superiority considered the teaching of the
English language an excellent way of civilizing other peoples. Newspaper columnist Peter Finley Dunne's amiable Irishman, Mr. Dooley,
made many a penetrating comment around the turn of the century,
including the following one on the nation's civilizing efforts in the
Philippines: "In ivry city in this unfair land we will erect schoolhouses
an' packin' houses an' houses of correction; and we'll larn ye our
language, because 'tis aisier to larn ye ours than to larn oursilves
yours. An' we'll give ye clothes, if ye pay f'r thim; an' if ye don't, ye
can go without."[16]

Just how successful was the democratizing mission? The impact
of the American model in Europe was generally disappointing. Only
the British appeared to be moving rapidly and irreversibly in the
direction of greater democracy during the nineteenth century. This
development brought the United States little pleasure as long as the
Americans considered Great Britain their most serious international
rival. Furthermore, although the American example did have a considerable impact, the British tended to follow their own path to a
more democratic society. By the close of the nineteenth century, the
British and American governmental structures had come to resemble
one another in intent, if not precisely in form. This development definitely helped the Americans to overcome their earlier enmity and
acknowledge a sense of kinship with their British cousins. After all,
the dispersion of people speaking English, whether with an Etonian
crispness or a midwestern American twang, was considered essential
to the progress of mankind and of civilization. The United States
frequently copied England's policies in instituting its colonial administrations, although the Americans felt they had definitely improved
on the model. If American democracy had lost its uniqueness by the
late nineteenth century, so too had its sense of mission. As William
Graham Sumner pointed out, "There is not a civilized nation which
does not talk about its civilizing mission just as grandly as we do. The
English, who really have more to boast of in this respect than anybody
else, talk least about it, but the Phariseeism with which they correct

[16]Quoted in Robert L. Beisner, *Twelve Against Empire* (New York: McGraw-Hill,
1968), p. 275.

and instruct other people has made them hated all over the globe."[17] The Americans also had to compete with Germans, Frenchmen, Russians, Japanese, and even Spaniards in pursuing their civilizing mission. An arrogant belief that the United States was the best and greatest enabled Americans to discount the fact that the citizens of other nations might believe as fervently in their own destiny to civilize the world.

While the United States naturally had some interest in the impact of its model upon Europe, it also favored keeping the New World separate from the Old. The Western Hemisphere should adopt from the outside only what had intrinsic merit, and thus escape the corruption and decay Americans perceived in Europe. Advocates of hemispheric isolation in the United States particularly hoped that their southern neighbors would follow the lead of the United States, rather than cling to European traditions and examples. During the first two decades of the nineteenth century, this hope was greatly encouraged as one Spanish colony after another followed the United States' example in throwing off its ties to the mother country to create a democratically-governed republic.[18]

Unfortunately, for one reason or another, the Latin American peoples experienced difficulty in trying to maintain stable governments. While many northerners viewed the American Civil War as a forge that had tempered and strengthened the Union, they ridiculed Latin American civil strife as petty and devoid of virtue. The United States' increasingly frequent interventions in Caribbean affairs after 1900 often stemmed from an American desire to nudge warring, misguided Latinos back toward a semblance of responsible government. The American mission had traditionally been concerned with such democratic devices as free elections, constitutions, and widespread suffrage. Particularly after the turn of the century, however, the United States became more concerned with evaluating the use and misuse of these devices. Responsible leaders and stable governments often seemed more desirable than the tumult and turmoil of pure democracy. A mismanaged Latin American republic represented a failure of the American mission, so the United States felt called upon to institute coercive repair measures.

This use of idealism to justify a repressive policy opened American diplomats and statesmen to charges of cynicism. After all, many

[17]Sumner, *Conquest*, p. 145.

[18]Arthur A. Ekirk, Jr., *Ideas, Ideals, and American Diplomacy* (New York: Appleton-Century-Crofts, 1966), p. 31; Dexter Perkins, *The Evolution of American Foreign Policy* (New York: Oxford University Press, 1966), p. 35.

nations cloaked their diplomatic initiatives in moralistic rhetoric. Historian Charles Beard dismissed as hypocritical the American policy formulations which alluded to the nation's moral obligations. He claimed these allusions were designed solely to win domestic approval.[19] There was much more to it than hypocrisy, however. The moralistic sentiments or rationalizations that were used to defend a particular policy had a way of developing a life of their own. However egotistical, hypocritical, or self-serving it might have been originally, the rhetoric of the democratic mission had been in use for so long that it had become a powerful force for shaping and legitimatizing the nation's actions. The mission sentiments had already become a traditional theme in American foreign policy when William H. Seward proclaimed that "the practice of this government, from the beginning, is a guarantee to all nations of the respect of the American people for the free sovereignty of the people in every other state. . . . It is in reality the chief element of foreign intercourse in our history."[20]

The three major, traditional themes that underlay all policy in this period are, then, a desire for economic expansion, a drive to extend American political influence far beyond the national borders, and an effort to fulfill America's self-assumed democratic mission to the rest of the world. Not every action taken involved all three themes; sometimes only one or two were readily apparent. But no analysis of American foreign policy from 1880 to 1914 can be complete without consideration of all of these underlying themes. Taken together, they can clarify and categorize virtually everything that took place. No one of them was brand new; each had traditionally influenced American foreign policy formulations. Consequently, they provided guideposts for those encountering new difficulties as the nation's external interests expanded and became more complex.

Musing on the difficulties inherent in formulating foreign policy in a democratic country late in 1904, President Theodore Roosevelt wrote: "It would be well-nigh impossible, even if it were not highly undesirable, for this country to carry out any policy save one which had become part of the inherited tradition of the country, like the Monroe Doctrine."[21] In other words, the American public would re-

---

[19]Beard, *National Interest*, p. 275.

[20]Quoted in Frank Tannenbaum, *The American Tradition in Foreign Policy* (Norman: University of Oklahoma Press, 1955), p. 62.

[21]Elting E. Morison, ed., *The Letters of Theodore Roosevelt*, 8 vols. (Cambridge, Mass.: Harvard University Press, 1951–1954), 4:1084.

ject any policy that could not directly or indirectly be tied to some long-standing, widely accepted precedent. Roosevelt's example was apt. Few Americans would criticize a policy linked to so venerable a tradition as the Monroe Doctrine, even if that policy dealt with an issue or crisis only tangentially related to the historic circumstances that had led to its issuance. Appeals to or comparisons with traditional modes of behavior characterized almost every foreign policy formulated around the turn of the century.

Because of the American people's traditional acceptance and support for the three expansionist themes just described, they could serve as rationalizations for new initiatives, guaranteeing public support for the diplomats. Although it boasted of its democratic heritage and its free press, the United States government sometimes found these elements less than helpful in dealing with foreign problems. Aroused popular disapproval could easily destroy an intricately balanced set of initiatives. Or, as in the case of California's anti-Japanese behavior after 1906, public sentiment could force policymakers into hazardous situations which their own natural caution would never have permitted. While the public might object to dramatic or radical new departures, American statesmen found the people much less likely to criticize initiatives based upon traditional beliefs. Any policy that could be successfully defended on the basis of tradition and precedent would not arouse much public alarm.

Public attitudes mattered, but the actual implementation of American foreign policy remained in the hands of a relatively few individuals. Having closely examined the decisions made during the Spanish-American War about colonization, historian Ernest R. May concluded that only a few Americans played influential roles in foreign policy formulation.[22] Presidents and politicians frequently appealed to the public for support, or newspaper editors, hoping to win a circulation war, pounded away at a particular issue until the public was thoroughly aroused. The policymakers only had to placate the electorate when the public was upset, however, and in the late nineteenth century, the American people remained largely indifferent to foreign problems. Normally, foreign policy was determined by only a few individuals: presidents, secretaries of state, and a handful of State Department officials. These policymakers enjoyed a great deal of freedom. They could even make unpopular decisions as long as their attitudes coincided with those Secretary of State Walter Q.

[22]May, *American Imperialism*, pp. 223–24.

Gresham expressed: "After all, public opinion is made and controlled by the thoughtful men of the country."[23] Gresham firmly believed his policies to be correct; he was equally certain that thoughtful men would approve of them.

Statesmen could usually pursue a particular foreign policy without much interference, unless it involved a treaty or required an appropriation. Then senators and representatives had an opportunity to alter or reject anything they found distasteful. Some policymakers ran up rather sorry records in their sparring with Congress. Even though historians and most of his contemporaries considered John Hay a respectable and responsible secretary of state, he did not fare well in his skirmishes on Capitol Hill. After fighting congressional review for seven years, Hay resignedly wrote in his diary that "a treaty entering the Senate, is like a bull going into the arena: no one can say just how or when the final blow will fall—but one thing is certain—it will never leave the arena alive."[24] Actually, the irascibility of the Senate was only partially to blame. Hay's successor at the State Department, Elihu Root, won Senate approval for all but three out of over one hundred treaties he submitted. He amassed this impressive record by taking the senators into his confidence and by attending Senate Foreign Relations Committee hearings whenever possible. He thus worked in tandem with the legislative branch for the ultimate benefit of American foreign relations.[25]

The diverse nature of the problems and personalities involved would invalidate any general statement about the impact of public and congressional opinion on foreign policy. A high level of popular excitement, an inept policymaker, or a partisan group of legislators could substantially influence policy. On the other hand, a practical, prudent secretary of state like Root could serve his country well without ever running seriously afoul of public opinion. An excellent way to avoid serious pitfalls was to design policies based upon America's traditional expansionist economic, political, and moral themes. How well or how poorly each policymaker did will become apparent when American foreign relations from 1880 to 1914 are reviewed.

[23]Walter Q. Gresham to Carl Schurz, 6 October 1893, Papers of Walter Quintin Gresham, Library of Congress Manuscript Division (cited hereafter as LCMD).

[24]Quoted in William Roscoe Thayer, *The Life and Letters of John Hay*, 2 vols. (Boston: Houghton, Mifflin, 1915), 2:393.

[25]Philip C. Jessup, *Elihu Root*, 2 vols. (New York: Dodd, Mead, 1938), 1:544; Richard W. Leopold, *Elihu Root and the Conservative Tradition* (Boston: Little, Brown, 1954), pp. 51–52.

2

The First Stirrings
of Expansionism, 1880-1892

On 23 May 1865, solid ranks and files of blue stretched out along Washington's Pennsylvania Avenue as the neatly uniformed brigades and corps of the Army of the Potomac thundered past in a triumphal celebration of the Union's grand victory. The next day, the raw-boned, homespun, and tattered troops of Sherman's Army of the Tennessee straggled by, their pride and fierceness more than offsetting what they lacked in discipline and elegance. European observers remarked on the awesome size of the armies, well aware that a great many more Americans had served their time in the trenches and the wildernesses of the American battlefields. No other nation could have called together so large, so well-trained, and so experienced a mass army at that moment. Through a sanguine, agonizing, self-destructive exercise, the United States had created the world's pre-eminent military machine.[1]

Some Americans advocated sending elements of these armies into Mexico to chase out the French soldiers who trespassed on the continent in violation of the honor of the Monroe Doctrine. Others hoped to loose hoards of troops on the defenseless Canadians to the north. Neither invasion was to occur. The vast army being reviewed was already in the process of demobilization. The blue uniforms would be stripped of insignia and worn to rags on hardscrabble farms in New England, in factories and coal mines in the Northeast, and in the forests and prairies of the West. The citizen army of the United States would go home, hang up its swords and medals, and turn its

[1]Margaret Leech, *Reveille in Washington* (New York: Harper & Row, 1941), pp. 414-17.

attention to plowshares and steel rails. Before the end of the year the vast armies had ceased to exist except as ghosts at Grand Army of the Republic rallies.

The disbandment and dispersal of the army ruled out for the time being any capitalizing upon America's potential as a great world power. The nation would maintain a low profile in international affairs as it dealt with a multitude of postwar dislocations. Domestic reconstruction engrossed the attention of civil and military leaders, carpetbaggers and local politicos, and southern businessmen and northern investors, leaving them with little inclination and less time to dwell on the world overseas. The few foreign policy initiatives that occurred in those crowded years were generally the work of single individuals. Secretary of State William H. Seward purchased Alaska from a Russian government eager to dispose of what it considered a worthless property. President Ulysses Grant became infatuated with the concept of annexing the island nation of Santo Domingo but handled the transaction so ineptly as to permanently foreclose the project. Meanwhile, his secretary of state, Hamilton Fish, dextrously managed to obtain a settlement of all outstanding American claims against Great Britain which proved satisfactory to almost everyone on both sides of the Atlantic.[2]

After that triumph, Fish kept the State Department in low gear; William Maxwell Evarts, his successor under President Rutherford B. Hayes, was equally reserved. During the dark years of depression in the 1870s, interest in foreign affairs lagged far behind economic concerns although a few publicists emphasized the connection between the two. For example, David A. Wells hammered away at the theme that protective tariffs in the United States and in Europe stymied the operation of the natural economic forces which would clear up the worldwide depression.[3] Obviously responding to the glut theory, others called for increased exports to help siphon off the nation's surplus production. President Hayes himself noted in his 1877 inaugural address that "the long commercial depression in the United States has directed attention to the subject of the possible increase of our foreign trade and the methods for its development, not only in Europe but with other countries, especially with the States

[2]For fuller coverage of these events, see Charles S. Campbell, *The Transformation of American Foreign Relations 1865–1900* (New York: Harper & Row, 1976), chaps. 1–2.

[3]David A. Wells, *Recent Economic Changes* (New York: Appleton, 1890), pp. 70–71, 260.

and sovereignties of the Western Hemisphere."[4] Unfortunately Great
Britain continued to expand its control of the Latin American and
Far Eastern markets that Americans hoped would solve their glut
problem. Presidential statements alone had little effect on trade patterns, so American goods represented only a small fraction of those
shipped into these areas.

   The first American statesman who did more than simply talk
about the development of Latin American markets was Evarts's successor at the State Department, James Gillespie Blaine. Blaine bustled
into office with an overabundance of plans, but the fatal wounding
of his chief, President James A. Garfield, gave Blaine a scant few
months to implement them. His first tour at the State Department
showed him to be antagonistic, impulsive, energetic, and fully aware
of the nation's growing capabilities. Although he stridently claimed to
be a "realist," his policies frequently foundered due to his clumsy
efforts at execution. An older, more sensible, and reserved Blaine
returned to the State Department in 1889 under President Benjamin
Harrison. Yet he never abandoned his exuberance in pursuing initiatives designed to strengthen American foreign policy commitments
along the lines of the three traditional expansionist themes.

   Blaine easily assumed dominance of the direction of United
States foreign policy since there were only a few experienced officers
working on the diminutive State Department staff. The most notable
was third Assistant Secretary Alvey A. Adee who served as second
or third in command at the State Department from 1878 to 1924.
Adee's constant presence insured that policymakers would always
have ready access to American traditions and precedents. His ency-
clopedic mind was stuffed with information about previous policies
and appropriate approaches. Although he never tried to impose his
own ideas upon a superior, he executed decisions with a maximum
of diplomatic grace. He drafted countless State Department documents including the courtesy notes the presidents exchanged with
the heads of other nations. He had become such an institution in
Washington that the newspapers expressed great surprise when
Woodrow Wilson composed his own presidential Thanksgiving proclamations rather than simply promulgating the ones Adee had been
drawing up on an annual basis.

---

[4]James D. Richardson, *A Compilation of the Messages and Papers of the Presidents,* 10
vols. (Washington, D.C.: Bureau of National Literature, 1911), 8:5874.

Adee's responsibility and rectitude were unique in the United States foreign affairs establishment. Diplomatic posts and departmental positions were routinely parceled out as rewards for prior political service rather than for any diplomatic experience or capability. Even after the 1883 Pendleton Act created a professional civil service system for much of the federal government, the State Department remained a bastion of the spoils system. Fortunately, the amount of business the department conducted in the late nineteenth century was relatively small, enabling the secretary and his few top assistants to keep track of it fairly easily. Furthermore, much of it was not of earthshaking importance. In the 1880s, for example, most of the departmental correspondence with continental European nations dealt with a series of import restrictions they had levied against American pork.

The president and his secretary of state played a direct role in all decision-making, so the American posture at any given moment frequently reflected the character of these individuals. Seldom has a secretary's personality had a greater impact on the style of American foreign policy than did that of James G. Blaine. Although he was impressive beneath a full, graying beard and head of hair, Blaine's face seemed somewhat blank, with the exception of his heavy-lidded, canny eyes. His oratorical skill had won him popular acclaim; his phenomenal memory for names and faces made many an undistinguished citizen consider him a personal friend. Indeed, few public men could rally such an army of dedicated admirers—and few stirred such venomous attacks from his personal and political enemies. Blaine was a very private man, secretive to a degree unusual for the age. He scrupulously pursued the policy his notorious correspondence had advocated: "Burn this letter!" A man of wide acquaintance, with countless business associations, he must have kept his fireplace going full blast because so very few of his personal papers survived him.

Representing the state of Maine, Republican Blaine played one faction off against another to claw his way up to the position of Speaker of the United States House of Representatives in the tumultuous 1870s. Then, just as serious questions arose about his political integrity, he moved over to the relative security of the Senate. Considered solid presidential timber in every election from 1876 on, Blaine finally won the Republican nomination in 1884, only to lose to Grover Cleveland by a narrow margin. Blaine possessed an extraordinary talent for spotting and emphasizing popular issues. An outspoken critic of Great Britain, his Anglophobia won him dividends from Irish- and German-American voters. He created the role William McKinley would star in a decade later, that of an uncompromising advocate of protective tariffs. While in the Senate in the late 1870s, he spoke out strongly in favor of federal action to revive the decrepit merchant marine. Having clearly perceived a relationship between exports and national prosperity, he stridently advocated trade expansion.[5]

He was just beginning to take full command at the State Department when the tragic assassination of his friend in the White House threw his own public career off course. Blaine well knew he could not remain in the cabinet for long; he and the new president, Chester A. Arthur, were leading members of opposing factions within the Republican party. Nevertheless, he clung to his position even after Arthur had chosen a successor, in order to ram through his plans and to tie the Arthur administration to his policies. Furthermore, Blaine hoped to make his few months at the State Department so impressive that voters would flock to his banner in the upcoming 1884 presidential race.

The fate of Blaine's foreign policy initiatives lay with those who took charge in late 1881. Chester Arthur had never seriously entertained presidential ambitions prior to his politically-inspired nomination to the vice-presidency in 1880. Like everyone else who has unexpectedly been catapulted into the White House, Arthur developed an intense desire to win the presidency in his own right. Like Blaine, he hoped to build a foreign policy record on which to run in 1884. To implement his policies he chose Frederick T. Frelinghuysen of New Jersey as his secretary of state. Frelinghuysen was a rather colorless, straight party-line politician with absolutely no prior experience relevant to the responsibilities he assumed at the State Department. As neither he nor Arthur intended to share credit with Blaine for any diplomatic triumphs he (Blaine) might have engineered, the new administration devoted its early efforts to sabotaging any initiatives associated with the man from Maine. So enthusiastically did he pursue his anti-Blaine purge that Frelinghuysen had little time left to get his own program into operation before Arthur lost the Republican nomination in the summer of 1884. Piqued when the convention chose Blaine, his bitter rival, Arthur and his secretary of state engaged in the same sort of last-minute grandstanding Blaine had done in order to leave behind a record of dynamism in diplomacy.

[5]David M. Pletcher, *The Awkward Years* (Columbia: University of Missouri Press, 1962), p. 18.

Actually, Frelinghuysen and Arthur should have let Blaine's record stand, as he had frequently acted as his own worst enemy through his bungled administration of his foreign policies.

After he had left office, Blaine publicly ticked off his foreign policy goals as, "First, to bring about peace, and prevent future wars in North and South America; second, to cultivate such friendly commercial relations with all American countries as would lead to a large increase in the export trade of the United States."[6] Blaine's commitment to United States trade domination of Latin America dovetailed with his hatred of Great Britain, America's chief commercial competitor, as well as his desire to increase the international prestige of the United States. Even before Blaine had entered the State Department he had developed an interest in expanding American trade to the south. Thus he had already turned away from strict protectionism to advocacy of the more flexible and sensible plan of promoting reciprocal trade agreements. Reciprocity would encourage trade with Latin America while simultaneously protecting it from European (British) competition.

Ironically, Blaine's most spectacular failure in his first tour as secretary of state occurred in Latin America, the very area he had intended to impress with his skill and finesse. The War of the Pacific provided him with the opportunity to fall flat on his face. The war had begun in 1879 as the result of a border dispute involving Chile, Peru, and Bolivia. Bolivia quickly dropped out of the ensuing fight which Chile exploited as a showcase for its racy new naval vessels and superior military organization. The disputed boundaries lay in a desert region that all three countries had considered totally worthless until the discovery that it was tremendously rich in nitrates. Intending to make the most of this valuable natural resource, Chile sent its armed forces smashing into southern Peru and then demanded Peruvian recognition of the Chilean territorial conquest. Until Blaine took charge, all Secretary of State Evarts had done was to express American willingness to mediate among the three South American governments. Not one of them took up this offer.[7]

Why was Blaine so eager to get the United States involved? After he had left office, Blaine made the far-fetched claim that the War of the Pacific was actually a British war, with England using Chile to ruin Peru. As he favored any and every United States move against Brit-

[6]Ibid., pp. 77–78.

[7]U.S., Congress, Senate, *Affairs in Chili, Peru, and Bolivia, Papers Relating to the War in South America and Attempts to Bring about a Peace,* 47th Cong., 1st sess. (1882), Ex. Doc. No. 79, p. 107. Cited hereafter as *Affairs in Chili, etc.*

ain, Blaine claimed that he had hoped to prevent or at least limit the English intervention—a policy that might ultimately reduce the large financial and trade operations England conducted on the west coast of South America to the detriment of North American interests.[8] Blaine eventually had to testify before a Democratic-controlled House committee investigating allegations that his actions had been influenced by American businessmen who hoped to gain control of the nitrate bonanza if Peru won back her lands. The investigation proved inconclusive. All of this obscured the fundamental reason for Blaine's interest. While still secretary of state, Blaine had resolutely rejected a French government proposal for joint American, British, and French mediation, claiming that "the interests, commercial and political of the United States, on this continent, transcend in extent and importance those of any other power, and where these immense interests are deeply involved this government must preserve a position where its influence will be most independent and efficient."[9] Here the pugnacious secretary of state put forth a strongly-worded unilateral American declaration designed to assert United States supremacy in the Western Hemisphere. Blaine's words had the effect of implicitly extending American political influence by putting Europe on notice that his nation intended to take the lead in preventing outside interference in South American affairs. In addition, he sincerely did want peace in Latin America, because peaceful nations would be more valuable arenas for American commercial expansion.

Though his goals reflected traditional American impulses, Blaine proved extraordinarily inept at carrying them forward. A dedicated spoilsman, Blaine had insisted upon immediately recalling Evarts's inferior diplomatic representatives in Santiago and Lima. Unfortunately, his own choices, Generals Hugh Judson Kilpatrick and Stephen A. Hurlbut were even worse. Shortly after his arrival in Santiago, Minister Kilpatrick became gravely ill, leaving the control of United States affairs in Chile to his Chilean wife and her friends. Minister Hurlbut's health held up better, but his blunt, impulsive personality and his desire to make money out of his foreign appointment won few friends in Peru. Meanwhile, Blaine had concluded that Chile was unfairly obstructing peace by its refusal to relinquish the territories it had won on the battlefield. Having conveniently forgotten his own country's history of expansion, he self-righteously wrote Kilpatrick that "territorial changes should be avoided as far as possi-

---

[8]Pletcher, *The Awkward Years*, p. 42.
[9]*Affairs in Chili, etc.*, p. 598.

ble; . . . they should never be the result of mere force."[10] But, being a
realist, he simultaneously advised Peru that "the United States cannot
refuse to recognize the rights which the Chilian Government has acquired by the successes of the war, and it may be that a cession of
territory will be the necessary price to be paid for peace."[11] Neither of
the ministers paid any attention to Blaine's carefully framed instructions. The secretary of state was acutely embarrassed when the
impetuous Hurlbut concluded an agreement with the beleaguered
Peruvian government granting to the United States a naval coaling
station at Chimbote in return for support against Chile. While Blaine
personally had few reservations about American expansion, he could
clearly discern the impropriety of American diplomats negotiating for
a territorial enclave in Peru while simultaneously criticizing Chile for
refusing to relinquish the territory it had won in the war. The whole
affair hardly squared with Blaine's stated purpose of having the
United States act as a benevolent neutral concerned only with the best
interests of the belligerents. He speedily reprimanded Hurlbut.[12]

Unable to pursue a rational policy with the overzealous Hurlbut
and the dying Kilpatrick, on 1 December 1881 Blaine sent William
Henry Trescot and his son, Walker Blaine, on a special mission to the
two South American republics. He told Trescot to warn Chile that
unless it acquiesced to United States mediation, Blaine would issue a
call to other American nations to join the United States in forcing
peace upon the warring parties. A few days later Blaine resigned. The
new secretary of state, Frelinghuysen, immediately canceled this implied war threat by sending a message to Trescot, telling him to drop
any suggestion of enforced United States mediation. When the Senate
requested all communications relating to American peace efforts,
Frelinghuysen sent copies of his own notes and all of Blaine's correspondence to Congress, which published them. The Chilean minister
in Washington then relayed them to Santiago. Because his journey
had cut him off from contact with his own government, Trescot first
learned from the very Chilean officials whom he had come to con-
front that Frelinghuysen had torpedoed his mission.[13]

[10]Ibid., pp. 158–59.
[11]Ibid., p. 501.
[12]Ibid., pp. 577–79; Pletcher, *The Awkward Years*, p. 49; Frederick B. Pike, *Chile
and the United States 1880–1962* (Notre Dame, Ind.: University of Notre Dame Press,
1963), p. 56.
[13]*Affairs in Chili, etc.*, p. 187; Herbert Millington, *American Diplomacy and the War of
the Pacific* (New York: Columbia University Press, 1948), p. 122; David Saville Muzzey,
James G. Blaine (New York: Dodd, Mead, 1934), pp. 214–15.

By 1883, Frelinghuysen had scrupulously abandoned all United States efforts to prevent Chile's conquest of the nitrate lands. Blaine's widely publicized plan to bully Chile into mediation did little but strengthen an already prevalent anti-United States attitude throughout Latin America. If Blaine had dispatched responsible, unselfish diplomatic representatives to the warring nations, he might well have hammered out a more reasonable settlement than that to which Frelinghuysen acquiesced. Instead, the War of the Pacific fiasco fatally undermined Blaine's ambitious schemes to bring North and South America closer together.

Blaine hoped to bring about a commercial and cultural marriage between the north and south. He intended to court the favor of his southern neighbors at a Pan-American conference. Blaine insisted that the United States would behave as an equal in such a conference and never attempt to foist its own wishes on the conferees. Yet he never doubted that the United States would be the first among equals in any Pan-American endeavor. Critics promptly labeled his proposed conference as a selfish plan to increase American trade and impose United States political control over the area, but the invitations Blaine issued on 29 November 1881 claimed that the meeting's "sole aim shall be to seek a way of permanently averting the horrors of cruel and bloody combat between countries, oftenest of one blood and speech, or the even worse calamity of internal commotion and civil strife."[14] Of course, a peaceful, prosperous Latin America would obviously offer increased trade opportunities for the United States. Despite widespread public interest, Blaine's successor robbed him of credit for devising such a conference by canceling the invitations.

Blaine thus had little to show for his drive for American unity. On a more limited scale, he favored a proposal to form a union out of the five poor and chronically unstable Central American republics. Writing of the proposed union, Blaine cogently expressed his whole Latin American policy:

> Precluded both by sentiment and interest from the indulgence of any desire for increased territory and anxious to open to its commerce beneficial interchange with foreign products, and to give to such commercial relations the freest extension; taking a profound interest and a just pride in the system of republican government which its own example had introduced and encouraged on the American continent, the Government of the United States would do all in its power to foster

[14]Richardson, *Messages and Papers*, 6:4685.

the growth of stable and strong institutions in its sister republics of the South.[15]

In this brief statement, Blaine alluded specifically to two of the United States' traditional foreign policy themes, economic expansion and the democratic mission. His equally virulent desire to expand American political interests in the Western hemisphere is evident in his outburst over French efforts to cut a canal through the Isthmus of Panama.

Blaine was hardly the first American statesman to express an interest in encouraging and protecting travel and communication across the land connection between North and South America. In fact three historical documents figured prominently in his assertions of United States concern. The first was the Monroe Doctrine. Next came an 1846 treaty with New Granada (later Colombia), involving a United States guarantee to keep the trade route across Panama open. Meanwhile, the potential canal route through southern Nicaragua had attracted the attention of both the United States and Great Britain. In 1850, after each had striven to seize or control strategic advantages over the other, the two nations agreed in the Clayton-Bulwer Treaty that neither would begin work on a canal without consulting the other. This controversial treaty also prohibited the fortification of any canal that might be built as well as an agreement that neither nation would expand its territorial holdings in the isthmus. Both the 1846 and 1850 treaties were designed primarily to clear the air as the digging of an isthmian canal was beyond the technological competence of any nation at that time. With the passage of three decades, at least one man felt the time had come to tackle the job.[16]

Having won international acclaim for his construction of the Suez Canal, Ferdinand de Lesseps found it easy to raise capital in France to finance work on a Panamanian canal beginning in 1878. Those workers who survived the tropical living conditions and deadly diseases found that the project overtaxed their technical and financial capabilities, but the Panama Canal Company stubbornly refused to abandon its project until well into the 1880s. President Hayes re-

[15]U.S., Department of State, *Papers Relating to the Foreign Relations of the United States* (Washington, D.C.: Government Printing Office, 1889), p. 102. Cited hereafter as *Foreign Relations.*

[16]Pletcher, *The Awkward Years,* p. 26; U.S., Congress, Senate, *Compilation of Reports of the Committee on Foreign Relations, 1789–1901,* 56th Cong., 2d. sess. (1901), Ex. Doc. No. 231, 8 parts (volumes), 4:109; Dexter Perkins, *The Monroe Doctrine 1867–1907* (Baltimore: Johns Hopkins University Press, 1937), pp. 66–67; Alice Felt Tyler, *The Foreign Policy of James G. Blaine* (Minneapolis: University of Minnesota Press, 1927), p. 27.

sponded to this threat to United States hemispheric supremacy by hastily entering into negotiations with Nicaragua for an alternative route, and publicly claiming: "Our merely commercial interest in [the canal] is greater than that of all other countries, while its relation to our power and prosperity as a nation, to our means of defense, our unity, peace and safety, are of paramount concern to the people of the United States."[17] Each succeeding president made equally unequivocal proclamations about American rights and interests in a canal.

Predictably, the State Department exploded when that zealous champion of American supremacy, James G. Blaine, heard rumors that an alliance of European governments would be formed to guarantee the neutrality of the canal and protect it from outside interference. Disregarding de Lesseps's insistence that his was a purely private business operation, Blaine reacted patriotically to these unfounded rumors.[18] The circular letter he fired off to all the European capitals on 24 June 1881 was a brassy assertion of America's growing political influence. It alluded to the tremendous growth of the western states of the Union, insisting that they needed a canal in order to ship the enormous agricultural surplusses they produced. Blaine also noted that the 1846 treaty with Colombia had guaranteed to the United States "'positively and efficaciously' the perfect neutrality of the isthmus and of any interoceanic communications that might be constructed upon or over it for the maintenance of free transit from sea to sea; . . ."[19] Finally, he implicitly brought in the Monroe Doctrine, saying that "it is the long-settled conviction of this government that any extension to our shores of the political system by which the great powers have controlled and determined events in Europe would be attended with danger to the peace and welfare of this nation."[20]

Most European nations disdainfully ignored Blaine's nationalistic fulminations, but Great Britain took pains to indicate its total disagreement. The British response on 11 November lectured Blaine on the American responsibilities inherent in the Clayton-Bulwer Treaty. Blaine retaliated with a long, abrasive note in which he once again referred to the developments on the American west coast and dismissed British interest in a canal as "inconsiderable" in comparison with those of the United States. Then Blaine ripped into the Clayton-

---

[17]Dexter Perkins, *The United States and the Caribbean*, rev. ed. (Cambridge, Mass.: Harvard University Press, 1966), p. 100.

[18]*Foreign Relations* (1881), pp. 356–57, 441, 885.

[19]Ibid., p. 537.

[20]Ibid., p. 540.

Bulwer Treaty's prohibition against American fortification of any isthmian canal built. After pointedly alluding to the awesome military strength the United States had exhibited during the Civil War, he admitted that his nation would never need a huge navy like that of Britain. Blaine considered it only fair, however, that America build land fortifications along the canal. The canal would then be in safe hands, Blaine insisted, because the United States had no involvement whatever in European power struggles and was therefore less likely than any other great power to become involved in a war. He concluded his peroration by calling upon Great Britain to agree to remove the Clayton-Bulwer Treaty's prohibition against fortifications, while leaving untouched its provisions denying either nation the right to acquire territory in Central America.[21]

In response to Blaine's self-righteous assertions, the *London Times* admitted on 17 December 1881 that the United States was certainly the major power in the Western Hemisphere and predicted that it would eventually absorb much of North America. The general English reaction was much less charitable. The British government had no intention of writing off as inconsequential its extensive territorial holdings in North America nor of recognizing the United States as a great power. In his official reply, outraged Foreign Minister Lord Granville insisted that the British Dominion of Canada certainly had as great an interest as California and Oregon in the building of a canal.[22] He also firmly defended the Clayton-Bulwer Treaty. Far from agreeing to weaken its provisions, he insisted that an international conference be called, as Hamilton Fish had suggested in 1877, so that all of the maritime nations could "participate in an agreement based on the stipulations of the convention of 1850."[23]

Blaine's chauvinism was catching because it galvanized the normally reticent Frelinghuysen into a strident defense of American honor. He continued to send off presumptuous notes to the British foreign office well into 1883, reiterating America's assertion that it had the preeminent commercial and defense interests in the proposed canal. North America had changed dramatically since the ratification of the Clayton-Bulwer Treaty; the document was not "responsive" to existing conditions. After all, Frelinghuysen charged, the British themselves had already subverted the treaty by extending their power in Central America. The secretary of state threatened

[21]Ibid., pp. 554–58.
[22]Ibid., p. 549; *Foreign Relations* (1882), p. 303; Pletcher, *The Awkward Years*, p. 67.
[23]*Foreign Relations* (1882), p. 304.

that he would consider any attempt to create a European protectorate over the canal as a violation of the Monroe Doctrine's insulation of the Western Hemisphere from outside encroachment. If Britain disregarded Monroe's dictums, the United States could justifiably abandon the doctrine's principle of American noninterference in European affairs. And, Frelinghuysen noted ominously, "no well-informed statesman doubts the ability of this nation to raise a powerful navy."[24] Understandably, the British showed no dread of a potential American navy. Granville summarily dismissed the Monroe Doctrine arguments as being neither applicable (a sentiment many Americans then and more recently have shared) nor as having any international standing. Frelinghuysen's final petulant salvos were equally ineffective, and the exchange petered out, having had no effect whatsoever on either the Clayton-Bulwer Treaty or the nonexistent canal. The whole affair is illustrative, however, of the European attitude toward any United States assertions of its increasing political prominence in the 1880s.[25]

Because the British had refused to take up the gauntlet Blaine had so dramatically flung down, Arthur and Frelinghuysen took more direct action on the canal issue. Throughout the year 1884 Frelinghuysen saw to the negotiation of a treaty with Nicaragua which assigned control of a five-mile-wide canal zone to the United States. Such a provision would clearly violate the Clayton-Bulwer Treaty's prohibition against territorial aggrandizement in Central America. Nevertheless, when President Arthur submitted the completed treaty to the Senate for approval, he noted: "The negotiation of this treaty was entered upon under a conviction that it was imperatively demanded by the present and future political and material interests of the United States."[26] The senators were not so sure, and their debates raised as many questions as they answered. Heated discussions over alternative routes, financial schemes, and political arrangements for the proposed isthmian canal would persist until long after American steam shovels had begun digging in Panama in 1904. Few complained, therefore, when Arthur's successor, Democratic President Grover Cleveland, simply recalled the Frelinghuysen-Zavala Treaty from the Senate in 1885 and never again presented it for approval.

A similar Draconian fate befell the Arthur administration's other diplomatic initiatives. Believing in the glut theory, Arthur had hoped to resolve the nation's economic sluggishness by encouraging arbitra-

[24]Ibid., pp. 272–82.
[25]*Foreign Relations* (1883), pp. 421, 477, 490.
[26]Richardson, *Messages and Papers*, 7:4893.

tion and reciprocity with Latin America in order to increase trade. Consequently, he had the State Department set about negotiating reciprocal trade agreements. In such an arrangement, one nation would lower its customs duties on specific items imported from another nation in return for special privileges for its own merchants. Thus, the United States might reduce or eliminate its import taxes on coffee, sugar, or other exotic products, while a tropical nation would provide similar reductions in its taxes on steel, wheat, or any other commodity the United States had to export. Best of all, reciprocity would give United States exporters access to Latin American markets on a favorable basis while leaving intact the domestically popular high protective tariff rates. Indeed, the higher the listed rates were, the more bargaining room the secretary of state had in negotiating reciprocal trade agreements. Frelinghuysen successfully concluded reciprocity treaties with Spain (to gain access to her colonies of Cuba and Puerto Rico) and the Dominican Republic, but his term of office elapsed before he could complete his arrangements with El Salvador, Colombia, and Great Britain (to gain access to the British West Indies). It did not matter. Cleveland withdrew from the Senate the Spanish and Dominican reciprocity treaties along with the one for a Nicaraguan canal zone, preferring to work out his own tariff policy.[27]

Despite his efforts to place his own stamp on his foreign policies, Arthur's actions differed significantly from Blaine's in only one realm. In 1883 he expressed interest in the commercial development of the central region of Africa under the leadership of King Leopold of Belgium. The president warned his countrymen that they could not remain indifferent to the work of Leopold's International Association of the Congo, ostensibly dedicated to keeping the area politically neutral and open to free trade. The American minister to Germany, John A. Kasson, had triggered this presidential interest, which he hoped to exploit in order to increase American prestige abroad. When a conference on the Congo convened in Berlin in late 1884, Kasson convinced Frelinghuysen to let him attend as the American delegate with a virtually free hand. The American representative alluded to the American sense of mission as he spoke in favor of measures that would preserve to the native Africans their hereditary rights. When the conference agreed upon an "open door" commercial arrangement granting all nations' merchants equal trading rights in the Congo River Basin, Kasson and his superiors in Washington were quite pleased. Consequently, the American representative unhesitat-

[27]Pletcher, *The Awkward Years*, pp. 177–80, 284–333.

ingly signed the general act of the conference on 25 February 1885, recognizing King Leopold's association as the Congo Free State.[28] When news of the agreement reached this side of the Atlantic critics expressed concern that it might commit the United States to assist in policing the enforcement of its terms. This particular issue never needed to be resolved because President Cleveland's assumption of office a short time later insured that the United States would never ratify the general act. As the European powers did not yet recognize the United States as an important power, the lack of American ratification was of no consequence in world affairs.

Like rivers running into a desert, most Republican foreign policy initiatives seemed to dry up once they encountered the unsympathetic Cleveland. Bluff, truculent, ponderous, and deliberative, the Democratic president perceived himself a rock of rectitude and responsibility. "Public office is a public trust," Cleveland declared, and he had no intention of handling this trust casually or recklessly. No Blaineite fireworks would add brilliance to his policies; no hasty, ill-conceived proposals would be forthcoming. His lack of aggressiveness gave the American people a breather before they were to be plunged into more adventurous times. The man Cleveland chose to handle foreign affairs shared his moderate views.

Thomas Francis Bayard served as secretary of state throughout Cleveland's first term, 1885 to 1889, and as the United States' first ambassador to England, 1893 to 1897. Of all the American diplomats one encounters in the late nineteenth century, Bayard left behind the most complete record. He kept everything. In addition to official correspondence, his letter books contain a vast number of personal letters which enable one to gain an intimate acquaintanceship with this member of a Delaware political dynasty. A life-long Democrat, Bayard had barely missed becoming a presidential candidate on several occasions. Some refused to forget his forgiving attitude toward his southern neighbors as they stormed out of the Union in 1861. Basically, however, his Delaware constituency was far too small to matter in the tally of electoral votes. Bayard's modesty matched the unpretentiousness of his home state, and he never overcame a degree of small-mindedness. A dependable politician, he handled the multitude of patronage problems he encountered with the same concern

---

[28]Ibid., pp. 315–20; Richardson, *Messages and Papers*, 7:4763; U.S., Congress, Senate, *Independent State of the Congo*, 49th Cong., 1st sess. (1886), Ex. Doc. No. 196, p. 15; Edward Younger, *John A. Kasson* (Iowa City: University of Iowa Press, 1955), p. 333.

and thoroughness he devoted to his governmental responsibilities. Criticism angered and saddened him; he once whimsically asked a friend to find him "some respectable occupation in which the 'half-pennies' are more abundant, and the kicks less plenty than in the Secretaryship of State."[29]

Like Cleveland, Bayard detested the thought of American imperialism. Firmly committed to the American democratic mission, any form of colonial injustice distressed him. After reading a friend's description of the Caribbean colony of British Guiana, Bayard responded emotionally: "What a picture you draw of the results of governing colonies from a distance—by which all faculty of self-government is deprived of the exercise by which alone it can be kept alive or developed and the distant ruler can neither know nor care for the real wants or sufferings of the people."[30] Furthermore, Bayard disapproved of attempted compulsion by any great power, including the United States. He acted on his sentiments in 1888 by criticizing the American minister to Haiti for his frequent requests for the dispatch of American war vessels to Haiti's troubled waters.[31]

Though their conservative attitudes did not cause them to seek confrontations, both Cleveland and Bayard defended any of America's traditional foreign policy objectives which seemed threatened. Here, Great Britain was the perennial antagonist. The Cleveland administration worked hard to regain the American fishing rights in Canadian waters that Congress had thoughtlessly abrogated early in the decade. When the Republican-controlled Senate stubbornly refused to approve the treaty Bayard had hammered out with Britain, President Cleveland retaliated with proposed economic sanctions against Canada that were so severe that all sides gratefully agreed to the modus vivendi Bayard worked out with the Canadian government which kept American fishermen at sea. Although the fishing rights controversy had little popular appeal outside of New England, Bayard took pride in his success in defending American desires and honor on this issue.

The restrained policymakers in the first Cleveland administration benefitted from the United States' still minor position in international relations which allowed them largely to ignore external developments, and it produced an undistinguished, unsurprising, and uncluttered foreign policy record. In particular, these conservative

---

[29]Bayard to Schurz, 3 March 1888, Papers of Thomas F. Bayard, LCMD.
[30]Bayard to Wells, 18 April 1887, Bayard Papers, LCMD.
[31]*Foreign Relations* (1888), p. 900.

statesmen seemed content to ignore the hemispheric ambitions both Blaine and Arthur had pursued. Except for the relatively minor complications with regard to Hawaii, to be dealt with separately in the following chapter, only the Samoan question gave Cleveland and Bayard real trouble. On that issue, however, the Democrats resolutely responded in line with America's traditional foreign policy themes. Thus, when Cleveland became convinced that Germany intended to eliminate United States influence in Samoa in the mid-1880s, he acted stubbornly and zealously. The Samoan situation represented the first substantial test of the United States commitment to the expansion of its commercial, political, and moral influence as an emerging great power.

The Samoan Islands lie some 2,700 miles to the southwest of Hawaii, a location which had made them important stopover points for ships sailing around Cape Horn on their way to China and Japan. In addition, their tropical products attracted American, German, and British settlement and investment. The Samoan Islands were in fact in the fringe area where United States and European commercial interests overlapped. Therefore, an early indication of how the United States would respond when its expansion directly conflicted with that of powerful European nations occurred in Samoa. Had the United States been as ready for colonial expansion in 1880 as it would be twenty years later, American policy might well have been clear-cut and bold. Instead it developed tentatively and awkwardly.

The American government's interest in the islands had begun stirring as early as the Grant administration. Although his work was never ratified, Commander Richard W. Meade of the United States Navy had worked out a trade treaty with the local ruler in 1872. A key provision of the treaty was a cession of exclusive rights for the United States in the superb harbor at Pago Pago on the island of Tutuila. President Grant was also responsible for the dispatch of Colonel A. B. Steinberger as a special agent to Samoa. By the mid-1870s, Steinberger had become deeply involved in native politics, at one point serving as the king's prime minister. His disruptive influence among the natives discredited his enthusiastic calls for American annexation of the islands. Eventually the American and British consuls arranged for the commander of a British naval vessel to deport him.[32]

---

[32]Muzzey, *Blaine*, p. 396; Tansill, *Thomas F. Bayard*, pp. 13–14; Paul M. Kennedy, *The Samoan Tangle: A Study in Anglo-German-American Relations* (Dublin: Irish University Press, 1974), p. 9; George Herbert Ryden, *The Foreign Policy of the United States in Relation to Samoa* (New Haven, Conn.: Yale University Press, 1933), p. 72.

Fearing British or German encroachments, the weak native government in Samoa appealed several times to the United States for protection. The most President Hayes's administration would consider was a revival, in 1878, of the commercial treaty with its grant to the United States of a right to maintain a naval base at Pago Pago. Though it fell short of the protectorate they had sought, the Samoans were most pleased with Article V of the 1878 treaty which promised that the United States would employ its good offices to assist the Samoan government if it encountered difficulties with another foreign power. Following Senate approval, the American consul, Thomas M. Dawson, felt a certain sense of responsibility to protect native rights. He therefore instigated discussions with the British and German consuls at Apia. The three officials eventually drew up a "municipal convention" on 2 September 1879, providing for formal consulations among the three nations' representatives whenever any problems arose. This consultive agreement helped preserve relative tranquility for the next few years. President Hayes never requested Senate approval for the agreement, certain it would encounter serious opposition on the basis that it represented an entangling alliance with European powers. But, informally at least, the United States had expanded its political influence far out into the Pacific, where its representative was being treated as an equal by those of two major European nations.[33]

The Samoan consultative arrangements fell victim to an epidemic of imperialism that soon began sweeping Germany in so virulent a form that Chancellor Otto von Bismarck reluctantly agreed to seek colonial dominions. Germany's 1884 decision to enter the imperialist race created an abiding fear in the United States of German advances in its own neighborhood. Samoa represented the first focus for a paranoia that would persist well into the twentieth century. German settlers were more numerous and wealthier than the citizens of any other foreign nation residing in Samoa, so the German government naturally considered taking complete control of the island group. A master of personal diplomacy, Bismarck coerced the British government into defining a separation of British and German colonial zones in the Pacific. Then the Germans could attempt to consolidate their control of Samoa—with implicit British support. The United States found itself friendless and threatened with expulsion. Secretary of

[33]Kennedy, *Samoan Tangle*, pp. 21–25; Richardson, *Messages and Papers*, 6:4563; Ryden, *Foreign Policy*, pp. 193–201, 234–35.

State Bayard stoutly denied Germany the right to any additional or exclusive political influence in the islands.[34]

The United States possessed limited political leverage in Europe, and, recognizing his weak bargaining position, Bayard fell back upon the democratic mission sentiment, telling his consul at Apia, Berthold Greenebaum, that "the moral interest of the United States with respect to the islands of the Pacific . . . would counsel us to look with concern on any movement by which the independence of those Pacific nationalities might be extinguished by their passage under the domination of a foreign sovereign."[35] Greenebaum responded with considerably more zeal than Bayard had intended the following year when he raised the American flag and announced that the United States was establishing a protectorate over the islands. Bayard hastily reprimanded his over-enthusiastic consul, who unrepentently insisted he had only been acting in response to a Samoan request based on Article V of the 1878 treaty.

The German strategy was to stir up discontent among various native factions, hoping to use the resulting instability to broaden its own control. Unimpressed with America's mission impulse, the Germans ruthlessly ignored Bayard's criticism of their interference with native self-rule. Frustrated by the American secretary of state's apparent refusal to do more than issue rhetorical objections, the Samoans desperately toyed with the idea of allying with the Kingdom of Hawaii. Such a union of weaklings could only spread the problem throughout the Pacific, so Bayard finally called for representatives of the three foreign powers to confer in Washington, D.C., in the summer of 1887. The conferees immediately found themselves at loggerheads. The Germans wanted approval for a mandate which would give a single nation (Germany) control of the islands; Bayard favored a strengthening of the Samoan government by providing it with foreign advisers, a plan which would probably operate much like the discarded tripartite consultative arrangement. The conference expired without resolution.[36]

To Bayard's dismay, the United States had become enmeshed in a sticky international crisis. Some American officials were becoming insistent about the need to protect their nation's commercial and political influence abroad. Alvey Adee gathered these sentiments to-

[34]Kennedy, *Samoan Tangle*, pp. 43–50; Ryden, *Foreign Policy*, pp. 277–78; Tansill, *Thomas F. Bayard*, pp. 22–24; *Foreign Relations* (1883), p. 354.

[35]Tansill, *Thomas F. Bayard*, p. 27.

[36]Kennedy, *Samoan Tangle*, pp. 64–66; Ryden, *Foreign Policy*, pp. 346–47, 365.

gether in a note to Bayard which outlined why he considered a continuing American presence in Samoa crucial, including a contention that a German takeover would pose a threat to the United States' west coast.[37] Bayard himself cared little about commercial and strategic interests, imbued as he was with an altruistic desire to bring an end to all foreign interference with the local government. As he wrote early in 1888:

> But, for the reason that the native Government is weak, it has seemed all the more clear to the United States that the control of the islands by any strong foreign power, or its representatives, would defeat the great object of securing native independence and autonomy, and the practical neutralization of the group.[38]

Bayard self-righteously told Germany and Britain that the United States could, much earlier, have made an American protectorate out of the islands, because the Samoan people had requested such action on several occasions. Yet he insisted that they should remain independent, self-governing, and neutral.

In the wake of the inconclusive 1887 conference, the three great powers continued to pursue their dissimilar and contradictory policies unilaterally. The energetic Germans deported Samoan King Malietoa, whose election all three powers had recognized in 1881, and tried to replace him with their own puppet, Mataafa, in an effort to gain complete control of the native government. Meanwhile, Bayard fretted about the prospect of a naval confrontation because he was well aware that the United States Navy in 1889 was hardly capable of defending itself, much less the country. Despairingly, he notified Cleveland on 5 January 1889 that if the Germans decided to annex or form a protectorate out of Samoa, the United States could do little but request that Bismarck's government respect American treaty rights in the islands.[39]

President Cleveland decisively overruled his intimidated foreign policy adviser. With the encouragement of Navy Secretary William C. Whitney and Assistant Secretary of State George L. Rives, Cleveland sought support from Congress, which possessed the option of declaring war. As a lame-duck president in January 1889, Cleveland was acting from a mixture of motives, among them a desire to avoid bequeathing an ongoing war to the incoming Harrison administra-

---

[37]Tansill, *Thomas F. Bayard*, p. 27.
[38]*Foreign Relations* (1888), pp. 607–8.
[39]Bayard to Cleveland, 21 January 1889, Bayard Papers, LCMD; Kennedy, *Samoan Tangle*, pp. 68–69; Tansill, *Thomas F. Bayard*, pp. 96–102.

tion. Cleveland used the mission impulse to justify the thrust of his policy:

> Acting within the restraints which our Constitution and laws have placed upon Executive power, I have insisted that the autonomy and independence of Samoa should be scrupulously preserved according to the treaties made with Samoa by the powers named and their agreements and understandings with each other. In addition to my protests, during the existence of internal disturbance one or more vessels of war have been kept in Samoan waters to protect American citizens and property.[40]

Both the German and British navies had also sent ships to Samoan waters. Fortunately, an act of God interfered. A terrific tropical storm slammed through the area in March 1889, grounding or destroying all the German and American ships stationed at Samoa. The sailors worked so hard to rescue one another that any thought of conflict dissipated.

Cleveland's rhetorical blasts were no less effective in bringing about a diplomatic reassessment. Bismarck concluded that American friendship rated higher than German control of Samoa, so he called for a renewal of three-way discussions in Berlin. Bayard hoped for formal acceptance of his earlier proposal of tripartite control which would preserve the neutrality of the islands without weakening the American position. He could do little but hope, however, as James G. Blaine once again took control of the State Department on 4 March 1889. Although he was enthusiastic about the nearby Hawaiian Islands, Blaine personally considered Samoa too remote for protection by United States forces. Furthermore, as a star-spangled nationalist, he had a violent aversion to any scheme that would lock the United States into an agreement with either Germany or Great Britain. Blaine could dream up no reasonable alternative, however, so the three commissioners he sent to Berlin promoted the Bayard proposal.[41]

The veteran of the 1884 Congo Conference, John A. Kasson, once again represented the United States at an international conference in Berlin. Neither Bismarck nor the British representatives liked Bayard's tripartite scheme, but when the United States stubbornly refused to consider partitioning the islands or allowing any single power to predominate, they reluctantly acquiesced to the American proposal. The final act of the Berlin Conference called for the re-

[40]Richardson, *Messages and Papers*, 7:5390.
[41]Ryden, *Foreign Policy*, p. 426; Tyler, *Foreign Policy*, pp. 232–33; Younger, *John A. Kasson*, pp. 350–54.

enthronement of King Malietoa and a return to the status quo that had existed in the early 1880s. A formal, consultative alliance of the three great powers' representatives would guarantee the implementation and preservation of this arrangement. Although it represented a serious divergence from normal American foreign policy, the announcement of American participation in the tripartite governing scheme evoked little unfavorable comment at home.

Blaine never really warmed to the arrangement. He felt that neither the American commitments to so remote a group of islands nor the formal cooperation with Germany and Great Britain were wise, and he was hardly surprised when the so-called condominium agreement on Samoa proved to be a failure. The three nations seldom found common grounds for agreement. Even though the Germans did drop their unilateral drive to conquer the islands, the archipelago seethed with unrest for the next decade. But unworkable as it was, acceptance of the condominium was as far as the United States could go at the time. The international commitments strained American traditions nearly to the breaking point. The United States had forcefully maintained its negligible political influence in the islands; it had protected the minor American economic interests there; and it had incessantly championed the concept of self-government for the natives. But it was too soon for colonialism. Ten years had to pass and a wealth of changes had to occur before the United States would be ready to agree to the partition of the islands, enabling it to annex those with the greatest appeal.

When Republican President Benjamin Harrison called James G. Blaine out of retirement to head his cabinet in 1889, he insured a revival of more aggressive Latin American policies. To his great satisfaction, Blaine resumed control of the Department of State just in time for the opening of the Pan-American conference he had planned eight years earlier. The concept of a hemispheric conference had continued to grow more popular, so much so that even Democrats were calling for one. In 1888, therefore, the Cleveland administration had issued new invitations to a meeting scheduled to begin in the fall of 1889. Although these invitations suggested the discussion of such topics as how the American republics could institute arbitration agreements or increase their prosperity, the conference also had a decidedly commercial orientation. The conferees were to consider several specific trade measures, including the establishment of a customs union, uniform customs regulations, uniform weights and measures, copyright and trademark regulations, and a common silver coinage system.[42] The United States Department of State arranged for the visiting delegates to spend several weeks touring major American industrial centers in what turned out to be a vain hope that they would return home convinced of the United States' capability to provide all the imports their countries might desire. The conference had little perceptible effect on United States trade with Latin America, and it generally failed in other commercial areas as well. The American delegation was pleased in one area—the lack of action on a proposal Brazil and Argentina put forward to have the conference stipulate that no American nation could acquire territory from any other. The move was designed to embarrass both the United States for its Mexican cession and Chile for its more recent capture of southern Peru. The only permanent result of the conference was the Pan-American Union, headquartered in Washington, D.C., which subsequently worked to encourage trade and cultural exchanges among its member states. The conference did establish a precedent for amicable discussion that the Latin American governments found beneficial. Consequently, every few years, another conference would meet, having about as few tangible results as the first. Blaine's friendly gestures toward Latin America thus brought the United States no rewards from the southern republics either in the form of increased trade or political influence.

Never at a loss for stratagems, Blaine determined to pursue these goals on a bilateral basis. President Cleveland had stunned the nation in 1887 by devoting his entire annual message to arguments in favor of lowering the nation's high protective tariff rates. Republican Benjamin Harrison considered his presidential election victory over Cleveland the following year as a mandate not only to retain the existing protective system his party had fathered, but to adjust certain rates upward. William McKinley, a prominent Ohio Republican representative firmly committed to high protective rates, drafted a new tariff bill which the Fiftieth Congress approved in the spring of 1890. Blaine had made sure that the McKinley Tariff included authorization for the State Department to work out reciprocity arrangements with other countries. He spent the next couple of years superintending the negotiation of several reciprocal trade agreements. All his efforts went for naught, however, when Cleveland recaptured the presidency in 1892 and thereby discredited the entire Republican tariff position including reciprocity. United States–Latin American trade might have blossomed under Blaine's reciprocity program, but

---

[42]*Foreign Relations* (1888), p. 1658.

the concept failed to get a fair chance to prove its effectiveness until well into the next century.[43]

Blaine's interest in Latin America had never been wholly commercial; he also hoped to expand American political influence and prestige in that area. Starting with President Garfield in 1881, the nation's leaders had gradually assumed a bipartisan commitment to upgrade the United States Navy with at least a token fleet of modern, steel, steam-powered war vessels. When Blaine returned to Washington in 1889, the new vessels either completed or under construction had become a factor in foreign-policy planning. They might, for example, require overseas naval bases for coaling and refitting. When another of Haiti's frequent revolutions flared up in 1888 and 1889, Blaine exploited the instability by attempting to lease the harbor of the Mole St. Nicholas. Thwarted, he shifted his attention to the Dominican Republic's Samana Bay on the southeastern side of the island, but Dominican national pride prevented the signing of an agreement. In late 1891, the Peruvian government once again offered Blaine an opportunity to establish a naval station at Chimbote, this time in return for a large sum of money Peru needed to pay claims awarded to Chile. Blaine held out for a better price, but the offer was not repeated.[44]

Aside from a desire to establish bases, the United States Navy had begun to influence America's foreign policy in other ways. A serious confrontation with Chile in the early 1890s illustrated the danger of the naval element in diplomacy. Running true to form, Blaine had sent a thoroughly unsatisfactory minister named Patrick Egan to Chile in 1889. A naturalized Irish-American and a dedicated foe of the British, Egan proved to be an extremely inappropriate emissary to a nation with friendly ties and substantial trade with England. When a rebellion swept Chile in 1891, Blaine routinely advised Egan to ignore the rebels. As luck would have it, the dissident forces won a smashing victory shortly afterward, and several members of the ousted regime took refuge in the American legation. Egan resolutely held out against the new government's demands that he turn over those who had sought sanctuary. Both Blaine and President Harrison stoutly backed him up, badly straining relations between the two governments by the fall of 1891.[45]

[43]Tyler, *Foreign Policy*, pp. 185–89.

[44]Ibid., pp. 97–98; Albert T. Volwiler, ed., *The Correspondence Between Benjamin Harrison and James G. Blaine 1882–1893* (Philadelphia: American Philosophical Society, 1940), pp. 223, 227.

[45]*Foreign Relations* (1891), pp. 146–47, 159; Muzzey, *Blaine*, p. 415; Pike, *Chile and the United States*, p. 67.

A very dangerous practice which major governments typically followed in this period was to dispatch warships to the harbors of nations suffering from governmental instability. The ostensible purpose was to protect foreign citizens and interests from damage. Consequently, the United States had duly stationed the U.S.S. *Baltimore* at Valparaiso during the Chilean disturbances. On 16 October 1891 a Chilean mob attacked and beat some of the ship's sailors who had unwisely been granted shore leave. Two Americans were killed, another sixteen wounded. United States Navy Captain W. S. Schley conducted a hasty investigation which, not surprisingly, concluded that the attack had been completely unprovoked. Meanwhile, President Harrison convinced himself that the men's uniforms indicating their nationality had triggered the riot. Taking the attack as an insult to his nation, the enraged former general contemplated taking stern steps to avenge American honor.[46]

Secretary of State Blaine had become a tired old man, and he was greatly distressed at the prospect of seeing naval broadsides blast apart all his efforts to draw North and South America together. Apparently the only moderate in Harrison's cabinet, Blaine found his position severely undermined when Chile's unrepentant foreign minister, Manuel A. Matta, bombastically ordered his minister to the United States to uphold Chile's honor. Although the Chilean envoy exercised his own discretion and did not deliver Matta's volatile message to Blaine, the foreign minister was so proud of it that he publicly read it to the Chilean Senate. As war clouds gathered, Egan immediately suspended relations.[47] President Harrison sent a blistering note to Congress to the effect that the United States, as a great power, would not suffer ill-treatment lightly:

> It must, however, be understood that this Government, while exercising the utmost forbearance towards weaker powers, will extend its strong and adequate protection to its citizens, to its officers, and to its humblest sailor when made the victims of wantonness and cruelty in resentment, not of their personal misconduct, but of the official acts of their Government.[48]

Fortunately, Blaine's moderation won out. The Chilean government disavowed Matta's antagonistic statement, and Blaine negotiated

---

[46]U.S., Congress, House, *Relations with Chile*, 52d Cong., 1st sess. (1892), Ex. Doc. No. 91, pp. v–vi, ix–x. Cited hereafter as *Relations with Chile*.

[47]*Foreign Relations* (1891), p. 269; Muzzey, *Blaine*, pp. 419–20; Pike, *Chile and the United States*, p. 76.

[48]*Relations with Chile*, p. xiii.

a monetary compensation. The $75,000 that Chile provided for the relief of the victims of the attack and their survivors ended the *Baltimore* crisis, but it did little to heal the rift in the United States–Chilean relations. The incident did prove that Blaine had matured substantially in the decade since he had petulantly castigated the British government over the Clayton-Bulwer Treaty. But his was an outdated viewpoint; Harrison's stirring rhetoric caught the new spirit of the times. By the early 1890s the United States was flexing its muscles, intending to force others to recognize it as a great power. Had the United States actually stumbled into a war with Chile and won (an outcome by no means certain given the Chilean navy's experience and equipment), it clearly would have established American supremacy throughout the Western Hemisphere. Instead, that supremacy remained unproven until 1898.

3

The United States
Sidesteps an Empire, 1890–1896

On 27 April 1893, nearly twenty-eight years after the Union armies had paraded through Washington on their way home, a different sort of military review took place in New York Harbor. President Cleveland and his cabinet observed the assembled international fleet of warships from the deck of the rakish, half-sail, half-steam dispatch boat *Dolphin,* commissioned in 1884 as the first of the American navy's new generation of all-steel naval vessels. Ridiculed as a "junketing" boat by its critics, the *Dolphin* did seem more suited to service as a mobile reviewing stand than to war. Fortunately war was far from the minds of the onlookers who braved the drizzle for a glimpse of the review's thirty-four ships from nine nations, ranging from the 388-foot German protected cruiser, *Kaiserin Augusta,* down to the tiny wooden replicas of the *Pinta,* the *Nina,* and the *Santa Maria* Spain had built to honor the 400th anniversary of Columbus's discovery of America.

As the *Dolphin* glided by, each ship fired its cannons to salute the high office Grover Cleveland had resumed less than two months before. The review gave the president a momentary respite from the hoards of office seekers who had hounded him relentlessly since his election victory. But the naval display held dangers of its own. Cleveland was acutely aware that it might stimulate demand for additional naval construction to bring the American navy up to par with the grim warships riding the windswept, gray waters of the Hudson River. More ominous still was the thought that the nation's naval expansion would fire its expansionist desires; Cleveland had only just begun dealing with the Hawaiian annexation treaty, a measure of which he totally disapproved.

Hawaii, office seekers, and naval appropriations all loomed large in the spring of 1893, but as yet Cleveland had no inkling of two great calamities, one personal and one national, which were about to descend on him. He would not notice for another week or so the irritating lump in the roof of his mouth, a lump which grew so rapidly that by the end of June he had agreed to a major operation. In order to insure absolute secrecy, his advisers arranged for a medical team to perform the surgery aboard a private yacht. Thus, just two months after the naval review, Cleveland was once again afloat in New York Harbor, ostensibly for a pleasure cruise. The operation to remove the cancerous part of his upper jaw was short, successful, and left him outwardly little changed. Unfortunately, he could find no such quick and certain remedy for the financial panic and economic collapse that devastated the American economy in the fall of 1893.

Coming as it did after twenty years of grueling hard times, the depression that engulfed the nation from 1893 to 1897 seemed like an apocalyptic cataclysm. The glut theory's explanation for depressions attracted new armies of supporters. Populists, free-silver advocates, free-trade spokesmen, and manufacturers joined in criticizing the existing system for its failure to cope with persistent economic adversity. Significantly, all four groups believed that capturing foreign markets would lead to recovery. Populist farmers produced enormous surpluses that had to be disposed of abroad. Silverites claimed their program would increase exchange with the many foreign nations on the silver standard. Free traders had for years assailed high tariffs as restricting international trade. In 1895, a group of industrialists founded the National Association of Manufacturers to coordinate efforts designed to encourage the export of American manufactured goods. Historian Walter LaFeber argues that in the last decade of the nineteenth century the nation's traditional commitment to expansion changed its emphasis, away from landed settlement and in favor of commercial empire.[1]

Not everyone agreed just where a commercial empire should lie. Until well into the twentieth century, most American agricultural exports went directly to Great Britain and Germany. But, as the percentage of United States industrial exports climbed relative to agricultural shipments, the nation's trade patterns tended to swing away from Europe and toward nonindustrialized areas. Americans anticipated that new markets for both agricultural and industrial goods

---

[1] Walter LaFeber, *The New Empire: An Interpretation of American Expansion 1860–1898* (Ithaca, N.Y.: Cornell University Press, 1963), p. 69.

could be captured in the Far East and Latin America. Political philosophers like Brooks Adams and Alfred Thayer Mahan constantly emphasized the market potentialities of the vast, heavily-populated Chinese Empire. Many trade expansionists in the 1890s expressed an almost religious faith that the Far East would ultimately prove to be America's greatest market area. Another potential market area lay directly to the south. British manufacturers and merchants had Latin American trade sewed up, of course, but that fact only convinced advocates of increased trade that the United States would profit enormously if Americans could develop customers in this area.[2]

Proponents of trade expansion often favored political expansion as well. By the mid-1890s, a group of younger Republicans including Henry Cabot Lodge and Theodore Roosevelt had become vocal proponents of the "large policy," which called for the United States to enlarge its political and economic influence throughout the world. Carried to their logical conclusions, the arguments developed in conjunction with the large policy would justify outright colonization. Colonies, in turn, would provide protected markets for American traders, and American annexation of Hawaii in the Pacific or Cuba in the Caribbean would create stepping-stones to the anticipated great markets in the Far East and Latin America. Not incidentally, the large policy group felt colonial possessions would boost United States prestige worldwide.

An obvious way to encourage respect for American political and economic initiatives was through the development of effective armed forces. As one American bluntly put it, "We need to be armed as becomes a great Power."[3] The haphazard program of naval construction in the 1880s shifted gears when Congress finally approved the building of battleships in 1890. Navalism came into vogue in the 1890s with political, popular, and intellectual spokesmen all taking part in the debate over naval building strategies. Alfred Thayer Mahan began to gain a popularity in his own country commensurate with that which he had achieved overseas. Although it had not deliberately been planned that way, the 1893 Naval Review showed how far behind other nations the United States Navy was, and it did stimulate still more enthusiasm for ships.

This fascination with naval construction was symptomatic of a growing United States interest in foreign relations and opportunities

---

[2]Ibid., pp. 84–88, 186; Thomas J. McCormick, *China Market* (Chicago: Quadrangle, 1967), p. 53.

[3]Murat Halstead, "American Annexation and Armament," *Forum* 24 (September 1897): 66.

in the 1890s. Seizing colonies, expanding trade, digging a canal, even fighting a war began to appeal to the American people. In many ways, however, the United States continued to behave like the clumsy adolescent in foreign affairs it had shown itself to be in the 1880s. The agonizing indecision Americans displayed over whether the United States should annex the Hawaiian Islands showed that the nation had a long way to go before it could be considered a decisive, responsible world power. The Hawaiian annexation controversy provided an essential service, however, in that it forced the American people to thrash out and codify all of the arguments and rationalizations they would need to justify future colonial expansion.

American involvement in the Hawaiian Archipelago had a long history. Early in the nineteenth century American settlers and their descendants had begun the informal colonization of the islands by dispossessing the native Hawaiians of their lands in order to establish large plantations. This informal empire had prospered and might have gone on doing so, largely ignored on the mainland, had the American settlers remained free of fears of foreign domination on the islands or had the native rulers not become disenchanted with their economic bondage.

The federal government had long since officially recognized the preeminence of American interests in Hawaii. Serving under President John Tyler in 1842, Secretary of State Daniel Webster had proclaimed that

> . . . the President [is] quite willing to declare, as the sense of the Government of the United States, that the Government of the Sandwich Islands ought to be respected; that no power ought either to take possession of the islands as a conquest, or for the purposes of colonization, and that no power ought to seek for any undue control over the existing Government, or any exclusive privileges or preferences in matters of commerce.[4]

Webster could only take such a bold stand because American economic dominance was already well established in the 1840s. Hawaii's economy had become thoroughly intertwined with that of the United States by the 1860s; no other nation could offer Hawaii similar economic advantages. American influence in Hawaii continued to increase during the last half of the nineteenth century, at the same time the wealth, power, and even the health of the native monarchy de-

---

[4]Charles Callan Tansill, *The Foreign Policy of Thomas F. Bayard 1885–1897* (New York: Fordham University Press, 1940), pp. 364–65.

teriorated. The royal blood lines thinned out, and each succeeding monarch's reign seemed shorter than the last. The Americans who reaped great profits from their island holdings generally supported the monarchy, however, because the Hawaiian royalty favored them, depending upon their economic success to provide tax revenues for their profligate ways. This symbiosis survived a considerable number of shocks over the years until it collapsed completely in 1893.[5]

The attempted formalization of the relationship between the United States and Hawaii with a reciprocal trade treaty fell through in 1855, largely due to American disinterest. Reciprocity would benefit Hawaii so much more than it would the United States. A reciprocal trade agreement would reduce or eliminate payment of normal American customs duties on sugar, while American exports to Hawaii would enjoy similar advantages. To Hawaii's dismay, the United States could obtain sugar from a number of sources, whereas the dependent Hawaiians would continue purchasing American products whether or not a tariff existed. Reciprocity would essentially force the United States to pay for the privilege of buying Hawaiian sugar through lost import tax revenues.

The islands' economic health depended upon the maintenance of a foreign market for Hawaiian products, so the government went to drastic lengths to do so. During a period of instability which followed the death of King Kamehameha V in December 1872, desperate Hawaiian officials seriously debated whether to ask the United States to annex the islands, but they ran into opposition from Secretary of State Hamilton Fish.[6] Fish, however, was willing to consider a commercial treaty in order to help the Hawaiian government survive, but he knew he could not sell Congress on any arrangement which lacked political provisions beneficial to the United States. As the negotiations dragged on into 1875, King Kalakaua briefly considered offering to lease to the United States government the mouth of the Pearl River for a naval base. American and Hawaiian negotiators finally settled upon a provision that would forbid any European power from gaining special political privileges in Hawaii. So important were the political as opposed to the commercial advantages of the

[5]U.S., Department of State, *Papers Relating to the Foreign Relations of the United States,* Appendix II: *Affairs in Hawaii* (Washington, D.C.: Government Printing Office, 1894), p. 135; Sylvester K. Stevens, *American Expansion in Hawaii 1842–1898* (reprint ed., New York: Russell & Russell, 1968), p. 85; Merze Tate, *Hawaii: Reciprocity or Annexation* (East Lansing: Michigan State University Press, 1968), p. 104.

[6]Stevens, *American Expansion,* p. 115; Merze Tate, *The United States and the Hawaiian Kingdom* (New Haven, Conn.: Yale University Press, 1965), pp. 29–33.

1875 reciprocity treaty that the Senate Foreign Relations Committee later claimed it had been "negotiated for the purpose of securing political control over those islands, making them industrially and commercially a part of the United States and preventing any other great power from acquiring a foothold there which might be adverse to the welfare and safety of our Pacific coast in time of war."[7] Once ratified, the reciprocity treaty greatly benefited the American planters on Hawaii while it served to sanction the United States' informal colonization of the islands. Thus nearly a quarter of a century before its decision actually to take overseas colonies in 1899, the United States had extended its political influence to an insular area, strengthened its economic position in the Pacific, and assumed a position of defiance against possible European intervention.

As expected, the 1875 treaty contained few economic benefits for the United States. When he came to deal with Hawaii, James G. Blaine continued to emphasize the importance of the United States' political influence in Hawaii, not its commercial stake. In a representative example of the rhetorical means through which Americans attempted to extend American influence during this period, Blaine boldly reaffirmed Webster's claim of an informal American protectorate over Hawaii. Ever vigilant for any indication of British insidiousness, Blaine dashed off a blistering note in response to a false rumor that the British government intended to encourage the emigration of coolie laborers from India to Hawaii, hoping thereby to create a population which would favor British annexation. "The United States regards the Hawaiian group as essentially a part of the American system of states," he asserted, "and the key to the North Pacific trade, and, while favorably inclined toward the continuance of native rule on a basis of political independence and commercial assimilation with the United States, we could not regard the intrusion of any non-American interest in Hawaii as consistent with our relations thereto."[8] Some historians have insisted that here Blaine was deliberately extending the Monroe Doctrine to Hawaii. Actually, he was simply calling attention to the already extensive American political influence in the islands. Although his message paid homage to the mission theme with its praise of Hawaiian self-government, few would deny that Blaine expected the Hawaiian Islands would soon be formally brought into "the American system of states" through outright annexation.

[7]Stevens, *American Expansion,* pp. 126–27.
[8]*Foreign Relations* (1881), p. 570.

As the 1875 reciprocity treaty had an initial term of seven years, Secretary of State Frelinghuysen had to see to its renewal in 1882. He scrupulously sidestepped the annexation issue, while noting that, "in fact, able men of our time have not hesitated to assert that our acquisition of Hawaii is a public necessity and a question of time. While I do not share in such advanced views, I should be loth to see the influence we have in Hawaii weakened, and the control we have of its commerce abandoned . . . or lost through the active machinations of elements hostile to us as a nation."[9] Frelinghuysen definitely favored the retention of the Hawaiian agreement because it exemplified the sort of reciprocity policy he hoped to use to promote American trade. The renewal process dragged on, however, so that not until 6 December 1884 did Frelinghuysen sign an agreement providing for a continuation of the 1875 reciprocity agreement.

Significantly, newly inaugurated President Cleveland did not withdraw the Hawaiian treaty from the Senate as he did Frelinghuysen's other reciprocity measures. The maintenance of American interests in Hawaii and the protection of the islands from foreign encroachment had won solid bipartisan support. Even the moderate Bayard favored the Hawaiian connection, hoping it would keep the newly imperialistic Germany at arm's length in Hawaii. He was also annoyed when Canada granted special privileges to the Hawaiians in an effort to create Pacific trade for the government-owned Canadian-Pacific Railroad. But, like his predecessors, Bayard ranked commercial interests well behind the maintenance of American political influence in the islands, warning a Democratic representative not to "allow a commercial question to outweigh political considerations so important as I believe the control of these contiguous islands on our Pacific Coast to be now, and still more so to be in the near future."[10] In fact, the Cleveland administration showed as great a concern as it did on any other foreign policy issue over obtaining Senate approval for the renewal of the reciprocity treaty and its prohibition against European interference in the islands. President Cleveland touched on both the economic and mission themes when he urged Congress to act in late 1886:

As a result of the reciprocity treaty of 1875, those islands, on the highway of Oriental and Australasian traffic, are virtually an outpost of

[9]Frelinghuysen to Chairman, House Committee on Foreign Affairs, 20 December 1882, Drafts; Diplomatic of Frederick Theodore Frelinghuysen, LCMD.

[10]Tansill, *Thomas F. Bayard*, p. 374.

American commerce and a stepping-stone to the growing trade of the Pacific. The Polynesian Island groups have been so absorbed by other and more powerful governments that the Hawaiian Islands are left almost alone in the enjoyment of their autonomy, which it is important for us should be preserved.[11]

The old problem of the lack of economic benefits for the United States proved to be the major stumbling block in the Senate. Some political advantages simply had to be added to the renewal agreement to generate wider support. Senator George F. Edmunds of Vermont, temporarily serving as chairman of the Foreign Relations Committee in April 1886, proposed an amendment that would grant to the United States an exclusive right to construct a naval base at Pearl Harbor. Although Republican Edmunds provided no explanation for his amendment, it was obviously designed to sweeten the package. The Hawaiians themselves had once considered offering a lease to Pearl Harbor; eleven years later such an inducement had become essential. The United States Navy was growing, as was interest in American colonization in the Pacific. Both factors legislated in favor of the establishment of naval bases at strategic points. The Edmunds Amendment won over several senators who had objected to the lack of economic benefits for the United States, and the renewal agreement gained congressional approval.[12]

Secretary of State Bayard was furious at the senatorial meddling in diplomatic affairs, particularly as no one on the Foreign Relations Committee had consulted with him. He definitely wanted the United States to maintain the upper hand in Hawaii, if for no other reason than his heartfelt wish to avoid an international tangle reminiscent of the one in Samoa, and he warned that the demand for Pearl Harbor would cause the Hawaiian government to back down, killing the whole reciprocity agreement. His forebodings were at least partly justified because no one in the island government wanted to be responsible for giving away so valuable a concession. Ultimately, the economic importance of the treaty to Hawaii overrode such hesitancy. On 20 October 1887, nearly a year after the Senate had completed its action, the Hawaiian government ratified the renewal agreement which now included a cession of rights to Pearl Harbor to the United

[11]James D. Richardson, *A Compilation of the Messages and Papers of the Presidents*, 10 vols. (Washington, D.C.: Bureau of National Literature, 1911), 7:5085.

[12]U.S., Congress, Senate, *Compilation of Reports of the Committee on Foreign Relations, 1789-1901*, 56th Cong., 2d. sess. (1901), Ex. Doc. No. 231, 8 parts (volumes), 8:244; Stevens, *American Expansion*, p. 170; Tansill, *Thomas F. Bayard*, pp. 377-78; Tate, *Hawaii*, p. 185.

States. No base was constructed, but the reciprocity treaty thus officially renewed remained in force until the islands were annexed in 1898.[13]

Americans dealt with Hawaii in the 1870s and 1880s in line with the traditional foreign policy themes. Private citizens had already extended United States commercial influence so effectively that the islands functioned as an integral part of the American economy. Blaine, Frelinghuysen, Cleveland, and Bayard unequivocally warned the other great powers of the United States' intention to prevent anyone else from seizing the islands. The cession of Pearl Harbor gave this implicit American protectorate a tangible base from which to operate. Because of the mission theme, the fact that the Hawaiians were independent and governing themselves in a partially democratic manner made an outright American annexation of the islands unlikely. Furthermore, the Hawaiian political structures had hardly inhibited the commercial success of the Americans who had moved to the islands. Unless these structures changed dramatically, American policymakers would not seriously contemplate annexing Hawaii.

Ironically, the reciprocity arrangements the Hawaiian government had sacrificed so much to obtain inexorably led to the government's demise. Reciprocity with the United States encouraged the consolidation of vast sugar plantations under American control. Increased sugar exports brought the islands a glow of prosperity which the United States Congress snuffed out with the passage of the McKinley Tariff in 1890. The new tariff legislation canceled all duties on the importation of foreign sugar, substituting a bounty for domestic sugar producers. Hawaii's reciprocity arrangements were meaningless once the sugar duty had been abolished.

When the price for their sugar plummeted a ruinous 40 percent, those with large economic holdings on the islands began to reevaluate the worth of their allegiance to the feeble Hawaiian monarch. Annexation to the United States would bring the planters the benefit of the two-cent per pound bounty the federal government now paid all domestic sugar producers. Equally important, annexation would lead to a responsible, stable government for the first time in years. In order to counter growing annexation sentiment on the island, the monarchy thought of bargaining with the United States for the economic support it needed. But, having already given up Pearl Harbor in 1887, Hawaii had little to offer. Besides, any further concessions to

[13]*Foreign Relations* (1887), p. 591; Bayard to Cleveland, 11 January 1887, Bayard Papers, LCMD; Tansill, *Thomas F. Bayard*, p. 395; Tate, *Hawaii*, pp. 190–95.

the United States would weaken native support for the monarchy, and the Hawaiian people were in an emotional, nationalistic mood in the early 1890s.[14]

King Kalakaua died in 1891, leaving the royal family without a male heir. The throne thus fell to Queen Liliuokalani, a vocal proponent of Hawaiian nationalism. Uneasy over the queen's accession, the wealthiest men on the islands, most of them Americans or the descendants of American missionaries, formed a secret organization known as the Annexation Club. Any movement in the direction of American annexation had to start in Hawaii, because the United States had so little to gain from it. To sound out the American government's attitude, the Annexation Club sent Lorrin A. Thurston to Washington, D.C., in late March 1892. President Harrison prudently avoided seeing him, but Thurston did manage to confer with the secretaries of state and navy. He returned to Hawaii convinced that Harrison's cabinet would favor annexation given the right opportunity. Meanwhile, the club brought United States Navy Captain G. C. Wiltse, stationed at Honolulu, and American Minister John L. Stevens into its confidence. Soon both American officials were sending reports emphasizing how strong annexationist sentiment was on the islands.[15]

Minister Stevens became the American official most responsible for encouraging the annexation movement. He had been a political crony of Blaine's in Maine, and the two men apparently agreed on most major foreign policy issues. Shortly after his arrival in Hawaii, Stevens shocked his host government by publicly stating his conviction that Hawaii would ultimately be annexed to the United States. Although Stevens sent prodigious amounts of correspondence to Washington, little went the other way, prompting some historians to assume that Stevens's messages were simply filed and ignored. A more likely explanation is that Stevens was, at that time, the man articulating United States policy with respect to Hawaii. Not until after the revolution in 1893 did the State Department express even the slightest official displeasure with the outspoken minister's activities.[16]

[14]Stevens, *American Expansion*, pp. 202–3; Tate, *U.S. and Hawaiian Kingdom*, p. 114; William Appleman Williams, *The Roots of the Modern American Empire* (New York: Random House, 1969), p. 36; Julius W. Pratt, *Expansionists of 1898* (c. 1936, reprint ed., Chicago: Quadrangle, 1964), p. 160.

[15]*Foreign Relations* (1894) Appendix II, p. 185; Pratt, *Expansionists of 1898*, p. 57; Tate, *U.S. and Hawaiian Kingdom*, p. 116.

[16]Tate, *U.S. and Hawaiian Kingdom*, p. 141; Pratt, *Expansionists of 1898*, pp. 50–51; Alice Felt Tyler, *The Foreign Policy of James G. Blaine* (Minneapolis: University of Minnesota Press, 1927), pp. 208, 216–17.

Stevens's comments were blunt and unequivocal:

> There are increasing indications that the annexation sentiment is growing among the business men as well as with the less responsible of the foreign and native population of the islands. The present political situation is feverish and I see no prospect of it being permanently otherwise until these islands become a part of the American Union or a possession of Great Britain.[17]

Stevens doubtless knew that any mention of British advances was like waving a red flag before the Anglophobic Blaine. If the British themselves were not interested, Stevens went on, the Canadians might be. Actually, no foreign power ever seriously contemplated wresting economic and political control of Hawaii from the United States, but Stevens and others frequently suggested it in order to rouse support for American annexation.[18] Stevens constructed an elaborate and persuasive list of reasons for annexation in a long message he sent Blaine's successor at the Department of State, John W. Foster. Stevens contended that annexation was almost inevitable in view of the long history of Hawaiian dependence upon the United States. In a section entitled "What Should Be Done?" the imperialistic minister outlined his plan for action: "One of two courses seems to me absolutely necessary to be followed, either bold and vigorous measures for annexation or a 'Customs Union,' an ocean cable from the California coast to Honolulu, Pearl Harbor perpetually ceded to the United States, with an implied but not necessarily stipulated protectorate over the islands."[19]

Stevens naturally favored speedy annexation, and his opinions won sympathetic consideration in Washington. The general public seemed only marginally interested in foreign affairs prior to 1893, but those who did take an interest favored the formal extension of American political influence to Hawaii. In 1891, long before Stevens's correspondence could have influenced his attitudes, Secretary of State Blaine wrote President Harrison that he considered "only three places of value enough to be taken, that are not continental. One is Hawaii and the others are Cuba and Porto Rico. Cuba and Porto Rico are not now imminent and will not be for a generation. Hawaii may come up for decision at any unexpected hour and I hope we shall be pre-

---

[17]*Foreign Relations* (1894), Appendix II, p. 353.
[18]Ibid., p. 379; Tate, *U.S. and Hawaiian Kingdom*, p. 150; E. Berkeley Tompkins, *Anti-Imperialism in the United States* (Philadelphia: University of Pennsylvania Press, 1970), p. 48.
[19]*Foreign Relations* (1894), Appendix II, p. 194.

pared to decide it in the affirmative."[20] Navy Secretary Benjamin Tracy, who exerted more pressure for naval expansion than had any of his predecessors in office, wanted Hawaii colonized to guarantee his forces the Pacific bases and coaling stations his ambitious plans called for. Many navy officers saw the possession of Hawaii as fundamental to creating defense arrangements in the North Pacific for the American west coast.

President Harrison, not Blaine or Tracy, would make the ultimate decision about annexation. The Chilean episode had driven the president and his secretary of state apart; the resulting estrangement had caused Harrison to assume personal control over his administration's foreign policies. The president had originally favored a protectorate arrangement for Hawaii, but he gradually came around to the view that only outright annexation could resolve the nagging economic and political troubles on the islands. He cemented this decision by choosing a committed advocate of annexation to succeed Blaine when the man from Maine retired in the summer of 1892. Secretary of State John W. Foster was an erudite and skilled negotiator who had previously served the United States as an international troubleshooter. Colonialism ran rampant overseas, and Foster's frequent travels abroad had convinced him that the United States could not safely stand aloof. His presence at the head of the State Department insured, as Blaine had hoped, that at the unexpected hour when Hawaii came up for decision, the Harrison administration was ready to decide in favor of annexation.

Although the administration was willing to act, the timing of that hour of decision could hardly have been less opportune. Harrison had lost his reelection bid to Democrat Grover Cleveland in November 1892. Worse still, the Democrats had simultaneously captured control of both houses of Congress, and they had no intention of letting any Republican party policy slip through without close scrutiny once they took over. The Hawaiian revolution occurred in mid-January 1893, and another month elapsed while a treaty of annexation was worked out. The Harrison administration thus had a scant three weeks in which to push the treaty through the Senate. Even a noncontroversial measure would have had a slim chance of winning approval in such a short time, and there was certainly no more controversial issue than Hawaiian annexation.

[20]Quoted in Albert T. Volwiler, ed., *The Correspondence Between Benjamin Harrison and James G. Blaine 1882–1893* (Philadelphia: American Philosophical Society, 1940), p. 174.

Those who captured control of Hawaii in early 1893 had a great many other things on their minds than the rapidly approaching expiration of Harrison's term. The revolution resulted from the growing Hawaiian nativist resentment against white exploitation combined with the American minority's increasing distrust of native rule. Newly enthroned Queen Liliuokalani heightened both the American distrust and her subjects' nativism by canceling the constitution that had given the minority of American and American-descended citizens a disproportionately large share of control over governmental affairs. The members of the Annexation Club and their friends countered with a coup in mid-January 1893, setting themselves up as a "Committee of Public Safety." The committee could not guarantee public safety, however, without the support of the marines and sailors aboard the United States Navy vessels stationed at Honolulu. The committee beseeched Minister Stevens for help, and Stevens peremptorily ordered Captain Wiltse to send ashore a large number of his men "in order to protect American lives and property."

The deployment of the heavily armed, disciplined American naval forces made resistance futile, and the queen agreed to surrender—but not to the Committee of Public Safety. Defiantly, she proclaimed that she was giving in to "the superior force of the United States of America." Having accomplished by American proxy its goal of assuring its own as well as the public safety, the committee transformed itself into a provisional government which immediately dispatched several commissioners to the United States to work out an annexation agreement. Stevens did not feel constrained to wait for instructions from Washington. In addition to speedily recognizing the provisional government, he raised an American flag over the Hawaiian government house and announced that the islands had become a protectorate of the United States. The whole episode recalled Consul Greenebaum's precipitate actions in Samoa in 1886. Unlike Greenebaum, however, Stevens received only a mild rebuke from the secretary of state. Although he did feel the declaration of the protectorate was uncalled for, Foster backed up Stevens's extension of recognition to the revolutionary government, and he did not criticize the landing of American troops. After all, similar landings had occurred in Hawaii during previous instances of internal instability.[21]

Stevens cared little whether his personal acts brought disapproval. On 1 February 1893 he urged Foster not to dally: "The Ha-

[21]*Foreign Relations* (1894), Appendix II, pp. 199, 406–7; William Adam Russ, Jr., *The Hawaiian Revolution (1893–94)* (Selinsgrove, Pa.: Susquehanna University Press, 1959), pp. 95–96, 121–22.

waiian pear is now ripe, and this is the golden hour for the United States to pluck it."[22] If the United States did not, Stevens warned, the British would surely do so. The Hawaiian commissioners commandeered the fastest ship in Honolulu at that time to speed them to San Francisco; then they raced to Washington on the transcontinental railroad to confer with Secretary Foster. The government they represented existed solely as a device to fill the interregnum until an annexation treaty could be ratified. President Harrison expressed concern about the provisional government's nonrepresentative nature and pressed Foster to insert something in the treaty which would indicate that the temporary arrangement had some popular support. Foster brushed aside Harrison's desire to work the democratic mission theme into the final document as impractical in the time available.[23]

On 15 February 1893 the secretary of state signed a straightforward treaty that would permanently attach Hawaii to the United States. Foster glossed over the question of exactly what status—whether colony or territory—Hawaii would have, claiming that that could be arranged after annexation had been ratified. To stimulate speedy action on the treaty in the Senate, President Harrison once again trundled out the specious argument that another great power might take over if the United States did not act expeditiously.[24] The importance tradition and precedent play in United States foreign policy is nowhere more evident than in the Harrison administration's defense of its actions with regard to Hawaii. Secretary Foster included with the treaty a lengthy report describing all of the previous occasions annexation had been contemplated when United States interests in Hawaii had been threatened. He hoped the report would make the acquisition of the islands appear to be the natural and logical fulfillment of historical inevitability.[25]

The expiring, lame-duck Senate refused to be rushed into a heedless confirmation of the treaty. President Cleveland took the oath of office on 4 March 1893, settled back into his old job, and reminisced about his first action as president eight years earlier. It seemed an apt precedent, so, as he had done with Frelinghuysen's treaties in 1885, he now withdrew the Hawaiian annexation treaty from the

[22]*Foreign Relations* (1894), Appendix II, p. 402.

[23]Pratt, *Expansionists of 1898*, pp. 119-20.

[24]Richardson, *Messages and Papers*, 8:5783.

[25]U.S., Congress, Senate, *Correspondence Respecting Relations between the United States and the Hawaiian Islands from September, 1820, to January, 1893;* 52d Cong., 2d sess. (1893), Ex. Doc. No. 77, pp. 1-24.

Senate. Cleveland's action precipitated a bitter, partisan battle that would persist to the end of the century. The leaders of the two major political parties simply did not agree on the question of political expansion. To the dismay of the nation's imperialists, a cautious, anti-imperialistic Cleveland administration was back in charge.

During his second term as president, Grover Cleveland continued to regard himself and to be regarded as a conservative in foreign affairs. Fortunately, his restraint was at least tempered by a better understanding of international relations than he had brought to the presidency in 1885. As in his first term, Cleveland devoted the majority of his attention to domestic problems, of which he encountered a great many. Not wishing to recall Thomas F. Bayard to the State Department, Cleveland was pleased when Congress created the first American ambassadorship which allowed him to pack his former secretary of state off to London. There Bayard served out his term in considerable awe of his English hosts and increasingly out of touch with the Cleveland administration's initiatives. Bayard's attitudes about foreign relations affected policy formulation much less from London than they had in Washington.

Cleveland surprised the nation by choosing as his chief of cabinet Walter Quintin Gresham. A federal judge from Illinois, Gresham had never wavered from his lifelong allegiance to the Republican party until he became fed up with its high tariff platform in the 1892 presidential race. In fact, at Republican presidential nominating conventions Gresham had frequently attracted votes from delegates in the party's reform wing. In addition to doubts about his political suitability for a Democratic cabinet position, many Americans questioned whether his dedication to informality might not alienate the disciplined, standoffish diplomatic corps. Gresham blithely ignored the rules of etiquette and, as he had throughout his life, persisted in wearing shirt sleeves and munching on a dilapidated cigar when meeting those who came to his State Department office. Gresham's down-home, straight-shooting attitudes were apparent in his policy initiatives as well.

The new secretary of state's antiimperialist attitudes nicely matched Cleveland's own reluctance to annex Hawaii. In addition to their general opposition to colonization per se, both Cleveland and Gresham disliked the haste with which the treaty had been drafted. Gresham decided to emphasize what he viewed as the immorality of the whole affair, hoping thereby to deflate popular support for annexation. As evidence of his commitment to America's democratic mission, Gresham continued to express doubt that the provisional administration in Hawaii represented popular self-government, even though Minister Stevens assured him that "the present government is supported by all the more responsible citizens and by seven-eighths of the property of the country. By all the best citizens it is regarded as the best government the islands have had for many years."[26] The idealistic Gresham hardly cared whether the wealthy, upper class favored the provisional government; indeed, that sort of support probably guaranteed that the poorer people hated it all the more intensely.

Those who advocated annexation on practical rather than philosophical grounds treated Gresham's moralistic sentiments with contempt. Republican Henry Cabot Lodge, for example, insisted that strategic considerations alone far outweighed any conceivable moral scruples against annexation. Ambassador Bayard, too, worried about losing the islands he considered crucial to the United States Navy. Alfred Thayer Mahan agreed, authoritatively declaring that Hawaii was essential to the defense of the West Coast and the proposed isthmian canal. Annexationists stressed Hawaii's importance both as a buyer of American exports and as a stepping-stone for Far Eastern trade, conveniently neglecting to mention the existing treaty relationship which assured Americans unencumbered use of Hawaii as a market and as a trading station. Having thoroughly examined the evidence available to him at the State Department, Gresham knew that no other power intended to take over the islands. Consequently, the Cleveland administration did not fear for American security because of the Hawaiian Islands, nor did it worry about losing their economic benefits to American merchants.[27]

Totally distrustful of the news Stevens was providing, Cleveland and Gresham decided to send their own man, James H. Blount, as a special emissary to Honolulu. A Democrat from Georgia, Blount had just retired from the chairmanship of the House Committee on Foreign Affairs, and he was believed to favor expansion. Although Cleveland's opponents charged the president with overstepping his authority in sending off an emissary without Senate approval, most Americans would agree that more information on the Hawaiian situation would be useful. Gresham instructed Blount to investigate

[26]*Foreign Relations* (1894), Appendix II, p. 419.

[27]LaFeber, *The New Empire*, pp. 200–201; Tansill, *Thomas F. Bayard*, p. 408; John A. Garraty, *Henry Cabot Lodge* (New York: Alfred A. Knopf, 1953), p. 151; John A. S. Grenville and George Berkeley Young, *Politics, Strategy, and American Diplomacy* (New Haven, Conn.: Yale University Press, 1966), p. 109; A. T. Mahan, "Hawaii and Our Future Sea-Power," *Forum* 15 (March 1893): 8–10.

all facets of the recent revolution and current conditions in Hawaii, and in particular, "the sentiment of the people towards existing authority."[28]

Blount quickly concluded that the provisional government did not enjoy anything approaching majority support. "If the question of annexation by the United States should be made to depend upon the popular will in these islands, the proposition had as well be abandoned at once," he wrote Gresham in May 1893.[29] Two months later Blount predicted that the provisional government would collapse if its annexation efforts failed. The annexationists had been pleased that an old-line southerner like Blount had been sent, expecting him to approve of a white minority ruling a "colored" native population, but he apparently left his racial prejudices at home. As Cleveland had invested him with full authority over all American officials in the islands, he ordered the American admiral in Honolulu to haul down the American flag Stevens had raised as symbolic of the protectorate the impetuous minister had proclaimed. Finally, Blount talked to Liliuokalani who insisted that, because she had abdicated only in the face of overwhelming American force, the American government must restore her to her throne.[30]

Blount's secret reports solidified Gresham's resolve to undo "this great wrong" which the United States had perpetrated.[31] His suggestion to Cleveland's cabinet called for the United States to sever relations with the provisional government and to reinstate the queen. Attorney-General Richard Olney wrote a long critique of Gresham's proposals on 9 October 1893, warning of possible pitfalls in the restoration scheme. The most important was his contention that force had been used to overthrow the queen's movement and, therefore, the United States might have to resort to force to restore her. Gresham's policy thus carried with it a substantial element of risk. Sure that he was idealistically correct, the secretary of state ignored Olney's practical considerations and pressed ahead. Responding to the mission theme, Gresham maintained that Americans should not interfere with the right of citizens of other countries to govern themselves. His final, official recommendation to Cleveland on 18 October chided his countrymen by asking, "Can the United States consistently insist that other nations shall respect the independence of Hawaii

---

[28]*Foreign Relations* (1894), Appendix II, p. 567.
[29]Ibid., p. 533.
[30]Ibid., pp. 868–69.
[31]Matilda Gresham, *Life of Walter Quintin Gresham 1832–1895*, 2 vols. (c. 1919, reprint ed., Freeport, N.Y.: Books for Libraries Press, 1970), 2:836.

while not respecting it themselves? Our Government was the first to recognize the independence of the Islands, and it should be the last to acquire sovereignty over them by force and fraud."[32]

The man designated to implement Gresham's impractical plan was the Cleveland administration's new minister to Hawaii, Albert S. Willis. Gresham instructed Willis to extract from the former queen a promise not to punish the members of the provisional government. Liliuokalani balked at first and insisted upon exercising her royal prerogative of executing traitors to her government. Ultimately, she realized that she would have to treat the white leaders with reasonable gentility in order to get American support. When Willis then ordered the head of the provisional government, Sanford Dole, to step down, however, Dole angrily refused. He was furious with the administration's decision not to annex the islands. The Hawaiian-American leader maintained that Cleveland was out of step with the American people, and he intended to rule Hawaii until the president changed his policy or was voted out of office. Cleverly exploiting America's own mission theme, Dole proclaimed that "We do not recognize the right of the President of the United States to interfere in our domestic affairs. Such right could be conferred upon him by the act of this Government, and by that alone, or it could be acquired by conquest. This I understand to be the American doctrine, conspicuously announced from time to time by the authorities of your Government."[33]

Surveying the wreckage of his restoration policy, Cleveland decided to shift the responsibility for annexation if it were to occur to Congress. With his long message to the legislators on 18 December 1893 he included a full compilation of all of the documents relating to the case including Blount's heretofore secret reports. Cleveland took the opportunity to express his personal dismay that Foster had ever signed an annexation treaty. He also revealed his firm dedication to antiimperialism, insisting that the taking of the islands would violate the nation's traditions of expanding only into contiguous territory.[34] Meanwhile, Gresham's friends praised his quixotic attempt to restore the queen. The Democratic secretary of state felt certain Congress would vindicate his actions. "I am not at all disturbed about the Hawaiian question," he wrote in January 1894.

> My action has been with sole regard to justice and our national honor, and I have no doubt that the thoughtful people of the country view the

[32]*Foreign Relations* (1894), Appendix II, pp. 459–63.
[33]Ibid., pp. 1276–77.
[34]Richardson, *Messages and Papers*, 8: 5893–98.

question as I do. It is not true that the democrats are seriously divided on the question; indeed the party in the House stands practically as one man in support of the Administration. I do not look for serious trouble in the Senate.[35]

Despite Gresham's expressions of confidence, several senators, including Alabama Democrat John T. Morgan, then chairman of the Senate Foreign Relations Committee, sniped away at the administration's Hawaiian policy. Although the committee plowed through all the documentation Cleveland had presented and called many witnesses to testify, its final report proved anticlimactic. It tamely concluded, for example, that Stevens had not overstepped his legal authority in ordering American troops ashore to protect American lives and property during the revolution. On the other hand, it found nothing illegal in Cleveland's efforts to use his good offices to try to restore the queen. The committee made only one unequivocal decision: the United States could not rescind its formal recognition of the provisional government. A few Republicans authored a minority report that praised Stevens and criticized Cleveland, while a couple of loyal Democrats called for Stevens to be punished for his part in the revolution. Most significantly, however, the committee did not recommend immediate annexation.[36]

The report and various senators' public comments illustrated the themes Americans saw as important in the Hawaiian affair. Mission sentiments appeared prominently. The Hawaiian situation was so complex, however, that divergent interpretations of the relevance of this traditional doctrine emerged. As it had overturned a monarchy, some commentators praised the revolution as an outpouring of republican spirit. The Foreign Relations Committee's report noted that "civilization and constitutional government in Hawaii are the foster children of the American Christian missionaries." It went on to praise the American style of the provisional government and to reaffirm that the United States had "at least a moral suzerainty over Hawaii."[37]

The blatantly nondemocratic nature of the provisional government itself left it open to moral criticism. Senator George Vest of Missouri, an opponent of annexation, explained his view of the United States' democratic mission as:

[35]Gresham to Mrs. Bertha Honore Palmer, 15 January 1894, Walter Q. Gresham Papers, LCMD.

[36]Senate, *Reports of the Committee on Foreign Relations*, 6:363–64, 390, 396.

[37]Ibid., pp. 364, 374; U.S., Congress, *Congressional Record*, 53d Cong., 2d sess., p. 2993.

its traditional and established policy, not to interfere with the internal
or governmental affairs of another people; . . . our Government being
based upon popular sovereignty, we should encourage and acknowledge and respect that principle throughout the world, always letting it
be understood that our sincere sympathies went with popular government in every clime and every place.[38]

Blount's reports undeniably proved that the majority of the Hawaiian
population had no voice in the provisional government. They might
be too weak, divided, or disinterested to overturn it, but they certainly did not support it. No one denied that Minister Stevens's immediate extension of recognition to the rebel government definitely
deviated from the standard American procedure of withholding recognition from new governments until they had achieved a semblance
of popular support. The provisional government added to the con-
fusion by calling itself a "republic" in order to differentiate itself
from the overturned Kingdom of Hawaii. This semantic legerdemain
spurred Connecticut Representative Robert E. De Forest to protest:

A republican form of government forsooth! Let the gentlemen set up
any other pretense, than that, any shift, any evasion, any subterfuge,
but by all that is sacred in the sanctuary of freedom, let them not
attempt to screen the ridiculous and impudent pretensions of this little
coterie of autocrats under the honorable title of a republican form of
government.[39]

President Cleveland himself was deeply concerned about squaring
American behavior with its mission theme. "I am sorry that the vast
Hawaiian situation was talked today," he wrote Wisconsin Senator
William F. Vilas. "The thing I care the most about is the declaration
that the *people* of the islands instead of the *Provisional Government*
should determine the policy, etc."[40]

Some opponents of annexation looked beyond the current situation and despaired of any future improvement. Democratic Senator
John W. Daniel of Virginia complained not only that the current
government was undemocratic, but that Hawaii's "heterogeneous
population from all parts of the earth are not so advanced as to admit
of republican institutions unless they be maintained by the over-
lordship of some superior hand."[41] Senator Daniel's point was a very

[38]*Congressional Record,* 53d Cong., 2d sess., p. 1402.
[39]Ibid., p. 2379.
[40]Quoted in Allen Nevins, ed., *Letters of Grover Cleveland: 1850–1908* (Boston:
Houghton Mifflin, 1933), p. 353.
[41]*Congressional Record,* 53d Cong., 2d sess., p. 2897.

touchy one. The islands' heterogeneous racial composition caused even some of the most ardent proponents of annexation to worry whether the Hawaiian population could ever become integrated with that of the United States. At the time of the revolution Americans or American descendants made up less than 3 percent of the islands' 80,000 inhabitants. About half, or 40,000, were of native Hawaiian stock, and another 9,000 were of Portuguese or other European blood. Plantation owners had eagerly imported nearly 30,000 other inhabitants from China and Japan to work in their fields. Racism has always figured prominently in American thinking, and the prospect of adding a large bloc of nonwhite people definitely blunted the drive for annexation. Racial considerations also crept into the debate over what governmental structure the islands should have if they were annexed. A common suggestion was to consign them to a permanent territorial status similar to that of New Mexico with its mixed Anglo, Mexican, and Indian population. Proannexationist Senator John Sherman of Ohio proposed an ingenious solution to guarantee white control: he would simply make the islands a county of the state of California.[42]

Most advocates of annexation, however, dismissed as irrelevant any consideration of whether the Hawaiian people wanted to be annexed or of what status they would have in the Union. After all, annexation of Hawaii was clearly a part of the destiny God had mapped out for the nation, the natural culmination of its traditional process of territorial aggrandizement. Colorado Senator Henry M. Teller captured this new manifest destiny spirit by boldly affirming that

> I am in favor of the annexation of the islands. I am in favor of the annexation of Cuba; I am in favor of the annexation of the great country lying north of us. I expect in a few years to see the American flag floating from the extreme north to the line of our sister Republics to the south. I expect to see it floating over the isles of the sea—not only these, but in the Great Gulf and in the West India seas.[43]

Teller had thus eloquently restated the great dream of the expansion of American political influence throughout the hemisphere. He and his fellow annexationists ignored what they considered petty political and constitutional technicalities, seeing Hawaiian annexation as only the beginning of a series of territorial acquisitions. The imperialists

---

[42]Ibid., p. 1405; *Foreign Relations* (1894), Appendix II, p. 876; Russ, *Revolution*, pp. 192–93.

[43]*Congressional Record*, 53d Cong., 2d sess., pp. 1770–71.

found inconceivable Cleveland's refusal to carry out the expansionist policy his predecessors going all the way back to John Quincy Adams had favored. The United States simply must politically formalize the union with the Hawaiian Islands that commercial and strategic links had already forged.

As this first, full-scale debate over the annexation of a well-populated, noncontiguous area went on month after month, it provided ample opportunity for the airing of almost every argument ever to appear in discussions about whether the United States should take colonies. The strategic argument cropped up when annexationists claimed Hawaii would act as a sentinel to protect our western coast from naval attack. Opponents of annexation countered, reasonably enough, that the cost of defending the islands themselves from some never-specified menace might well be prohibitive. Economic arguments were not so prevalent as they would be in other debates over colonization simply because the Hawaiian and American economies were already linked to such a degree that annexation would bring few major economic changes. Similar strategic, economic, and moral discussions as well as controversies over racial problems, constitutional technicalities, and ultimate political relationships would erupt whenever the American people considered colonization anywhere in the world.

The exhaustive yet inconclusive annexation debates showed that the nation was not yet emotionally prepared to take positive action on the Hawaiian question in 1893 or 1894. The whole Senate finally approved a resolution, in the late spring of 1894, which stated that the United States would make no effort to restore the queen, thus leaving the provisional government in charge for the time being. At the same time, the resolution warned other foreign governments not to interfere in Hawaiian affairs.

With annexation temporarily ruled out, the provisional government had to restructure itself for an indefinite future. Sanford Dole had wisely anticipated such a contingency and had called for the convening of a constitutional convention in mid-March 1894. Well aware of the American criticisms that Hawaii was not truly a republic, the provisional government intended to draw up an American-style constitution. Taking its cue from the southern states, then engaged in revamping their own basic structures in order to limit the participation of the blacks, the planter aristocracy in Hawaii made sure the constitution kept the vast, antiannexationist majority of the population disfranchised. The native population thus had good reason to object, and the Hawaiians finally organized an attempt at rebellion in early 1895. It failed ignominiously. The white government controlled most of the weapons and trained manpower on the islands, so the uprising fizzled out without substantial loss of life or property damage.[44]

Gresham decided to maintain normal relations with the existing government in Hawaii. Consequently, with the promulgation of the constitution, he had Minister Willis in Honolulu recognize the new regime. Meanwhile, a revival of prosperity for the sugar planters helped smooth relations between the two countries. Recalling his forthright stand in the late 1880s, Cleveland put his ample weight behind a Democratic party move to overturn the McKinley Tariff. The president was disappointed when Congress did not go as far as he had hoped, but the Democratic Wilson-Gorman Tariff of 1894 did substantially alter the United States tariff structure. Best of all for Hawaii, it reimposed a tariff on sugar which, in turn, reestablished the advantages the reciprocity treaty gave Hawaiian planters.

The imperialists continued to criticize Cleveland, but his resolve never buckled. In fact, he sometimes appeared to be teasing them in order to provoke agonized howls of dismay. In January 1895, for example, he stated that he favored the lease to Great Britain of one of the uninhabited islands in the Hawaiian group for an undersea cable station. Anti-British annexationists blasted Cleveland's stand as a sellout to the enemy.[45] The frustrated imperialists contemplated various schemes designed to circumvent the treaty-making powers of the president. Their best idea was to push through a joint congressional resolution; but the votes simply were not there. At best, they could comfort themselves with the knowledge that the emotional debate over Hawaiian annexation had stretched and strained America's traditional foreign policy attitudes; they would never be quite the same again. If a chance for annexation came up again, the nation would be that much further along the path toward accepting colonialism and seeking great-power status. As long as President Cleveland stood at the helm, however, the imperialist drive remained stalled. Cleveland personally considered his opposition to Hawaiian annexation a matter of principle. "Ever since the question of Hawaiian annexation was presented I have been utterly and constantly opposed to it," he as-

[44]Stevens, *American Expansion*, p. 270; Tate, *U.S. and Hawaiian Kingdom*, p. 258; William Adam Russ, Jr., *The Hawaiian Republic (1894–98) and Its Struggle to Win Annexation* (Selinsgrove, Pa.: Susquehanna University Press, 1961), pp. 33, 46, 51, 57.

[45]Pratt, *Expansionists of 1898*, pp. 200–201; Richardson, *Messages and Papers*, 8:5992; Russ, *Hawaiian Republic*, p. 256; H. C. Lodge, "Our Blundering Foreign Policy," *Forum* 19 (March 1895): 9–10.

serted after he had left office. "I regarded, and still regard, the proposed annexation of these islands as not only opposed to our national policy, but as a perversion of our national mission. The mission of our nation is to build up and make a greater country out of what we have, instead of annexing islands."[46]

Cleveland's dogmatic obstructionism did not necessarily include opposition to steps short of outright colonization. He was sufficiently in tune with the nation's traditions that he did not intend to overlook or denigrate United States interests abroad. His administration therefore dealt firmly with the disturbing incidents associated with American attempts to expand trade and political influence in Latin America. A revolution in Brazil in 1893 is a case in point.

A group of Brazilian naval officers commandeered their nation's warships and, using this power base, attempted to tie up the country's key port cities. The central government could not immediately subdue the maritime rebels, who, for their part, made almost no progress inland. The Cleveland administration routinely announced that the United States would treat the revolt with a strictly neutral policy—a policy which, in practice, meant that the United States made no political commitment either for or against the rebels. Instead, the United States intended to behave as though conditions in Brazil were normal, and American merchant ships continued to arrive at Rio de Janeiro. No other foreign nation had recognized the rebels as belligerents either; so any rebel attempt to enforce an embargo would be without legal sanction. In fact, such an enforcement attempt could be considered an act of piracy. The United States pursued the very policy which had nearly caused a war with Chile some three years earlier, that of stationing some naval vessels offshore. Tempers on both sides were red-hot when, on 30 January 1894, a rebel-held ship fired upon an American freighter heading for a pier at Rio de Janeiro. The U.S.S. *Detroit* fired warning shots in return, threatened to sink any interfering rebel vessel, and then convoyed the freighter safely to its berth. The rebel embargo was irretrievably broken. When it had finally brought the disturbance to an end, the Brazilian government awarded President Cleveland a gold medal for his "neutral" stance during the rebellion.[47]

The Brazilian incident showed the United States' willingness to exercise its growing political influence in the Western Hemisphere.

[46]Quoted in Nevins, *Letters of Grover Cleveland*, pp. 491–92.

[47]*Foreign Relations* (1893), pp. 98, 117, 120; *Foreign Relations* (1894), Appendix II, pp. 62–63; Richardson, *Messages and Papers*, 8:5867.

Cleveland's gold medal showed that such behavior did not automatically alienate South American people. In fact, some optimistic Latinos felt they might be able to turn the United States' desire to play the great power game to their own advantage. They certainly disliked the concept of European interference or colonization in their hemisphere. If they attempted to use the Colossus of the North to fend off Europe, however, they opened themselves to the danger inherent in hiring a powerful mercenary army: one can never be absolutely sure the hireling will not turn on his employer. Venezuela definitely got a mixed result when it sought United States assistance in the protracted Venezuela–British Guiana boundary dispute. The United States used the incident to issue a startling reinterpretation of the Monroe Doctrine and to strengthen its position relative to other great powers.

Eastern Venezuela merged into the western reaches of the colony of British Guiana along an undefined line. Neither side cared as long as the jungle region remained unexplored and unsettled. In 1842 Sir Robert Schomburgk surveyed a line that satisfied the British, but Venezuela never accepted it. Toward the end of the nineteenth century, British and Venezuelan settlers began filtering into the region, only to stumble onto an unexpected treasure trove. The largest gold nugget ever found, weighing 500 ounces, was dragged out of the Orinoco watershed. Suddenly, the exact boundary between the two territories became of more than academic interest. Furthermore, Venezuela wanted to prevent the British from controlling the mouth of the Orinoco River, the only means of communication with much of the Venezuelan hinterland. On the other hand, the British felt a responsibility to protect those who had settled in the region thinking they would remain under Britain's enlightened authority.

The British government insisted that the two nations jointly work out a mutually acceptable boundary. Venezuela favored arbitration of the issue, hoping thereby to minimize the effect of Great Britain's clear-cut naval and military supremacy. After the British had adamantly rejected arbitration in the mid-1880s, Venezuela appealed to the United States for help. Secretary of State Bayard duly wrote to his minister in London, alluding to the Monroe Doctrine and expressing American interest in the settlement because of "the sense of responsibility that rests upon the United States in relation to the South American republics. The doctrines we announced two generations ago . . . have lost none of their force . . . in the progress of time."[48]

---

[48]Tansill, *Thomas F. Bayard*, p. 636.

Bayard refused to go further than an offer of United States good offices to the two governments, a role which became crucial when Venezuela and Great Britain severed diplomatic relations over the boundary issue in 1887. Bayard steadfastly refused to pressure either side toward a compromise, however, leaving the matter to fester. The secretary of state realized that the British proposal for a joint agreement upon a line, with only minor deviations to be arbitrated, accorded with standard international practices. He also recognized the blatantly self-serving nature of much of the Venezuelan rhetoric.

When Blaine returned to the Department of State in 1889, its evenhandedness deteriorated. A champion of Pan-American solidarity and a longtime enemy of England, Blaine naturally sided with Venezuela. Meanwhile the Venezuelan government had found a clever way to goad the United States into action. It swore that Great Britain's real goal was to extend its colony's boundary, and then Venezuela convinced the Harrison administration that such an extension could be viewed as a violation of the Monroe Doctrine's strictures against further European colonization in the New World. The self-proclaimed knight-protector of the Western Hemisphere simply had to respond to this challenge.[49] President Harrison publicly called for the arbitration of the issue and warned that "this Government will continue to express its concern at any appearance of foreign encroachment on territories long under the administrative control of American States."[50]

The Chilean episode, Hawaiian annexation, and his 1892 election loss so distracted President Harrison that he did no more than complain about the situation before turning the case over to the more conservative Cleveland. Secretary of State Gresham had no intention of seeking an international confrontation, especially with England. Thomas F. Bayard, now American ambassador in London and becoming increasingly infatuated with his host country, was equally disinterested in Venezuela's plight. Meanwhile, Cleveland himself became absorbed in grappling with the domestic depression. They all might well have kept the issue on a back burner indefinitely had it not been for two factors, one domestic and the other foreign. Cleveland found himself and his party in deep political trouble at home by 1894, and he vainly hoped to recapture needed Irish-American votes for his party by standing firm against Great Britain. This resolve grew

[49]David Saville Muzzey, *James G. Blaine* (New York: Dodd, Mead, 1934), p. 436; Tyler, *Foreign Policy*, p. 88; Grover Cleveland, *Presidential Problems* (New York: Century, 1904), p. 244.
[50]Richardson, *Messages and Papers*, 8:5616.

stronger when he surveyed the popular outrage over an external incident: the Corinto Affair in Nicaragua.

Nicaraguan authorities gradually became intolerant of the self-righteous, bullying attitude of certain British commercial and political agents. Finally, in 1894, the exasperated Nicaraguan government arrested, imprisoned, and subsequently banished several British subjects including a vice-consul. Having failed to obtain redress for this indignity through normal diplomatic channels, the British government decided to take direct, forceful action. In the spring of 1895, a British fleet appeared off the east coast of Nicaragua, and the fleet's admiral sent the government at Managua an ultimatum demanding the sum of 15,000 pounds as a compensation for its anti-British actions. After the Nicaraguan government had peremptorily refused, Royal Marines stormed ashore and captured the port city of Corinto. The Nicaraguans hastily applied for assistance from the United States. The British government had taken the wise precaution of assuring the American government that its occupation of Corinto would last only until its demands for restitution had been met. Furthermore, the British added, they had no intention of extending their influence in Nicaragua, an action that would violate the Clayton-Bulwer Treaty. Satisfied with Great Britain's good faith, Gresham and Bayard refused to intercede, leaving Nicaragua no choice but to pay the indemnity.[51]

The American public was not nearly so tolerant of Britain's power play. The newspapers claimed England had grossly violated the Monroe Doctrine and pugnaciously called for an American response. President Cleveland thus had to deal with a major outbreak of jingoism. This warlike sentiment—part patriotism, part frustration, part militarism—would take on increasing venom in the next few years. In the aftermath of the Nicaraguan incident, the Cleveland administration felt it must stifle this jingoism, perhaps by evoking from England an admission that the United States was supreme in the New World. The Venezuelan boundary controversy provided just such an opportunity.

The apparent sudden arousing of American interest in resolving the boundary dispute in 1895 clearly reflected the growing domestic pressures on the president to assert American power. Both Republican Henry Cabot Lodge and Democrat John T. Morgan, the nation's leading foreign policy spokesmen, were criticizing Cleveland's failure

[51]*Foreign Relations* (1895), p. 1028; Gresham, *Walter Quintin Gresham*, 2:785; Tansill, *Thomas F. Bayard*, pp. 680–81.

to take action.[52] Meanwhile, the Venezuelan government had hired the former American minister to Caracas, William Lindsay Scruggs, to act as its agent in publicizing its position in the dispute. Scruggs kicked off his public relations campaign in 1894 with the publication of a pamphlet entitled "British Aggressions in Venezuela, the Monroe Doctrine on Trial." His premise was the same one Blaine and Harrison had acknowledged: any British claim to additional territory violated the Monroe Doctrine's anticolonization decree. Scruggs successfully lobbied in Congress to get a resolution favoring Venezuela's position passed in February 1895. He also sent Cleveland a copy of his pamphlet and, when Gresham died suddenly in May 1895, and Attorney General Richard Olney became secretary of state, Scruggs hastened to send the new man a copy as well.[53]

Richard Olney had risen from a modest background to a position as an extremely successful lawyer in Boston, intimately associated with the reorganization of several New England railroads. Although President Cleveland had met Olney only once, when he was casting about for names of good men to serve in his cabinet in 1893, Olney's work as a Democratic fund-raiser and his legal skills convinced the president to name him attorney general. The two dissimilar men fell into a very amicable working relationship; Olney's energy and ability to come to a decision quickly complemented Cleveland's plodding, cautious style. Indeed, so efficiently did he work that, unlike other officials in Washington, Olney seldom went home late and never let his work interfere with his leisure and vacation activities. Prone to impatience, Attorney General Olney had won national fame and not a little notoriety for his hasty decision to send federal troops to suppress the Pullman Strike in Chicago, in 1894. He exhibited the same forcefulness and self-confidence when Cleveland shifted him over to the State Department.

The impact a secretary of state's personality could exert upon the direction of policy in this period is nowhere more graphically apparent than in a comparison of Cleveland administration foreign policies under Gresham and then under Olney. The latter spelled out his conceptions of America's major interests in foreign relations in a lengthy article he wrote in 1898. He insisted that the United States

[52]Henry Cabot Lodge, "England, Venezuela, and the Monroe Doctrine," *North American Review* 160 (June 1895): 651–52; Nelson M. Blake, "Background of Cleveland's Venezuelan Policy," *American Historical Review* 47 (January 1942): 261.

[53]Grenville and Young, *Politics,* pp. 135–50; Dexter Perkins, *The Monroe Doctrine* (Baltimore: Johns Hopkins University Press, 1937), p. 143; Tansill, *Thomas F. Bayard,* p. 665; Scruggs to Olney, 17 June 1895, Richard Olney Papers, LCMD.

could not remain isolationist; it was a great power and would shortly take a leading position in the community of nations. He also favored the extension of American trade to new overseas markets.[54] Olney's attitudes thus comfortably matched the main currents of American foreign policy thinking in the late nineteenth century. He personally brought his president's policies into a much closer alignment with tradition than had his unpretentious predecessor at the State Department.

Characteristically, Olney left Washington for his summer home at Falmouth, Massachusetts, just after being named to the highest appointive post in the executive branch. Alvey Adee ran the department while Olney vacationed—and worked on his note concerning the Venezuela boundary dispute. He summarily scrapped the conciliatory proposals Gresham had been drawing up relative to the boundary controversy. Obviously influenced by the arguments from the Scruggs pamphlet, Olney drafted a stern message for Ambassador Bayard, in London, to deliver to the British government. The note revealed the rather startling way in which Olney apparently ranked the importance of the factors involved. Of least concern were the actual details of the boundary dispute itself. Olney showed considerably more annoyance with England's refusal to treat with sufficient respect the requests of an American republic, Venezuela. But the secretary of state's main point was that, because of the Monroe Doctrine, England's disrespect was a matter of paramount concern to the United States. He therefore managed to transform the venerated doctrine into a justification for American interference in virtually any hemispheric problem associated with a European country.

President Cleveland referred to Olney's 20 July 1895 note as a "twenty-inch gun."[55] After a rather superficial review of past British-Venezuelan negotiations over the boundary, Olney got to the source of the American concern: the Monroe Doctrine's admonition that no part of America was open to colonization. Ever since its issuance in 1823, Olney insisted, the doctrine had made the United States responsible for preventing European incursions in the Western Hemisphere. Referring specifically to the boundary dispute, he proclaimed that "Great Britain cannot be deemed a South American state within the purview of the Monroe Doctrine, nor, if she is appropriating Venezuelan territory, is it material that she does so by advancing the

[54]Richard Olney, "International Isolation of the United States," *Atlantic Monthly* 81 (May 1898): 577–88.
[55]*Foreign Relations* (1895), pp. 545–63 contains text of Olney's note.

frontier of an old colony instead of by the planting of a new colony."
Olney went even further, ridiculing all European colonization in the
New World: "That distance and three thousand miles of intervening
ocean make any permanent political union between an European
and an American state unnatural and inexpedient would hardly be
denied."

The secretary of state offered several additional justifications for
American interference. He pointed out that the frequent interposi-
tion of the United States in the dispute "has made it clear to Great
Britain and to the world that the controversy is one in which both its
honor and its interests are involved and the continuance of which it
can not regard with indifference." In addition to its honor, markets
were important to the United States. Olney claimed that United States
citizens were "friends of the States of America, commercially and
politically." A European takeover of even a part of one of the Latin
American nations would signify "the loss of all the advantages incident to their natural relations to us." Olney then touched on the
democratic mission theme:

> The people of the United States have a vital interest in the cause of
> popular self-government . . . and they are content with such assertion
> and defense of the right of popular self-government as their own secu-
> rity and welfare demand. It is in that view more than in any other that
> they believe it not to be tolerated that the political control of an Ameri-
> can state shall be forcibly assumed by an European power.

Because of its commitment to the ideals of democracy, the United
States could not stand idly by; it must act. And his nation could act,
Olney insisted, because of its supremacy in the New World.

> Today the United States is practically sovereign on this continent, and
> its fiat is law upon the subjects to which it confines its interposition.
> Why? It is not because of the pure friendship or good will felt for it. It is
> not simply by reason of its high character as a civilized state, nor because
> wisdom and justice and equality are the invariable characteristics of the
> dealings of the United States. It is because, in addition to all other
> grounds, its infinite resources combined with its isolated position ren-
> der it master of the situation and practically invulnerable as against any
> or all other powers.

In thus drawing support from all three of the traditional themes
underlying American foreign policy, Olney showed that he was definitely not acting in concert with Venezuela. He remained in contact
with the Venezuelan government, but he decided when and how to
move on the basis of strictly American considerations. Here, the pri-

mary problem was a British disregard of United States rights and honor. Olney's 20 July 1895 note was a direct descendant of the emphatic canal notes Blaine had fired off to London in 1881 and of Frelinghuysen's subsequent defense of the Monroe Doctrine. Weary of the constant barrage of Republican criticisms of his foreign policy, Cleveland expressed delight over this assertive initiative, telling Olney that "It's the best thing of the kind I have ever read."[56] The two Democratic statesmen could not immediately reap any partisan benefits from the note, however, because diplomatic proprieties forbid its publication until they had a British reply.

They waited in vain. British Prime Minister Lord Salisbury had just formed his government, retaining for himself the foreign office portfolio. He assigned a very low priority to the American fulminations over a minor boundary dispute. Salisbury personally considered the United States negligible, and he planned to treat the whole affair as disdainfully as Lord Granville had dealt with Blaine and Frelinghuysen. More than four months elapsed before Lord Salisbury deigned to respond, and his note took a couple of additional weeks to cross the Atlantic. It thus failed to arrive in the United States until after President Cleveland had delivered his annual message in early December 1895.

Salisbury began, reasonably enough, with an absolutely correct statement: "The disputed frontier of Venezuela has nothing to do with any of the questions dealt with by President Monroe."[57] After all, Great Britain had won its colony from the Dutch in 1814, before Venezuela had become independent of Spain and before President Monroe had even been elected. Consequently, British claims could hardly be construed as new colonization. In any case, Salisbury went on, as merely a unilateral statement on the part of an American president, the Monroe Doctrine had absolutely no standing in international law. The prime minister did not fear the United States; therefore, he chose to ignore any American assertion of power in the Western Hemisphere. Before concluding with a repetitive discussion of why the British could not and would not arbitrate with Venezuela, Salisbury vehemently denied Olney's implication that its political union with Canada was "inexpedient and unnatural."

Republican leaders had already begun to flay the president for his inaction in foreign affairs when Cleveland jolted them with a

---

[56]Cleveland, *Presidential Problems*, pp. 256–59; Henry James, *Richard Olney and His Public Service* (Boston: Houghton Mifflin, 1923), p. 111.
[57]*Foreign Relations* (1895), pp. 563–76 contains text of Salisbury's reply.

special message to Congress on 17 December 1895. The message included both Olney's note and Salisbury's reply, giving the public its first look at the new, aggressive Cleveland stance. The president unreservedly rejected the British contention that the Monroe Doctrine lacked relevance to the dispute; he also reiterated Olney's claim that the dispute was of prime importance to the United States. Cleveland's strident language tended to obscure the basic moderation of his actual proposal. He sought congressional sanction to create a United States commission to investigate the whole boundary dispute, determine an appropriate boundary line, and then report back to the president. Only then, if Britain and Venezuela had not yet reached an agreement, would Cleveland by implication attempt to impose the commission's decision upon them.[58]

Olney's audacious note and Cleveland's bold stand well suited the American temperament. Letters poured in from friends and even a few political rivals complimenting Olney for the vigor and tone of his note. Cleveland's defense of the Monroe Doctrine stole the Republican party's thunder. On 4 December 1895, Republicans Henry Cabot Lodge and Shelby Cullom had introduced separate resolutions in the Senate calling for the United States to formalize and define the Monroe Doctrine. "The time has come for a plain, positive declaration of the Monroe Doctrine by Congress," Cullom declared, "and then, if necessary, plain positive enforcement of it against all comers."[59] After Cleveland's 17 December message, Senator Lodge momentarily abandoned his partisanship in order to claim a position at the head of the line of Republicans supporting the president's Venezuela policy. Like the secretary of state himself, many of these nationalists obviously cared much more about America's prestige than about Venezuela's boundary.[60]

One American remained distinctly unimpressed: Thomas F. Bayard in London was quite critical. He disliked associating the United States' interests with those of Venezuela, a country he felt had been misruled for years. Bayard's discontent bothered President

[58]Richardson, *Messages and Papers*, 8:6088; Gerald G. Eggert, *Richard Olney: Evolution of a Statesman* (University Park: Pennsylvania State University Press, 1974), pp. 221–22; George B. Young, "Intervention Under the Monroe Doctrine: The Olney Corollary," *Political Science Quarterly* 57 (June 1942): 255–57.

[59]*Congressional Record*, 54th Cong., 1st sess., p. 109.

[60]Theodore Roosevelt to Olney, 20 December 1895, Redfield Proctor to Olney, 18 December 1895, Horace Lurton to Olney, 19 December 1895, John Hicks to Olney, 18 December 1895, Olney Papers, LCMD; Garraty, *Henry Cabot Lodge*, p. 165; Karl Schriftgiesser, *The Gentleman from Massachusetts, Henry Cabot Lodge* (Boston: Little, Brown, 1944), p. 144.

Cleveland, who took great pains to explain and justify his position. In a rambling, personal letter to the American ambassador, Cleveland emphasized how cautious his commission concept was in comparison to the more dangerous methods others had suggested for resolving the differences between the disputing nations. He definitely did not underrate the importance of defending the Monroe Doctrine, however, saying, "I am entirely clear that the Doctrine is not obsolete, and it should be defended and maintained for its value and importance *to our government and welfare,* and that its defense and maintenance involve its application when a state of facts arises requiring it."[61]

The great emotional outpouring of support for Cleveland's policy failed to impress the self-assured British prime minister. Lord Salisbury was confident his empire could take on the Americans anytime. The Monroe Doctrine actually mattered very little to the British government, however, so pressure came to bear on the prime minister to relent. At this crucial juncture, news spread of the unsuccessful Jameson raid on the Boers in South Africa. The German kaiser promptly sent a congratulatory note to the Boers. This evidence of German hostility toward England combined with the possibility of a war in South Africa added to the British cabinet's desire to defuse the Anglo-American confrontation. Salisbury had to back down. He grudgingly admitted that the United States had a legitimate interest in the boundary negotiations, and, eventually, accepted American aid in arranging for arbitration between Venezuela and Great Britain. Olney had thus achieved his primary goal of getting the British to recognize and implicitly accede to the United States' claim of preeminent political influence in Latin America.[62]

Europeans generally resented Olney's contention that the Monroe Doctrine justified American interference in any Western Hemisphere issue involving a European country. To get a more restricted definition of that doctrine, the British privately suggested to Bayard that the United States call a conference of all the European powers with colonies in the Western Hemisphere. At the conference, the Europeans would pledge never to expand their colonial holdings, giving the Monroe Doctrine's anticolonial restriction official standing in international law. Despite Bayard's enthusiasm, Olney torpedoed

[61] Bayard to the President, 18 December 1895, Olney Papers, LCMD; Nevins, *Letters of Grover Cleveland,* pp. 418–19; Tansill, *Thomas F. Bayard, p. 748.*
[62] Grenville and Young, *Politics,* pp. 170–75; James, *Richard Olney,* p. 134; Perkins, *Monroe Doctrine,* p. 218; Young, "Intervention," p. 159; Ernest R. May, *Imperial Democracy* (New York: Harcourt, Brace, 1961), p. 50; Richard W. Van Alstyne, *The Rising American Empire* (Chicago: Quadrangle, 1965), p. 164.

this attempt to restrict the Monroe Doctrine to an internationally sanctioned set of definitions by claiming that the United States was "content with the existing status" of the doctrine.[63] Of course Olney was content with its status: as long as the Monroe Doctrine remained the unilateral property of the United States, American policymakers could conveniently reinterpret it to fit new circumstances. It continued to be an extraordinarily useful rationalization for all facets of the United States' Latin American policy.

Another British initiative found a much friendlier reception in Washington. Throughout its interference in the boundary dispute, the United States had emphasized the wisdom of arbitration. The British called the American bluff by suggesting that the United States and England agree to a bilateral arbitration treaty. Olney did not object to arbitration per se, and he felt such a treaty would encourage the warming trend in Anglo-American relations discernable in the wake of the British retreat over Venezuela. Working with British Ambassador Julian Pauncefote, the secretary of state completed the arbitration treaty early in 1897, but, to Olney's great disappointment, the Senate refused to approve. The senators did not intend to relinquish their jealously-guarded control over foreign affairs to outside arbitrators.[64]

The actual boundary dispute was eventually settled through the mechanism of a bilateral arbitration treaty between Great Britain and Venezuela, a fact which Cleveland later noted saved it from the "risk of customary disfigurement at the hands of the United States Senate."[65] The United States' role was primarily that of keeping the two parties negotiating long enough to reach an agreement. Olney used the American commission's report as a goad to both sides. The British saw no point in delay, because Republican John Hay informed Lord Salisbury that even if his party won the presidential election in 1896, a Republican administration would pursue Olney initiatives. Having failed to consult seriously with Venezuela throughout the whole affair, the secretary of state exhibited little displeasure that the British government essentially won its maximum demands in the arbitration. His only regret seemed to be that this result tended to discredit the process of international arbitration which he personally favored.[66]

[63]Eggert, *Richard Olney*, pp. 230–32; James, *Richard Olney*, pp. 228–32; Perkins, *Monroe Doctrine*, pp. 221–22.

[64]*Foreign Relations* (1896), pp. 224, 237–38; Eggert, *Richard Olney*, pp. 250–53; James, *Richard Olney*, pp. 144–49.

[65]Cleveland, *Presidential Problems*, pp. 276–77.

[66]Eggert, *Richard Olney*, pp. 249–50; James, *Richard Olney*, p. 248; Young, "Intervention," p. 266.

The Venezuela boundary episode had profound effects in several areas. It hastened the day when the century-old anti-British resentment in the United States would subside and a general rapprochement begin. The Latin American countries exhibited a heightened respect for and fear of the United States, which now seemed powerful enough to dictate the course of events in the Western Hemisphere. The Monroe Doctrine's scope increased, giving the United States a good deal of freedom in its own sphere. But the most important result of the boundary dispute and its resolution was its effect upon the international reputation of the United States. Olney frankly admitted that concern for American prestige underlay the drafting of his note. Many years later he claimed that "the excuse . . . was that in English eyes the United States was then so completely a negligible quantity that it was believed only words the equivalent of blows would be really effective."[67]

These weighted words were delivered at a crucial moment. While Olney was bedeviling the British in 1895, the Cuban people were launching a war of liberation against their Spanish colonial masters. The vigor with which Olney defended the cause of self-government and his assertions about the preeminence of American power in the New World did not slip by unnoticed in Cuba. The rebels wondered if they could entice the jingoist American people into supporting their cause. The longer the war persisted, the more likely the American people were to involve themselves in its resolution.

[67]James, *Richard Olney*, p. 140.

4

The United States
Seizes an Empire, 1895–1899

Although Theodore Roosevelt considered his boss, Navy Secretary John D. Long, "a dear," the rambunctious assistant secretary also confessed he would like to "poison his mind so as to make him a shade more truculent in international matters."[1] For his part, Long distrusted his likable but volatile subordinate, despite Roosevelt's energetic and generally successful efforts to put the navy in fighting trim in early 1898. Everyone at the Navy Department was operating under a strain in late February. On the fifteenth, the U.S.S. *Maine* had exploded with great loss of life in Havana harbor. The department had just arranged for a naval court of inquiry to investigate. The newspapers clamored for revenge and retribution. On the twenty-fourth, Secretary Long had warned, in his diary, that "the slightest spark is liable to result in war."[2]

In fact the strain was so great that Long decided to go home for the afternoon of the next day to rest. "Do not take any . . . step affecting the policy of the Administration without consulting the President or me," Long ordered his impetuous assistant secretary. "I am not away from town and my intention was to have you look after the routine of the office while I get a quiet day off. I write you because I am anxious to have no unnecessary occasion for a sensation in the papers."[3] Blithely ignoring this injunction, Theodore Roosevelt, as

[1]Elting E. Morison, ed., *The Letters of Theodore Roosevelt*, 8 vols. (Cambridge, Mass.: Harvard University Press, 1951–54), 1:701–2.

[2]Margaret Long, ed., *The Journal of John D. Long* (Rindge, N.H.: Richard B. Smith, 1956), p. 216.

[3]Joseph Bucklin Bishop, *Theodore Roosevelt and his Time* (New York: Scribners, 1920), p. 86.

acting secretary of the navy, cabled Commodore Dewey of the Asiatic Squadron to "keep full of coal. In the event of war your duty will be to see that the Spanish squadron does not leave the Asiatic coast, and then offensive operations in the Philippines."[4] Needless to say, the secretary felt his assistant had rather broadly interpreted what was routine in the office. Roosevelt had, Long told his diary, "come very near causing more of an explosion than happened to the *Maine.* . . . The very devil seemed to possess him yesterday afternoon."[5]

This particular episode has been described and analysed exhaustively over the succeeding years, but two points in particular need to be stressed. First, whatever Long may personally have thought of Roosevelt's instructions to Dewey, he did nothing to rescind them. Even though a subordinate official in the Navy Department had choreographed the first step in the seizure of a Pacific empire, his superiors either intentionally or carelessly neglected to cancel the orders. In this, as in so many other instances associated with the Spanish-American War, major policy decisions just seemed to materialize in an ad hoc manner. It was easier to go along with the trend, to acquiesce to subordinates' decisions, to take another step forward rather than to turn back or even to pause for thought.

The second moral of the story is that, if the devil possessed Roosevelt on that long-ago February afternoon, the nation as a whole was also in the throes of a demonic possession. A great many Americans were eager to take up arms, to man warships, and to march off to war. But why was this so? How had the supposedly peace-loving, idealistic American people become so stirred up? Why were they seemingly violating their great national principles in this way? The answers lie in an examination of the workings of the three traditional foreign policy themes as the century drew to a close.

Viewed from a strictly diplomatic perspective, the Spanish-American War does not represent a startling departure in United States foreign policy except in the one respect that it was a war. The explanations given for American entry, the actions taken during the fighting, and the goals sought during the peace negotiations all directly related to what had gone before in American foreign policy. Obviously, the war and its consequences crucially affected the nation's future development, but, if one understands the emotions, attitudes, and precedents operating upon the United States' foreign policy prior

[4] Allen Westcott, *American Seapower Since 1775* (Chicago: J. B. Lippincott, 1941), p. 222.

[5] Long, *Journal of John D. Long,* pp. 216–17.

to the conflict with Spain, the postwar changes appear less jarring. The war gave vent to the pressures seeking to fulfill and enlarge upon the three major diplomatic themes of this period, serving to speed up tremendously the normally glacial processes of change in international relations. But, one must be careful to examine whether this acceleration process basically altered American outlooks and fundamentally changed America's international goals, or if it simply carried the United States further down the path it had already selected.

In 1899, A. Lawrence Lowell wryly noted that "our country has been suddenly placed in the position of a man who, intending to make a small bid at a foreclosure sale to protect the interest of a poor neighbor, finds himself unexpectedly the owner of a large estate subject to a heavy mortgage."[6] Lowell was hardly unique in his view that external events had manipulated the United States into a position it had never intended to occupy. Historian Ernest R. May provides the most lucid recent formulation of this explanation for the United States' emergence as a world power, suggesting that European events and European examples launched the United States on its imperialistic career. As he puts it, "Some nations achieve greatness; the United States had greatness thrust upon it."[7] The energetic proponents of American colonization and expansion in the 1890s would hardly agree that their strenuous efforts had all been for nothing.

Those who had been urging the nation to expand through the two decades prior to 1898 would definitely have sided with H. H. Powers. "We have not suddenly changed our ideals," Powers wrote during the war, "we have been slowly developing them for a century and have suddenly discovered their application to a new situation. The war is a revelation rather than a revolution. . . . It is the natural outcome of forces constantly at work in the race and exceptionally characteristic of the American people."[8] Contemporary journals published article after article pounding away at the theme that the war was only crystallizing and strengthening the sentiments and traditions that had gone before. Some claimed American colonization had begun as early as 1784, when the Continental Congress began administering the western lands won in the Revolution. Others drew

---

[6]A. Lawrence Lowell, "The Colonial Expansion of the United States," *Atlantic Monthly* 83 (February 1899): 145.

[7]Ernest R. May, *Imperial Democracy* (New York: Harcourt, Brace, 1961), p. 270.

[8]H. H. Powers, "The War as a Suggestion of Manifest Destiny," *Annals of the American Academy of Political and Social Science* 12 (September 1898): 3.

parallels between the insular imperialism of the 1890s and the nation's earlier territorial expansion to the west and south.[9]

Certainly, expansionist sentiments were not a new phenomenon in the United States; they had been circulating with increasing frequency before the war began. We have already seen how the three expansionist themes undergirded all American foreign policies, whether conservative Democrats or aggressive Republicans were in charge. Continuing domestic economic problems increased the popularity of proposed external solutions to internal difficulties. The glut theory had enjoyed wide circulation in the twenty years before the nation plummeted into another paralyzing depression in 1893; now overseas markets seemed even more essential. Populists, laborers, industrialists, and those engaged in commerce at every level were convinced of the efficacy of market expansion abroad. Even the return of prosperity in late 1897 and early 1898 could not reverse the trend, as avid trade-expansionists claimed that increased exports had brought the nation out of its enervating depression.

Universal support for market expansion did not resolve the question of exactly how that expansion ought to be achieved. American surplus goods could simply be dumped on the free markets in the Far East and Latin America. Although few would oppose this pursuit of the free enterprise system overseas, many Americans wondered if it would be enough. The European trading nations were actively pursuing imperialistic courses, and no one could guarantee that they might not seize the free markets, cutting them off from American trade. The United States might well have to capture its own colonies to insure areas for the extension of America's economic influence abroad. But, whether they advocated colonial or noncolonial trade expansion, the American people generally seemed willing to go along with the idea of using external means to resolve the domestic depression.[10]

Nationalism and pride also helped encourage the political expansion of the United States in the 1890s. Many Americans believed that the United States was equal or superior to those nations recognized as great world powers. If the United States took colonies it

[9]Henry Cabot Lodge, "Our Blundering Foreign Policy," *Forum* 19 (March 1895): 15; John R. Procter, "Isolation or Imperialism?" *Forum* 26 (September 1898): 15; Carl Schurz, "Manifest Destiny," *Harper's Monthly* 87 (October 1893): 740.

[10]Procter, "Isolation," p. 21; R. B. Bradford, "Coaling-Stations for the Navy," *Forum* 26 (February 1899): 747; Charles Denby, "Shall We Keep the Philippines?" *Forum* 26 (November 1898): 279.

would prove the nation capable of carrying its share of the "white man's burden" and force others to recognize American prominence. Consequently, spreading American political influence to distant areas through colonization would enhance the nation's prestige as well as its commercial importance. Even crusty old Independent Republican Carl Schurz, an outspoken opponent of colonialism and imperialism, admitted that

> to see his country powerful and respected among the nations of the earth, and to secure to it all those advantages to which its character and position entitle it, is the natural desire of every American. In this sentiment we all agree. There may, however, be grave differences of opinion as to how this end can be most surely, most completely, and most worthily attained.[11]

Schurz definitely did not feel that embarking on an imperialist crusade was the proper course, nor did he favor trying to win political prominence through success in war. Many other Americans felt quite certain that only a great military victory would guarantee the United States full recognition of its rightful place among the great powers. Some even went as far as Admiral Luce had in his article on the benefits of war, which claimed that conflict enabled mankind to advance civilization. Yet even the most enthusiastic jingoists were not necessarily bloodthirsty. They anticipated a short, relatively painless war; after all, the powerful and resourceful United States should be able to dispatch its enemies quite easily. No one in the 1890s viewed war as the unthinkable, cataclysmic act it has come to be considered after two devastating world wars and the proliferation of nuclear armaments. War should be avoided, to be sure, but not at the cost of national honor. As it turned out, the sort of decisive, exciting, relatively effortless war Americans contemplated was the sort of war they got in 1898.

Fueling the jingoism of the times were the aging members of the Civil War generation. Over time, veterans of the North and the South had managed to repress their memories of the carnage, the discomfort, and the boredom they had endured during the long sectional conflict. But their moments of glory stood out vividly. The old soldiers stirred envy among their sons and grandsons with their stories of great battles and acts of heroism—stories which became more legendary with each repetition. Younger men felt that they, too, must have an opportunity to prove their valor and manliness; they, too, deserved a baptism under fire. When 300,000 men stampeded off to volun-

[11]Schurz, "Manifest Destiny," p. 738.

teer for duty in the war in 1898 along with the impulsive Theodore Roosevelt, they did so for many of the emotional, self-seeking, and ill-considered reasons the future president was acting upon.

Jingoism and imperialist attitudes had been evident for years, but the nation's aggressive expansionism came to a crest only after some additional factors emerged in the 1890s. For example, the 1890 census concluded that no discernible frontier line existed in the continental United States, a conclusion which raised anxiety about the nation's future. Historian Frederick Jackson Turner tapped the sources of this anxiety when, in 1893, he propounded his famous thesis that America's frontier experience had been directly or indirectly responsible for making the nation unique. Unique meant better in many American minds, and they feared the United States might lapse into mediocrity or decay without the cleansing, enobling effects of the frontier. They hastened to accept the suggestion that the capture and development of noncontiguous colonies could serve as a substitute for the lost continental frontier.

A second internal development that helped Americans justify the taking of colonies in the 1890s was the rise of a particularly virulent and repellent strain of racism. With the abandonment of enforced reconstruction in the late 1870s, northerners generally turned their attention toward modernization and industrialization. Left to fester on their own, the former Confederate states became a laboratory for the development of ever more discriminatory laws, customs, and behavior. The ability of the whites to segregate and disfranchise the blacks eroded even the most dedicated abolitionists' faith in the equality of the races. A heavy dose of white supremacy tainted much of the American expansionist doctrine. The United States had become great, it maintained, because white Anglo-Saxons had been in charge from the beginning. The domestic acquiescence to racism implicit in the Supreme Court's landmark *Plessy vs. Ferguson* case in 1896, tended to infect the nation's foreign policy as well. Ironically, it tied in very comfortably with the idealistic American sense of mission. Americans must share their great democratic ideals with others less fortunate. But if they were, after all, innately superior, the Anglo-Saxons had a responsibility as well as a right to rule areas inhabited by those of lesser races.

An additional factor that added strength to the drive for American expansion in the 1890s was a nagging fear of external attack. Technological advances had occurred in the speed and armament of the world's navies. Strategic considerations associated with the isthmian canal project as well as concern for the defense of both Pacific and Atlantic coasts led many individuals both in and out of government to conclude that the taking of colonies was essential to United States security. Since the early 1880s, Congress had been providing funds for the building of modern naval vessels. These steam-powered ships required conveniently located coaling stations. The American people's fascination with naval growth and defense helped urge them toward a colonial policy at the same time it armed the nation's statesmen with the wherewithal to capture noncontiguous territories. By the late 1890s, the American public seemed as eager as the naval officers directly involved to find an excuse for testing their new implements of war.

Fortunately, the testing of American power in 1898 had other, more laudable aspects. "When the war was begun, most of the Continental nations failed to conceal their contempt of us," admitted the *Atlantic Monthly,* but "they now respect us as they never dreamed they should. Nor is it only our naval victories that have given the world a somewhat new conception of the United States. Quite as impressive has been the absence of the old-time barbarities of war and of warlike vindictiveness."[12]

The democratic mission strain which underlay American foreign policy enabled Americans to contend that the United States' victory over Spain and its acquisition of an empire could be considered intrinsically just and good. After all, the capturing of colonies must certainly be moral if it helped fulfill God's great destiny for the United States. Throughout the 1890s, exponents of the large policy for the United States stressed mission sentiments in justifying the country's expansion. Because of its commitment to idealism, they argued, the United States would create a colonial system morally superior to that of all other nations; only the British might possibly be able to approximate the virtuous colonial administration Americans would operate. In addition, the further the United States spread its democratic ideas, the more civilized the world as a whole should become.

By the 1890s, the passive phase of America's traditional democratic mission was ending. The world was in a bad way, and Americans could help by extending their selfless, republican spirit overseas. Americans imbued with democratic mission spirit saw the taking and running of colonies as a great opportunity to implement their ideal system abroad. There could be no tyranny in American imperialism, the *Atlantic Monthly* maintained, because "the nature of our institutions forbids that we should set up any form of government except

[12]"The War with Spain, and After," *Atlantic Monthly* 81 (June 1898): 432.

one that at the earliest possible moment shall become self-govern-ment."[13] Bringing democracy to the enslaved, providing aid for the downtrodden, giving hope to the despondent—all these sentiments were inherent in America's emotional imperialistic impulse.

Obviously, Americans had perceived a great many positive vir-tues in the expansionist philosophy prior to the Spanish-American War. The long, vociferous, but inconclusive debate over the annexa-tion of Hawaii had helped publicize these attractive features. At the same time, the debate had given the American people an opportunity to learn of the possible drawbacks of imperialism. A whole catalog of antiimperialist arguments had emerged, ready to be drawn upon during the postwar discussion over colonialism. So fundamental were the three traditional foreign policy themes, however, that the oppo-nents of expansion made frequent use of them. They simply inter-preted their effects differently.

The antiexpansionists, for example, might agree that overseas markets would provide important economic benefits for the nation, but they failed to share the optimism of the expansionists as to the availability of such markets. China remained an extraordinarily poor nation, they pointed out, and the Chinese peasants probably never would have the wherewithal to become significant consumers of American surpluses. Others suggested that simple changes in Ameri-can trade policy would bring far greater immediate economic benefits than wars or conquests in distant lands. William Graham Sumner claimed that, "If we want more trade we can get it any day by a reciprocity treaty with Canada, and it will be larger and more profita-ble than that of all the Spanish possessions."[14] Others disinterested in expansive economic adventures expected that the domestic economy would eventually be capable of absorbing America's surplus produc-tion. Besides, forceful seizures of markets did not square with the American ideal of rugged competitiveness. Good quality, cheap American products should be able to find markets abroad without any governmental or military assistance.[15]

Many antiimperialists passionately expressed their faith in the democratic ideal. Even if they agreed that the United States rep-

[13]"The End of the War, and After," *Atlantic Monthly* 82 (September 1898): 430.

[14]William Graham Sumner, *The Conquest of the United States by Spain and Other Essays* (Chicago: Henry Regnery, 1965), p. 161.

[15]Robert L. Beisner, *Twelve Against Empire: The Anti-Imperialists, 1898–1900* (New York: McGraw-Hill, 1968), p. 217; Worthington C. Ford, "New Opportunities for American Commerce," *Atlantic Monthly* 82 (September 1898): 326; Carl Schurz, "The Anglo-American Friendship," *Atlantic Monthly* 82 (October 1898): 439.

resented the apogee of civilization's political and social development, however, they felt more comfortable with the older, passive democratic mission. Those who failed to learn from the American example should not be subjected to coercion. Force would be futile in any case, if one believed as did Carl Schurz that, "It is a matter of universal experience that democratic institutions have never on a large scale prospered in tropical latitudes."[16] Not everyone agreed America ought to pursue its civilizing mission. In an extraordinarily bitter condemnation of the whole mission concept, Mark Twain concluded that the way great powers treated weaker peoples bore little resemblance to the ideals they supposedly cherished. "Is it, perhaps, possible that there are two kinds of Civilization," he asked rhetorically, "one for home consumption and one for the heathen market?"[17]

Worse still, colonialism might wreck the American system by tarnishing the democratic ideal at home. Many opponents of colonization considered it unconstitutional. How could imperialists speak in lofty terms about extending human rights and civilization overseas, the antiimperialists asked, if in doing so they violated the American constitution? It was incongruous to praise self-government at home while simultaneously denying it to colonial peoples. Americans had spent more than a century trying to define exactly how different— and better—the United States was than any nation in Europe; now it seemed bent on emulating the worst characteristics of the great powers. William Graham Sumner's essay entitled "The Conquest of the United States by Spain" emphasized the many autocratic and distasteful acts Americans had to perform in dealing with the realities of colonial rule.[18]

Aside from the moral costs, the antiimperialists took a hard look at the monetary outlays expansion would require. The war costs were only the beginning. Colonies would greatly extend the nation's defensive perimeter and require continuing and inflated military appropriations. The free security the United States had enjoyed because of its isolation from the other great powers would disappear if the country took on the responsibility of protecting distant, insular regions from external attack or internal dissention. Many antiimperial-

[16]Schurz, "Manifest Destiny," p. 740.

[17]Mark Twain, "To the Person Sitting in Darkness," *North American Review* 172 (February 1901): 167.

[18]Beisner, *Twelve Against Empire*, p. 216; Sumner, *Conquest*, p. 139; Arthur A. Ekirch, Jr., *Ideas, Ideals, and American Diplomacy* (New York: Appleton-Century-Crofts, 1966), pp. 94–95; William MacDonald, "The Dangers of Imperialism," *Forum* 26 (October 1898): 180.

ists doubted that the value of the increased trade colonies might generate for the United States could offset the costs of defending and maintaining them as dependencies.[19]

Mundane considerations like these never deterred those who wanted the United States to become the world's great civilizing nation. For them, emotional returns would far exceed any material costs. And, after all, it was emotionalism that inevitably drew the United States into the Cuban Revolution. The nation decided actively to pursue its traditional expansionist goals, ignoring the antiimperialists' carping and reticence. Indeed, had they succeeded in somehow halting American expansionism after the Spanish-American War, they would have been responsible for a dramatic aberration in American foreign policy. The nation had become accustomed to expanding throughout the whole of its existence. As seen, a few final adjustments were made to the expansionist course in the 1880s and 1890s, but nothing could stop the nation's drive to expand and to earn universal acclaim as a great power.

Cuba was the last major American colony of the Spanish Empire which, in its heyday, had encompassed two-thirds of one continent and half of another. Faithful Cuba had remained loyal to the mother country, but there had been moments of disillusionment. The most serious was a rebellion that broke out in 1868 and then ran for a full decade. The Cuban rebels abandoned the fight only when the Spanish government promised to abolish slavery on the island and to institute other reforms. No one was particularly surprised when the poverty-stricken and internally-divided government in Madrid failed to do all it had promised. This predictable failure mattered little, however, because the rebels could not rouse the population to renewed revolt. A large number of the most articulate supporters of independence for the island had fled to the United States during the ten-year rebellion. In due course they became naturalized American citizens, but, much like the latter-day Castroite exiles in Florida, many of them nurtured the dream of someday going home to free their island.

The United States had frequently eyed Cuba as a logical prospect for annexation. At the beginning of the century John Quincy Adams had predicted that Cuba would inevitably become a part of the United States. In 1854, three top-level American diplomats in Europe went

---

[19]Howard K. Beale, *Theodore Roosevelt and the Rise of America to World Power* (New York: Collier Books, 1962), p. 34; MacDonald, "Dangers," pp. 181–82; Schurz, "Manifest Destiny," pp. 743–44; Edward Atkinson, "Eastern Commerce: What is it Worth?" *North American Review* 170 (February 1900): 302–3.

so far as to issue the Ostend Manifesto, threatening that the United States would seize the island if Spain did not sell it. Sectional antagonisms in the United States prevented this threat from being carried out. After the Civil War, interest in annexing the island rose again. Some Americans attempted to persuade the United States to intervene during the 1868–1878 rebellion, but President Grant's fixation on Santo Domingo effectively distracted the nation's attention. Meanwhile, Cuban-American economic ties became quite close. The United States was the logical market for Cuba's tropical products, and American investment in the island became substantial. The 1890 McKinley Tariff's cancellation of the American tariff on sugar gave the Cuban economy a tremendous boost which Blaine's reciprocity treaty with Spain in 1891 reinforced. The heady vision of prosperity that the Cubans had entertained for the first time in their history was ruthlessly shattered when the 1894 Democratic Wilson-Gorman Tariff ended all reciprocity agreements and reimposed a duty on foreign sugar. Cuba's economy buckled. This renewed economic distress enabled the Cuban people once again to forge a revolutionary determination. José Martí led his freedom fighters into their first skirmishes in the spring of 1895.

The United States government did not immediately sympathize with the "Cuba Libre" movement. The rebels' guerrilla war tactics sometimes seemed more brutal and destructive than necessary. Until they had assumed the trappings of respectability by establishing a skeleton government and winning some important skirmishes, the official United States posture was at best equivocal. The American people, however, showed no such reluctance to express their sympathy with the rebellion. The rebels' bombastic and idealistic pronouncements made exciting reading, so the American press enthusiastically reprinted them and kept up a steady stream of criticism of Spain. The Spanish minister to the United States repeatedly pointed out that many of the top officials in the self-styled Cuban Republic were actually American citizens still living in New York City, but this made no difference.[20] After all, Americans had made heroes of the naturalized Irish-Americans who had returned to the Emerald Isle to fight the hated British. Why should they now criticize the naturalized Cuban-Americans who were fighting to throw off colonial chains?

[20]French Ensor Chadwick, *The Relations of the United States and Spain* (New York: Scribners, 1909), pp. 440–41.

The rebels cleverly exploited the American public's sympathy with their activities. The Cuban liberators desperately hoped that the United States government would, by one means or another, help them drive the Spanish out. To show American officials where their duty lay, the Cubans emphasized the democratic aspirations of their movement. Thus rebel diplomat Tomás Estrada Palma told Secretary of State Olney that as soon as the revolt had begun, its leaders had "issued a call for the selection of representatives of the Cuban people to form a civil government." Palma drove his point home with the claim that the Cuban people were fighting for "the noblest principle of man—independence."[21] The rebels' cultivation of a democratic image definitely had the desired effect if it could move Senator William V. Allen of Nebraska to urge American intervention, because he believed it to be "the true policy and the true doctrine of our country that wherever a people show themselves desirous of establishing a republican form of government upon any territory adjacent to us they should receive our encouragement and support."[22]

Sympathy with a democratic revolt was, of course, only one of several reasons for American concern over the fate of Cuba. American annexation was still very much a live topic of discussion. Furthermore, protection of the existing American investments on the island, as well as the expectation that a free Cuba would welcome still more investment, received frequent mention. President Cleveland himself insisted late in 1896 that the American people had a concern with Cuba "which is by no means of a wholly sentimental or philanthropic character. . . . Our actual pecuniary interest in it is second only to that of the people and Government of Spain."[23]

President Cleveland's natural caution prevented him from moving in any direction very quickly. The conservative Democratic leader feared that American jingoists might attempt to precipitate direct American military involvement, an involvement that would inevitably bring up the question of annexation. The president's previous actions as well as his statements after the war clearly indicate his opposition to any form of colonial expansion. In order to head off the annexation spirit, the Cleveland administration devoted its primary efforts toward getting the fighting in Cuba stopped, thus wiping out any

[21]U.S., Congress, Senate, Committee on Foreign Relations, *Affairs in Cuba,* 55th Cong., 2d sess. (1898), Report No. 885, pp. 9, 13. Cited hereafter as *Affairs in Cuba.*

[22]U.S., Congress, *Congressional Record,* 54th Cong., 1st sess., p. 36.

[23]James D. Richardson, *A Compilation of the Messages and Papers of the Presidents,* 10 vols. (Washington, D.C.: Bureau of National Literature, 1911), 8:6150.

excuse for armed interference by the United States. While working along these lines behind the scenes, the president publicly affirmed his intention to remain strictly neutral.[24]

Congress was much more willing to choose sides. The development of the first of several congressional attempts to force the president to recognize the rebels as belligerents occurred in the spring of 1896. In addition to intangible morale benefits, American recognition of this state of belligerency would permit the revolutionaries to purchase arms and supplies in the United States. Secretary of State Olney refused, insisting that the executive branch alone had the prerogative of making any decision about recognition. John Bassett Moore, a renowned American expert on international affairs, defended the administration's position by claiming that recognition of the state of belligerency would have little practical effect in any case. Actually, the problem was much more ticklish than either Moore or the congressmen who sympathized with the rebellion cared to admit. Any move that indicated official acknowledgment of the existence of a rebellion would obviously strain State Department relations with the Spanish government, perhaps to the breaking point. Furthermore, jingoes in the United States might then press for their government to defend the Monroe Doctrine's principle outlawing European colonization, with Spain now defined as a European colonizing power. For these and other reasons, even the more favorably disposed McKinley administration never extended any sort of recognition to the rebels.[25]

While Cleveland publicly insisted on neutrality, he privately allowed his secretary of state great latitude. The public learned of this only when the correspondence between Richard Olney and Spanish Minister Dupuy de Lôme was published in 1897. The American statesman touched upon all of the traditional themes of American foreign policy in his long note of 2 April 1896. Olney warned Spain that the United States habitually felt a natural empathy with any revolution designed to bring about freer political institutions. He re-

[24]Charles A. Beard, *The Idea of National Interest* (c. 1934; reprint ed., Chicago: Quadrangle, 1966), p. 68; Walter LaFeber, *The New Empire: An Interpretation of American Expansion 1860–1898* (Ithaca, N.Y.: Cornell University Press, 1963), p. 268; Allen Nevins, ed., *Letters of Grover Cleveland: 1850–1908* (Boston: Houghton Mifflin, 1933), p. 448.

[25]LaFeber, *The New Empire,* p. 298; May, *Imperial Democracy,* p. 90; Richardson, *Messages and Papers,* 8:6068; Henry James, *Richard Olney and his Public Service* (Boston: Houghton Mifflin, 1923), p. 168; John Bassett Moore, "The Question of Cuban Belligerency," *Forum* 21 (May 1896): 288–300.

ferred to the United States' substantial economic interests in Cuba, as well as to the detrimental effects the rebellion was having on other American interests in the Caribbean. To end the dispute, Olney proposed that the United States mediate between Spain and the rebels. The Spanish government unequivocally rejected this attempt to exercise American political influence in the matter, holding fast to its contention that the situation in Cuba was a purely domestic affair. In declining the American offer of mediation, however, the Spanish government had also thrown away its only chance to use the United States in its own behalf. From that point on, the Colossus of the North drew ever closer to the rebel side and to the possibility of armed intervention against Spain.[26] After the 1896 Democratic presidential convention had rejected his record and policies for William Jennings Bryan and free silver, Cleveland made no further moves. He had no intention of saddling his successor with a war.

Democrat Bryan lost in November to Republican William McKinley, a man who is something of a historical enigma because of his great political talent of seeming to reflect the views of whomever he encountered. A successful career politician from Ohio, McKinley definitely had fixed convictions, but he was prudent in expressing his views publicly as president, preferring his advisers to work out a consensus acceptable to him. This expertise at benignly manipulating those around him evoked loyalty from a diversity of individuals and support from a great variety of interest groups. It also complicates the historian's task of sorting out exactly what he personally believed and precisely when he adopted these beliefs.

One can learn little from the men he chose to advise him on foreign policy. In organizing his cabinet, president-elect McKinley made an incredibly poor choice for the State Department. John Sherman's fame has proved much more fleeting than that of his brother, William Tecumseh Sherman, who had ravaged Georgia in 1864. Particularly after the Civil War, however, when his brother had essentially retired, John Sherman came into his own. A power in Ohio politics, Sherman spent most of his long life in public office, serving both as a senator and as secretary of the treasury. His name is linked to the basic federal antitrust law, and his wisdom and political skills were

---

[26]Chadwick, *Relations of U.S. and Spain*, pp. 465–66; U.S., Department of State, *Papers Relating to the Foreign Relations of the United States* (Washington, D.C.: Government Printing Office, 1897), pp. 540–44; John A. S. Grenville and George Berkeley Young, *Politics, Strategy, and American Diplomacy* (New Haven, Conn.: Yale University Press, 1966), pp. 190–93.

widely recognized. He habitually received delegate votes at presidential nominating conventions, so he seemed a natural choice to head the cabinet when a fellow Ohioan, McKinley, became president.

Even before his inauguration, however, McKinley found himself forced to defend his appointment as rumors of the aging Sherman's senility and incompetence circulated. When the governor of Ohio appointed McKinley's political manager and mentor, Mark Hanna, to succeed Sherman in the United States Senate, vicious allegations about corrupt bargains swept the nation. Sherman was bound to fail. He was physically not up to the job, particularly when the nation seemed to be rushing pell-mell toward war. Almost at once, the president began working behind Sherman's back. The old man finally resigned in a rage just before the war began.

The man whom McKinley had relied upon from the beginning, Assistant Secretary of State William R. Day, then moved into the top spot. Day had no great political ambitions and in his own way was as uncomfortable heading the State Department as Sherman had been. McKinley needed him, however, and the two worked well together. A country lawyer and judge from the president's home town of Canton, Ohio, Day had known McKinley for years. He was a hard-working, pleasant man who found his legal and judicial skills useful in untangling the diplomatic complexities the war brought. He also found the services of the omnipresent Adee invaluable, both as he learned the ropes under Sherman and after he had taken over officially. Day had no clearly defined views on expansion, however, as he illustrated after he had resigned to join the peace commission negotiating with Spain in 1898.

McKinley's last secretary of State, John Hay, was the only one with any prior diplomatic experience. By the time Hay took over, however, many of the key decisions with regard to Cuba had already been made and the future was well mapped out, in part by fate. Hay soon came to exercise an enormous influence on the direction of American foreign policy, but his major contributions came after the Spanish-American War had ended.

By the time McKinley moved into the White House in March 1897, the American people had long since become aroused over the well-publicized, ruthless Spanish efforts to snuff out the revolutionary movement in Cuba. The president, however, had his own personal priorities, and he did not intend to waste his chance to use his election mandate to bring about changes in the tariffs and the domestic depression. He immediately called a special session of Congress, which passed the Dingley Act, a protective tariff program reminiscent of the one McKinley had authored seven years earlier. Coincidentally, the nation's economy finally began to recover. Consequently, by the fall of 1897, McKinley was ready to turn his full attention to the festering Cuban crisis.

Until that time McKinley had pursued a policy quite similar to the one Cleveland had favored: hoping that a peace or truce arrangement in Cuba would absolve the United States of any need for direct involvement. Also, like Cleveland, McKinley had warned Spain that his patience had a limit. Although he assured the government in Madrid he had no intention of annexing Cuba to the United States, he reserved his criticism for the Spanish government and never condemned the rebels' policies. McKinley's views thus matched those of the vast majority of Americans who considered Spain at fault. A dedicated advocate of the Americans' democratic mission, McKinley noted in his first annual message that "we have only the desire to see the Cubans prosperous and contented, enjoying that measure of self-control which is the inalienable right of man, protected in their right to reap the benefit of the exhaustless treasures of their country."[27]

Cleveland's neutral, moderate Cuban policy had been unpopular; McKinley's similarly cautious approach threatened to undermine his support in the Grand Old Party. By 1896 the expansionism some of the younger Republicans had been advocating for years had achieved respectability and widespread acceptance in the party. Meanwhile, popular pressures for some sort of resolution of the Cuban disturbance grew ever more insistent, but, as yet, the American people disagreed over what form that resolution should take. The yellow press, swept along by William Randolph Hearst's *New York Journal* and Joseph Pulitzer's *New York World,* urged the government to declare war against Spain immediately. Thousands of Americans stood ready to volunteer their services the moment war was declared. Historian Charles Beard referred to the Spanish-American conflict as a people's war, but the people were generally content to await the McKinley administration's decision as to when the war would start.[28]

The moral support the president received from those he most trusted helped confirm his intention to delay making that fateful decision. Prominent individuals like businessman Edward Atkins bombarded the administration with notes insisting that continued non-interference or even outright American support of the Spanish

[27]Richardson, *Messages and Papers,* 8:6255.
[28]Samuel Flagg Bemis, *The Latin American Policy of the United States* (c. 1934; reprint ed., New York: Norton, 1967), p. 136.

government's efforts would most effectively and quickly calm the situation.[29] The business community certainly did not want to tamper with the slowly improving economy in 1897, and a war might well nip this fragile prosperity in the bud. Eventually, however, the Cuban rebellion would appear to be disturbing hemispheric conditions sufficiently to interfere with American commercial and market expansion. At that point the business community would join those demanding any action which would end the conflict. For some time, however, this was not the case, and President McKinley enjoyed a good deal of support for whatever he chose to do.

Regardless of their conflicting views as to what, if anything, should be done, everyone agreed that the conflict in Cuba was vicious and sanguinary. The Spanish government had appointed tough, hard-headed Valeriano Weyler as governor-general in Cuba. Weyler ordered all of the population into well-defended villages or concentration camps. Those who ignored the Spanish governor's orders were assumed to be either rebels or rebel sympathizers, so the Spanish troops were told to fire upon any one outside of the concentration areas. Weyler's policy resembled the "strategic hamlet" concept applied in the 1960s in Vietnam, but in 1897 Cuba the wealthy United States government was not shipping tons of food and supplies into the concentrated population areas. Many Cuban peasants had been nearly destitute before the concentration order; cut off from their farms, relatives, and jobs, they were even less able to fend for themselves. American newspaper reports exaggerated the human costs of the concentration scheme, claiming it had caused the death of half a million or more people. Actually the figure was about 100,000, which seems appalling enough.

A devout, humane Christian, President McKinley found the Cuban suffering extremely disturbing. As humanitarianism and Christian charity became intertwined with the democratic mission theme, the American people felt duty-bound to help those emulating their own revolutionary example. Throughout the fall of 1897, while the United States badgered Spain to find a way to halt the war and its attendant suffering, the McKinley administration also emphasized its humanitarian and mission sentiments. On Christmas Eve, Secretary of State Sherman announced that the Spanish government had agreed to

[29]Edward Atkins to Day, 28 December 1897, William R. Day Papers, LCMD; Samuel B. Capen to Long, 28 March 1898, Henry C. Higginson to Long, 30 March 1898, John D. Long Papers, Massachusetts Historical Society.

allow Americans to contribute money and goods for the relief of the suffering Cuban people. President McKinley donated $5,000 of his personal funds to this cause.[30]

The administration's diplomacy was less successful on more important issues, as neither the Spanish nor the rebels ever admitted that they might not, ultimately, succeed. As long as the United States government remained officially neutral with regard to the conflict, it maintained its regular, formal diplomatic ties with Spain. In the fall of 1897, assassins murdered the Spanish prime minister who had dispatched Weyler to Cuba. The new Spanish ministry responded to American pressures and agreed to withdraw Weyler and replace him with a less cold-blooded governor-general. This step ended whatever slim chance Spain had of ending the rebellion through sheer force of arms. And it was far from the last step the Spanish took to avoid giving the United States cause for war.

The primary American goal remained the same: to bring a speedy end to the conflict. Spain could easily have done so by giving in to the rebel demands. To avoid having to grant the island its independence, however, the Spanish government developed an autonomy plan in the late fall of 1897. Under this plan, the Cuban people would have their own assembly to handle internal governmental affairs, but the island would remain in a sort of dominion status in the Spanish Empire. The autonomy scheme had been worked out with the advice of the American minister to Spain, General Stewart L. Woodford. He had promised the Spanish foreign minister that "if the autonomy when decreed should be such as would give the Cubans actual and honest self-government in local affairs," the United States would refrain from interfering until it had been given a fair trial.[31] Here the Spanish were playing to the American mission theme; they knew the United States government would favor any steps that appeared to be leading toward greater self-government. The autonomy scheme proved to be an unmitigated failure. The rebels continued to demand complete independence, and the Spanish loyalists in Cuba balked at sharing their power and influence with the local population in a popular assembly. Secretary of State Sherman and Minister Woodford also informed the Spanish authorities of the United States'

---

[30]Chadwick, *Relations of U.S. and Spain*, p. 529; *Foreign Relations* (1897), pp. 511, 514; H. D. Money, "Our Duty to Cuba," *Forum* 25 (March 1898): 19; Theodore Roosevelt, *An Autobiography* (New York: Scribners, 1913), p. 209.

[31]*Foreign Relations* (1898), pp. 600–602.

total disillusionment with the autonomy arrangement.[32] Recognition of the failure of the autonomy scheme coincided with the publication of the Dupuy de Lôme letter and the sinking of the U.S.S. *Maine*. All three events had the effect of live grenades lobbed into the arsenal of American resentment against Spain.

Spanish Minister Enrique Dupuy de Lôme had time and again sought to convince the United States of his personal sincerity and of his nation's rectitude and honor. Weary of this long and unrewarding struggle, he revealed his true feelings in a private letter to a Spanish official visiting in Cuba in December 1897. A rebel agent spotted the letter in the Havana post office and immediately recognized its propaganda value. The Cuban junta arranged for the New York press to give it front-page treatment on 8 February 1898. The Spanish minister resigned even before the State Department demanded his official recall. The most famous line in the letter characterized McKinley as "weak and a bidder for the admiration of the crowd, besides being a would-be politician who tries to leave a door open behind himself while keeping on good terms with the jingoes of his party." Although he had obviously not stated it in the most flattering manner, Dupuy de Lôme was really only describing a president struggling to find the appropriate policy as the leader of a democratic nation and of a party filled with men calling for war. The United States government also protested Dupuy de Lôme's suggestion that the Spanish government raise, "if only for effect, the question of commercial relations" as a way of distracting the United States government from the mess in Cuba. Woodford frostily informed the Spanish foreign minister that the first line insulted American honor and the second illustrated Spanish insincerity.[33] The American people vocally and emphatically expressed their impatience with Spain and their willingness to support a show of force in defense of their nation's honor.

Yet the furor the Dupuy de Lôme letter caused seems inconsequential when compared to the reaction that greeted the next tragic and unexpected incident. On the evening of 15 February 1898, the United States second-class battleship *Maine* exploded and sank in Havana harbor, killing over 260 officers and men. Why was an American ship there at all? The *Maine* had been dispatched to Havana for the same reason the U.S.S. *Baltimore* had been stationed at Valparaiso in 1891 and the U.S.S. *Detroit* had been sent to Rio de Janeiro in 1894.

[32]Ibid., pp. 666–67; Money, "Our Duty to Cuba," p. 24.
[33]*Foreign Relations* (1898), pp. 1007–13.

Any nation that considered itself a great power might send warships to protect its citizens' lives and property in rebel-endangered areas and not incidentally to provide tangible evidence of its strength and concern. Consul-General Fitzhugh Lee, the highest ranking American official on the island, had fired off message after message before Christmas, reporting on the riots and violence in the island's capital city which might result in damage to American property. By the time the Navy Department had detached the *Maine* from the Atlantic Squadron, however, Lee had to admit that the spate of violence in Havana had ended. Sending a battleship down seemed like a relatively safe way to quiet the calls at home for some show of American concern, however, so the United States dreamed up an excuse to send the ship anyway. Referring to the navy's usual practice of sending ships to visit foreign ports to show the flag and encourage American trade, the United States government announced that the *Maine* would make a peaceful visitation to Havana. Of course the ship's presence could not help but impress Spain with the United States' strength.[34] The Spanish were extremely annoyed at the ship's arrival. They had contended time and again that the continuing evidence of American concern kept the revolution going.

Exhaustive examinations and inquiries then and later failed to uncover the reason for the ship's explosion. The Americans eager to go to war hardly cared; they considered avenging the American deaths a matter of national honor. Spain was officially accountable for everything that occurred in Cuba; therefore, Spain must atone for the catastrophe. Senator Joseph B. Foraker's comments illustrate the intensity of emotions and the skewed nature of some of the thinking the *Maine* disaster triggered.

> The commanding fact remains that our ship and sailors were destroyed by a governmental agency of war for which Spain was as much responsible as she was for the guns in her forts. It, therefore, follows that not only the act of destruction, but also the act of placing us in danger without warning, was an act of war; and we would have been justified in opening fire on Morro Castle the moment we found the keel plates on the deck of the ship.[35]

Theodore Roosevelt summed it up more succinctly when he wrote Alfred Thayer Mahan: "Personally, I can hardly see how we can

---

[34]Ibid., pp. 1025–26; Richardson, *Messages and Papers*, 8:6278.

[35]Joseph B. Foraker, "Our War with Spain: Its Justice and Necessity," *Forum* 25 (June 1898): 389.

avoid intervening in Cuba if we are to retain our self-respect as a nation."[36]

Despite his own desire to hold off, President McKinley found himself in the position of a man trying to rein in a runaway team. The American naval court of inquiry did not issue its inconclusive report until the end of March, but no one bothered to wait for it. Early in March, Congress rushed through a special defense appropriations bill making $50 million immediately available to the armed services. Most of the funds were wisely earmarked for naval preparedness, since the army used its share to begin constructing useless land fortifications in the continental United States. The appropriations act had most important psychological effects, however. The Cuban rebels saw it as concrete proof of American sympathy for their stand, and it stiffened their resolve to hold out for full independence. Meanwhile, the Spanish began to recognize how truly desperate their condition was in relation to the United States. Minister Woodford happily reported from Madrid that the appropriations bill "has not excited the Spaniards—it has stunned them. To appropriate fifty millions out of money in the Treasury, without borrowing a cent, demonstrates wealth and power."[37]

As March drew on, the Spaniards continually lost ground in their effort to calm America's growing impatience over the Cuban situation. On 17 March, Senator Redfield Proctor of Vermont, a highly respected Republican, delivered to Congress a lengthy report on conditions in Cuba, which he had just visited in a private capacity. Before his trip, Proctor confessed he had distrusted the reports in the popular press, feeling they had exaggerated greatly the level of the suffering on the island. His own visit had convinced him otherwise: the situation was truly desperate. He reeled off fact after fact to prove his point. Proctor actually had favored the large policy for some time, but he had carefully kept his expansionist sentiments hidden from the public. Consequently, many Americans considered him a moderate spokesman, and his heartrending tales of anguish and suffering intensified the pressure on the McKinley administration to bring about some resolution to the inhuman conflict.[38]

With the United States apparently moving irreversibly toward intervention, the Spanish ministry once again sought support from the other European great powers. No European intervention could

[36]Theodore Roosevelt to Mahan, 21 March 1898, Papers of Alfred Thayer Mahan, LCMD.

[37]*Foreign Relations* (1898), p. 684.

[38]*Congressional Record*, 55th Cong., 2d sess., pp. 2916–19.

succeed without the cooperation of Great Britain, but it had no intention of bailing out the ramshackle Spanish Empire. The British government had a number of other more important commitments, and it hoped to embroider upon and strengthen rather than destroy its improving relationship with the United States. The British ambassador in Washington, Julian Pauncefote, misunderstood his government's views, however, and he agreed to lead an international conciliation attempt. On 6 April he and several other top-level European diplomats called upon the United States to refrain from warlike moves. The American government simply ignored this call for restraint. When Pauncefote's home government then disavowed his action, Spain was left to its own depleted devices.[39]

Throughout March and into April, the Spanish played a delaying game. If they could stave off American action until Cuba's rainy season began in May, the inclement weather might blunt the rebel drives and reduce the pressures for American intervention. Neither Woodford nor his superiors in Washington would permit such a delay. Forced to the wall, the queen of Spain proclaimed an immediate and unconditional suspension of hostilities in Cuba. Some contemporaries and many historians have argued that the Spanish had at that point given in to all of President McKinley's demands, and the subsequent American war declaration was unconscionable. The inadequacies of Spain's autonomy scheme, however, had given the United States little reason to believe a unilateral Spanish armistice proclamation would end the fighting. After all, the rebels, not Spain, had begun the hostilities, and they had no intention of stopping until they had won complete independence for Cuba. The Spanish refused to go that far. They apparently felt it would be more honorable to surrender to a great power than to a band of colonial rebels.[40]

William McKinley forthrightly mentioned the Spanish armistice decree when he finally requested Congress to empower him to take action on 11 April 1898. His annual message late in the year conveniently summarizes his reasons for seeking a war declaration:

> The grounds justifying that step were the interests of humanity, the
> duty to protect life and property of our citizens in Cuba, the right to
> check injury to our commerce and people through the devastation of

[39] May, *Imperial Democracy*, pp. 164, 175, 181; R. G. Neale, *Great Britain and United States Expansion: 1898–1900* (East Lansing: Michigan State University Press, 1966), pp. 15, 31–32.

[40] *Foreign Relations* (1898), pp. 665, 675, 734–35; Grenville and Young, *Politics*, pp. 262–63; Long, *Journal of John D. Long*, p. 223; H. Wayne Morgan, *America's Road to Empire* (New York: John Wiley, 1965), p. 59.

the island, and, most important, the need of removing at once and forever the constant menace and the burdens entailed upon our Government by the uncertainties and perils of the situation caused by the unendurable disturbance in Cuba.[41]

The president thus proposed that the United States declare war against Spain for reasons of its own, not because the Cuban revolutionaries had asked for help. Indeed, they had not. The rebels found themselves in the same position as the Venezuelans who had petitioned the United States for assistance in the boundary dispute: they could not direct or limit American actions or prevent the United States from pursuing its own interests first and foremost. It is not altogether clear that the Cuban rebels had anticipated a full-scale American invasion of Cuba; they certainly could not be sure of obtaining their goal of independence once the United States had intervened. McKinley himself strongly opposed the idea of having the United States formally recognize the Cuban revolutionary government either before or after it entered the conflict. Despite McKinley's wishes, this issue caused great controversy in the ensuing congressional debates.

The Senate Foreign Relations Committee was cleared for action. It quickly published a voluminous report dealing with the history of Cuban-American relations and reporting on its hearings about the *Maine* explosion and related events. The committee referred in passing to the Monroe Doctrine which, it claimed, had made the United States responsible for all colonial problems in the Western Hemisphere. More important, the report stressed that "the inalienable right of self-preservation" gave the United States the right to intervene. The war was causing too much turmoil in its vicinity, and Germany, Britain, and even France had at one time or another been rumored to be considering a takeover of Cuba. "That our safety demands that we should control the possession of that island is not to be questioned," the committee insisted. "That in controlling the government of the island we should protect its people in the enjoyment of life, liberty, and property is equally true. We can not keep Cuba in the possession of Spain without being responsible for Spain's government of its people."[42] In short, the United States was extending its political influence, as well as pursuing its democratic mission in interceding in Cuban affairs.

[41]Richardson, *Messages and Papers*, 8:6310–11.
[42]*Affairs in Cuba*, Part 2, p. 8.

Spicing the ensuing congressional discussion were allusions to humanitarian responsibilities, national honor (specifically with regard to the *Maine*), as well as duty to civilization and to the Cuban people. The question of what official relationship the United States should have to the Cuban guerrillas and their shadow republican government provoked strong disagreement. Many spoke out passionately in favor of extending recognition to the Cuban revolutionary government and then joining it as an ally. As Senator Foraker commented, "We ought to be willing to recognize it because of its form and character. It is a republican form of government. It is a government based on a written constitution."[43]

Those who opposed American recognition of the Cuban republic explained their reluctance in many ways. Some pointed out, reasonably enough, that the rebels had so far created only the barest beginnings of a governmental structure, one which could not possibly rule the war-torn country responsibly; others could not openly express their reason for opposing recognition of the rebels: they wanted Cuba annexed to the United States. Many of the expansionists urging the acquisition of the more distant Hawaiian Islands felt it would be only natural for Cuba, too, to join the Union. Although they might not favor direct annexation, other Americans wanted the United States to stay clear of any commitment to a particular Cuban faction until the war had ended and the political turmoil had died down.

Senator Henry M. Teller of Colorado finally developed a proposal acceptable to all but the most outspoken annexationists. He would amend the war declaration to include a promise that the United States did not intend to exercise "sovereignty, jurisdiction or control" over Cuba. The United States could thus remain consistent with its ideal of self-government without becoming allied to the Cuban republican government. To gain congressional approval, the war declaration simply had to include a clear statement of the traditional American mission sentiment. But that statement could not be so self-denying as to alienate the imperialists, and his amendment won wide support. After the war, the senator indicated that he had proposed the amendment in part simply to neutralize possible adverse European reactions. Whatever his personal motivations, Teller had enabled the United States to participate in the Cuban conflict with untarnished democratic missionary zeal.[44]

[43]*Congressional Record,* 55th Cong., 2d sess., p. 3779.
[44]Ibid., pp. 3898–99; Elmer Ellis, *Henry Moore Teller* (Caldwell, Idaho: Caxton Printers, 1941), pp. 308–13, 343.

The war resolution that both houses of Congress approved on 25 April 1898 began: "Resolved . . . that the people of the island of Cuba are and of right ought to be free and independent."[45] At that moment, the democratic mission theme seemed paramount, but the others had obviously paved the way for the long-anticipated war declaration. And, once the fighting began, the American people became aware of the exhilarating fact that the war itself could help fulfill all of the nation's expansionist foreign policy desires.

Barely a week later, news flashed around the world of a great American naval victory in a place so remote that President McKinley was reputed to have had to look up its location on a globe. Following his prearranged plan, Commodore George Dewey had filled the Pacific Squadron's bunkers with coal in Hong Kong, where news of the war declaration reached him. He immediately began steaming to the southeast, toward the Spanish colony of the Philippine Islands. The squadron slipped into Manila Bay during the night, and, at dawn on 1 May the Americans spotted the Spanish fleet lying at anchor under the shore batteries of the naval station at Cavite. Without pausing, the American warships swept past, raking the Spaniards from stem to stern. Back and forth the American squadron steamed while both sides blasted away so furiously that impenetrable clouds of smoke rose, forcing Dewey to call a temporary halt. He consulted with his captains and was astounded to learn that only a few minor injuries had occurred and that his ships were almost completely unharmed. When the veil of smoke lifted, the Americans discovered that the Spaniards had fared much worse. Their fleet lay helpless in the water, razed, burning, or sunk. The fateful Battle of Manila Bay was over.

More than the war declaration or the ultimate American victory over the Spanish in Cuba, this particular event riveted world attention. Virtually overnight the United States had muscled its way to a top ranking among the naval powers of the world. At home, Americans saw the ease and speed of Dewey's victory as proof that the United States had been correct in going to war. God was on our side for sure.[46] The nation's journals blossomed with articles pressing for

[45]Richardson, *Messages and Papers*, 8:6297.
[46]Grenville and Young, *Politics*, p. 290; May, *Imperial Democracy*, p. 221; Julius W. Pratt, *Expansionists of 1898* (c. 1936; reprint ed., Chicago: Quadrangle, 1964), p. 289; William Roscoe Thayer, *The Life and Letters of John Hay*, 2 vols. (Boston: Houghton Mifflin, 1915), 2:167; Albert K. Weinberg, *Manifest Destiny* (Baltimore: Johns Hopkins University Press, 1935), p. 288.

the administration to follow up Dewey's victory with steps to assure America's prestige and position in the Far East. As former United States minister to China Charles Denby enthused,

> Dewey's victory is an epoch in the affairs of the Far East. We hold our heads higher. We are coming in to our own. We are stretching out our hands for what nature meant should be ours. We are taking our proper rank among the nations of the world. We are after markets, the greatest markets now existing in the world. Along with these markets will go our beneficent institutions; and humanity will bless us.[47]

The full consequences of the expansion of American political power into the Far East were only dimly perceived immediately after this glorious triumph. Other triumphs followed. The popular press glossed over the misery and hardships the ill-trained American troops encountered while fighting a war with inappropriate clothing, outmoded equipment, and inadequate supplies. Furthermore, McKinley's hesitancy had delayed the American war declaration until the uncomfortable rainy season had begun. None of this seemed important to those who eagerly volunteered, hoping to grab some of the glory. They made the most of the limited opportunities available in a short, relatively painless war in which disease claimed more than fourteen times as many lives as the 379 combat-related deaths. Happily for the glory-seekers, the one major army skirmish involved a dramatic charge to capture San Juan Hill, which dominated Santiago de Cuba, on 1 July. Two days later the Atlantic Squadron got a chance to destroy another incredibly decrepit Spanish fleet as it attempted to escape from the American army closing in from the east. The Spanish troops in Cuba generally fought only long enough to salve their honor before capitulating. In retrospect, the actual fighting appears almost inconsequential when compared to the striking political changes the Spanish-American War set in motion.

At home, expansionist sentiments seized the upper hand. The Teller Amendment had not outlined a timetable for setting Cuba free, so the McKinley administration decided to hold on to the island for a while. Dewey's victory raised the possibility of American control over the entire Philippine archipelago. To keep that option open, McKinley ordered troops sent from San Francisco to help stabilize the American position in Manila. Some detoured to Guam in the Marianas, took the Spanish authorities by surprise, and occupied the island. Although the highest ranking general in the United States

[47]Charles Denby, "Shall We Keep the Philippines?" *Forum* 26 (November 1898): 281.

Army, Nelson A. Miles, arrived in Cuba after the Spanish had been defeated, he was able to lead a successful conquest of his own, easily seizing the Spanish colony of Puerto Rico. Thus, several strategic decisions had put the nation firmly on an imperialistic course even before the official cease-fire. Just as Assistant Secretary Roosevelt's overzealousness in February had presaged Dewey's victory in Manila, so did these strategic decisions herald the beginning of the United States experiment in colonialism. In a way, the American people never really had a chance to decide whether they approved of colonization per se. Particularly by 1899 the matter at issue in the great imperialist-antiimperialist debates had already essentially been determined by executive action.

Realizing the hopelessness of its position, Spain requested an armistice on 22 July, maintaining that it had only fought to protect its honor. The Spanish authorities expressed doubts that Cuba could govern itself, but Secretary of State William R. Day guilelessly reassured them that the United States stood ready to provide the "aid and guidance" necessary to prepare the island for independence.[48] The armistice was finally announced on 12 August, the day before the United States Army planned to expand its authority over Manila. Communications were slow, however, so the Philippine capital was safely in American hands before news of the cease-fire reached the city.

As the warring parties had conducted their diplomatic dealings through the good offices of the French government, a conference to work out peace terms was scheduled to meet in Paris. The United States had irrevocably removed Cuba, Puerto Rico, and Guam from Spanish control. The only major territorial topic left to be discussed at the Paris conference would be a possible transfer of the Philippine colony from Spain to the United States. For better or worse, the war had already helped bring about American annexation of Hawaii, and the fact that the United States already had one major colony in the Pacific definitely aided those seeking to establish another in the Philippines. In order to understand fully the moods and attitudes of the American people in the fall of 1898, one must drop back and examine the final stages of the Hawaiian annexation.

The Republicans still smarted at the cavalier treatment Democratic President Cleveland had given their party's 1893 attempt at Hawaiian annexation. Therefore, almost as soon as William McKinley

[48]*Foreign Relations* (1898), pp. 819–21.

took office in 1897, he had ordered a new treaty negotiated. Once the eager Hawaiian leaders had signed the treaty in the summer of 1897, the United States Navy assumed full responsibility for defending the islands. McKinley wanted nothing to distract the special session of Congress he had called to approve his tariff program, so he waited to submit the annexation treaty until the regular session convened in December 1897. Then the president threw his full weight behind it, calling it the natural culmination of three-quarters of a century of close relations. The treaty went first to the Senate Foreign Relations Committee which was so distracted by the Cuban rebellion that it did not produce its report favoring Hawaiian annexation until mid-March 1898. The chances for amassing the two-thirds majority required for approval looked doubtful, however, so the treaty was dropped in favor of a joint congressional resolution which would require only a simple majority in both houses. The Hawaiian government did not care what process was employed as long as annexation was the ultimate result.[49]

The delays in congressional action, made even longer due to the declaration of war against Spain, left plenty of time for another acrimonious debate about annexation. Economic advantages figured prominently in the discussions. Even before the crushing of Spanish power in Manila, proponents of annexation were looking beyond Hawaii to the teeming population of the Far East as possible customers for American goods. Honolulu was envisioned as a busy entrepôt for goods shipped to and from the Orient. On the other hand, the Hawaiian Islands themselves offered only limited market potential, a fact which the antiimperialists used to ridicule the economic benefits arguments. William Graham Sumner went one step further, pointing out that, as the United States already totally controlled the Hawaiian economy, it would be foolish to take on the unnecessary and onerous burden of ruling the islands as well.[50]

[49]John Hay to Day, 9 May 1898, William R. Day Papers, LCMD; Matthew Luce to Long, 15 October 1897, John D. Long Papers, Massachusetts Historical Society; Richardson, *Messages and Papers*, 8:6263; William Adam Russ, Jr., *The Hawaiian Republic (1894–98) and its Struggle to Win Annexation* (Selinsgrove, Pa.: Susquehanna University Press, 1961), p. 141; U.S., Congress, Senate, *Compilation of Reports of the Committee on Foreign Relations, 1789–1901*, 56th Cong., 2d sess. (1901), Ex. Doc. No. 231, 8 parts (volumes), 7:203.

[50]*Congressional Record*, 55th Cong., 2d sess., p. 6143; John T. Morgan, "The Duty of Annexing Hawaii," *Forum* 25 (March 1898): 16; John R. Procter, "Hawaii and the Changing Front of the World," *Forum* 24 (September 1897): 39–40; William Graham Sumner, "The Fallacy of Territorial Extension," *Forum* 21 (June 1896): 416–17; Stephen M. White, "The Proposed Annexation of Hawaii," *Forum* 23 (August 1897): 729.

The mission theme was equally subject to conflicting interpretations. The large-policy proponents hailed the islands as a great testing ground for American democratic principles, emphasizing their long years of training under American Christian missionaries as well as their constitutional experience under the white government which, by then, had existed for half a decade. Opponents of annexation downplayed the importance of the tiny white population and expressed fear that the Hawaiian majority and the hoards of Chinese and Japanese immigrants could never rise to American political standards. Americans got on poorly with the very few Japanese and Chinese living in the continental United States, the antiimperialists pointed out. Would they do better with islands heavily populated with such peoples? By 1897, the American labor movement was criticizing the continuing importation of cheap labor into the islands and was therefore opposing annexation. This racist opposition did have an effect on the wording of the joint resolution: it contained a provision calling for an immediate end to Chinese immigration if Hawaii were annexed.[51]

Contradictory opinions existed as to just how essential Hawaii was to the defense of the United States. The Hawaiian government had already granted the United States its chief strategic advantage at Pearl Harbor; consequently the islands really did not need to be annexed in order to serve American defense purposes. Discussion of Hawaii's strategic value shifted abruptly from the hypothetical to the practical level after the war against Spain began. Dewey's fleet at Manila was thousands of miles beyond Hawaii and in need of supplies and reinforcements. The balance of American opinion definitely turned in favor of annexation when the war brought two issues into sharp focus. First, Hawaii's usefulness as a staging area for American advances in the Pacific was put to an actual test. Second, the prospect of a major expansion of American political influence into the Far East made the American people intensely suspicious of the other great powers, particularly of their possible interest in seizing Hawaii for themselves.

Characteristically, the Hawaiian government responded to the first issue by playing its trump card before the game really got underway. Hawaii might have remained neutral in the Spanish-American War, forcing the United States to make a bargain on annexation in order to get its support. Instead, the government in Honolulu an-

[51]*Congressional Record,* 55th Cong., 2d sess., pp. 6156–57; Morgan, "Duty," p. 13; White, "Proposed Annexation," p. 729; U.S., Congress, Senate, *Hawaiian Commission,* 55th Cong., 3d sess. (1898), Doc. No. 16, p. 2; Merze Tate, *The United States and the Hawaiian Kingdom* (New Haven, Conn.: Yale University Press, 1965), pp. 289–90.

nounced that it would side with the United States even before news of Dewey's victory had reached the islands. When the United States decided to ship additional troops and supplies to Manila, the Hawaiians were particularly helpful. The antiimperialists logically pointed out that the islands were in no way essential to the American efforts in the Philippines, as the great circle shipping routes between San Francisco and Manila came much closer to the American-owned Aleutians than they did to Honolulu. Nevertheless, an unshakable conviction spread that Hawaii was the logical and essential jumping off point for American expansion into the Orient.[52]

The second, war-intensified issue that swung support behind the annexation movement had to do with Japan. Between 1893 and 1897 Japanese immigrants had continued to pour into Hawaii. Meanwhile, Japan won an easy victory over China and gained undisputed control of Korea. After their heady successes in the Sino-Japanese War, the Japanese considered expanding in other directions. Hawaii held a natural appeal. By the summer of 1897, Japan's attitudes and ambitions had thoroughly spooked the State Department. Secretary Sherman issued standing orders to the American minister in Honolulu to announce a provisional American protectorate pending annexation if the Japanese seemed too aggressive. When the Senate Foreign Relations Committee issued its report favoring Hawaiian annexation in March 1898, the Japanese appeared much less threatening. The committee's report boasted that President McKinley's firmness had frightened them off. In fact, the Japanese were extremely interested in attracting American investment for their Korean stronghold, so they would never have jeopardized their good relations with the United States by moving to acquire Hawaii. Rumors flew about Japanese threats, however, and they had an effect very much like the earlier warnings of a possible British takeover. When the conflict with Spain erupted, wartime skittishness intensified American susceptibility to rumors of foreign interest in Hawaii. American annexation of Hawaii would knock out any such threat and make more credible American expansion in the Philippines.[53]

[52]Pratt, *Expansionists of 1898*, p. 319; Russ, *Hawaiian Republic*, pp. 281–88; Tate, *U.S. and Hawaiian Kingdom*, pp. 289–90; Thomas A. Bailey, "The United States and Hawaii During the Spanish-American War," *American Historical Review* 36 (April 1931): 553–59.

[53]Senate, *Foreign Relations Committee Reports*, 7:196; Tyler Dennett, *Americans in Eastern Asia* (c. 1922; reprint ed., New York: Barnes & Noble, 1941), p. 614; Sylvester K. Stevens, *American Expansion in Hawaii 1842–1898* (New York: Russell & Russell, 1968), p. 287.

The stormy annexation debates culminated in both houses of Congress in July 1898. Allusions to the economic expansion, political expansion, and democratic mission themes punctuated the oratory. Many realized that Hawaiian annexation had suddenly become a test case of how the United States felt about insular colonization in general. The American victories over Spain had presented the United States with several opportunities to obtain territory far outside its immediate vicinity. "I assume . . . that the annexation of the Hawaiian Islands is to be followed by the annexation of the Philippines, Puerto Rico, and Cuba at least," said Senator William V. Allen of Nebraska, "and that any man who advocates or votes for the annexation of the Hawaiian Islands will be estopped from denying the applicability of his reasoning or doctrine to the other islands."[54] While some considered this an even more compelling reason to prevent the annexation of Hawaii, others were just as eager to vote for it precisely because it set a precedent for future expansion. They saw it as only the first step in the creation of a global empire which would extend the beneficent political and moral influence of the United States to all of mankind.

The House rushed the resolution through, and the final Senate vote was 42 in favor with 21 opposed and 26 not voting. Because the Senate approved the joint resolution by exactly a two-thirds majority, the expansionists smugly claimed a treaty would have succeeded as well. Fortunately the annexation of Hawaii had few of the dire consequences the antiimperialists prophesied. Racial harmony has been better on the islands than on the mainland. The costs of defending Hawaii could never be considered in isolation from other American commitments in its vicinity, and Pearl Harbor eventually became the nation's major naval base in the Pacific. Governing the islands proved quite easy. The United States absentmindedly left the existing minority white regime in control for a couple of years before developing a standard territorial governmental structure. In short, the Hawaiian Islands slipped under American political influence with much less difficulty than the United States had encountered in carrying out some of its earlier continental expansion. All of this might not have occurred under normal circumstances, but the expansionist emotionalism running rampant in 1898 made the takeover seem quite effortless and reasonable.

The antiimperialists, of course, considered the annexation a tragic mistake. Furthermore, it had the baneful effect of encouraging

[54]*Congressional Record*, 55th Cong., 2d sess., p. 6703.

the expansionists and of setting a precedent for the annexation of more distant insular territories. The obvious parallels between annexing Hawaii and acquiring the Philippines were frequently noted in the succeeding months. The opportunity to take over the Philippines proved to be the Spanish-American War's great surprise issue— unplanned, unexpected, and disconcerting. The decision to attack the Spanish naval forces at Manila had emerged from naval strategic planning sessions held prior to the war declaration. If the United States neutralized Spain's naval power there, the Pacific coast of the United States would be safe from attack. Theodore Roosevelt's famous message to Dewey had only been one step in the implementation of this plan. No one anticipated the utter collapse of Spain's authority in the Philippines or that the United States would succeed so quickly in Cuba. Just before he deserted the Navy Department to form his Rough Rider regiment, Roosevelt indicated his opposition to annexing the Philippines, claiming they fell far outside the United States sphere of influence and interest. Hardly anyone in the United States including even the highest-ranking officials knew much about the Philippines prior to Dewey's stunning victory.[55] As the American people learned more about the islands and about their position in the world's balance of power, making them an American colony began to seem the only rational course.

The attitudes of the other great powers were crucial. In dramatically demonstrating that Spain was far too weak to defend the islands, the United States had threatened to disturb the balance of power in the Far East. The Philippines suddenly became the hottest item the current imperial market had to offer. Like Brer Rabbit, the United States was stuck in a Tar-Baby; it could not simply order its navy to steam out of Manila Bay and leave a power vacuum behind. Advice poured in from all sides. Both Japan and Great Britain definitely wanted to limit Germany's Far Eastern presence, so they wanted the United States to retain control, to keep it out of German hands. The United States had no substantial, existing territorial or political interests in the Far East; consequently, it was the only nation that could take over the islands without significantly altering the power balance in the Orient.[56]

[55]Dennett, *Eastern Asia*, p. 618; Grenville and Young, *Politics*, pp. 268–76; David Healy, *US Expansionism* (Madison: University of Wisconsin Press, 1970), p. 60.

[56]Memorandum of Conversation with Japanese Minister, 15 July 1898, William R. Day Papers, LCMD; Dennett, *Eastern Asia*, p. 638; Neale, *Great Britain*, pp. 111–12; Pratt, *Expansionists of 1898*, p. 333; A. Whitney Griswold, *The Far Eastern Policy of the United States* (New York: Harcourt, Brace, 1938), p. 22.

At home, those in favor of retaining control over the islands emphasized the United States' responsibilities as a world power in the Far East. Along with these responsibilities, imperialists perceived great opportunities for spreading the benefits of the American system. "We are responsible to the world for order in those islands," Senator Teller announced. "We must give the Filipinos a chance to learn to govern themselves. Our duty goes further than saying to them, 'Start a government and take care of yourself.' We must aid them, and as soon as possible let them take care of their own home and municipal affairs."[57] An opportunity to spread the gospel of democracy and republicanism exerted a strong attraction on the American people who had just fought a war to help the Cuban people achieve these same benefits. Surely the United States should hang on to the Philippines long enough to replace the tyrannical and corrupt Spanish government with something more just and responsible. Many Americans who favored the takeover obviously believed that the United States would keep the islands only until the Filipinos had developed fully a capacity for self-government.[58]

Opponents of acquisition used the mission theme to score points for their side. They were not sure the islands' population could ever be democratized. In October, Admiral Dewey himself reported on the deterioration in the political situation on the islands: "Distressing reports have been received of inhuman cruelty practiced on religious and civil authorities in other parts of these islands. The natives appear unable to govern."[59] On the other hand, this very incapacity seemed to make American administration all the more necessary. Whether they advocated annexation or independence, the Americans were guilty of selective perception. Thus, annexation-minded Americans did not admit that the full-scale rebellion which broke out just prior to the American acquisition of the islands represented a righteous struggle to throw off an oppressive master. Instead, it was the barbaric act of people obviously not yet capable of responsible self-government.[60]

No one could deny that the annexation of the Philippines would expand the nation's economic opportunities. Some writers could not

[57]Quoted in Ellis, *Henry Moore Teller,* p. 315.

[58]Long, *Journal of John D. Long,* p. 229; Weinberg, *Manifest Destiny,* pp. 290, 295; Frank F. Hilder, "The Philippine Islands," *Forum* 25 (July 1898): 534.

[59]*Foreign Relations* (1898), p. 298.

[60]Weinberg, *Manifest Destiny,* pp. 283, 297, 300–301; Philip C. Jessup, *Elihu Root,* 2 vols. (New York: Dodd, Mead, 1938), 1:333; Charles W. Dilke, John Barrett, and Hugh H. Lusk, "The Problem of the Philippines," *North American Review* 168 (September 1898): 262.

say enough about the Philippines' market potential. "The world contains no fairer nor more fertile lands, no more promising field for commercial enterprise," rhapsodized one imperialist.[61] Others were less optimistic. The primitive state of the archipelago's economy meant that heavy investment might be required to improve the standard of living and, correspondingly, the Filipinos' capacity to buy American goods. Fortunately, tax revenues from the islands paid for their upkeep from their very first years under American control, but the Philippines never became a sponge to sop up the American glut.

A much more convincing case could be made for the use of the Philippines as an entrepôt—an American Hong Kong. Revisionist historians have uncovered a vast body of evidence to support their contention that the lure of the China market was chiefly responsible for the American acquisition of the Philippines in 1898. The four hundred million Chinese were obviously a much more important group of potential consumers than the eight million Filipinos. During the 1880s and 1890s, trade expansionists had enthusiastically advertised the advantages of Far Eastern trade. The argument for retaining the Philippines as a way station to Oriental markets thus reached a well-primed audience. The recent creation of several European spheres of influence in or near China underlined the importance of an American foothold in the Far East. Germany, Russia, France, Great Britain, and, of course, Japan were well ensconced in the area; a commercial base of operations at Manila might be essential if the United States hoped to capture a share of the China market. And many Americans had convinced themselves that the China market was crucial to their nation's continuing prosperity. The United States would be foolish not to solidify the opportunity already in its grasp of creating a staging area for expanded trade in the Far East.[62]

President William McKinley would make the ultimate decision on the Philippines because he had the final say over what the United States demanded of Spain at the Paris peace negotiations. In large measure, McKinley allowed himself to be swept along by the emotionalism which was in overabundant supply in the summer and fall of 1898. In fact, the president had already stacked the deck in favor of annexation when he selected the five commissioners who would

[61]Hilder, "The Philippine Islands," p. 545.

[62]Beard, *National Interest*, pp. 81–82; Procter, "Isolation," pp. 21–22; William Appleman Williams, *The Roots of the Modern American Empire* (New York: Random House, 1969), p. 440; Thomas J. McCormick, *China Market* (Chicago: Quadrangle, 1967), pp. 107–25; John Barrett, "The Paramount Power of the Pacific," *North American Review* 169 (August 1899): 168.

negotiate with Spain. Three of them, newspaper magnate Whitelaw Reid and Republican Senators William P. Frye of Maine and Cushman K. Davis of Minnesota, had already publicized their enthusiasm for imperialist expansion. Secretary of State William R. Day, who resigned to attend the peace conference, had serious misgivings. Only the fifth commissioner, Democratic Senator George Gray of Delaware was a firmly dedicated antiimperialist. The instructions McKinley wrote for the peace commissioners called for the complete banishment of Spain from the Western Hemisphere. Cuban independence and American control of Puerto Rico and Guam were not negotiable. Then McKinley mentioned the Philippines' commercial importance due to their location near Oriental markets. More important, "The march of events rules and overrules human action," he admitted, and "the war has brought us new duties and responsibilities which we must meet and discharge as becomes a great nation on whose growth and career from the beginning the Ruler of Nations has plainly written the high command and pledge of civilization."[63]

At the Paris discussions, the Spanish tried to save the remnants of their empire in the Far East. As yet, American troops only occupied Manila and its environs; Spanish officials still governed the rest of the archipelago. The American commissioners heard testimony from several persons who had recently been in the Philippines. Commissioner Day thought that, because the bulk of the Filipinos were reportedly incapable of self-government, they should not be taken under American control. The imperialistic commissioners, Reid, Davis, and Frye, used the same reports to justify their call for the annexation of the entire archipelago rather than just Manila or the island of Luzon. From Washington, Secretary of State John Hay requested each of the commissioners to report his own feelings, but no one was particularly surprised when McKinley ordered them to press Spain to relinquish control to the United States. "Duty and humanity appeal to the President so strongly," Hay wrote the commissioners on 13 November, that the entire archipelago must be brought under the control of the United States. The American commissioners broke Spain's resistance by offering to add to the treaty a provision for a $20 million payment to encourage Spain to transfer the colony to United States ownership.[64]

The reaction to the actual signing of the treaty on 10 December 1898 was understandably mixed. A group of prominent Americans

[63]*Foreign Relations* (1898), p. 907.
[64]Ibid., pp. 920–49.

including ex-Presidents Benjamin Harrison and Grover Cleveland, as well as Mark Twain, William Graham Sumner, and Andrew Carnegie had formed an "Anti-Imperialist League." Inalterably opposed to the acquisition of the Philippines, the League urged the Senate to reject the peace treaty, which included American annexation of the archipelago. The antiimperialists' familiar arguments pointed out the damaging effects annexation would have upon the constitution, the American character, and democracy at home. Despite the fame and reputation of these men, their efforts came too late. The drive to expand America's worldwide political influence was at full throttle, and the annexation of Hawaii had broken down the last barrier to insular colonization. Nothing the antiimperialists could have done would reverse the century-old tradition of expansionism, particularly in the aftermath of the exhilarating, victorious war with Spain.

Their one faint hope lay in the fact that rounding up a two-thirds majority in the Senate is never easy. Although the Senate debated the treaty in secret executive sessions, the introduction of a couple of general antiimperialist resolutions gave the senators ample opportunity to voice their opinions in public. The discussions ranged over every conceivable reason for or against colonization, but many senators chose to emphasize what they perceived to be the United States' duty. The nation had already committed itself to assuming a responsibility which translated itself into the old familiar democratic mission. As Senator Knute Nelson of Minnesota claimed, "We are all ready with one accord to give those people the blessings of a good government. . . . We come as ministering angels, not as despots."[65] Unfortunately, no one had asked the Filipinos themselves whether they wished to be annexed. Just two days prior to the Senate's final action on the treaty, Filipino freedom fighter Emilio Aguinaldo declared war, touching off a bloody two-year guerrilla campaign against the United States. Like the fulminations of the Anti-Imperialist League, Aguinaldo's dramatic declaration came too late; most American minds had long since been made up. On 6 February 1899, the senators approved of the peace treaty and the acquisition of the Philippines by a vote of 57 to 27.

The Philippine insurrection would sputter on for two years, tarnishing American idealism and trying American patience. Although Dewey had slapped military censorship on all news reports going out of Manila even before any occupation troops arrived, disquieting rumors and stories circulated about the brutality and violence associated

[65]*Congressional Record*, 55th Cong., 3d sess., p. 838.

with the American army's efforts to subdue the rebels. Like the Spaniards they had displaced in Cuba, the Americans in Luzon and Mindanao found themselves reduced to extreme, inhuman tactics in searching out the rebel guerrillas who could blend in with the native population whenever they chose. Allegations of ruthless torture, civilian casualties, indiscriminate killing, and individual savagery blackened the United States' image at home and abroad. Eventually, more than four thousand Americans had died and some $170 million had been spent in order to extend the American mission to the Filipinos. Many Americans came to question the fundamental wisdom of their nation's becoming a great power if a bloody, debilitating, and costly guerrilla war was to be the chief reward.

For most Americans, however, the insurrection on those distant islands hardly impinged upon their perceptions. For years, they had been itching for a chance to show their stuff, and the Spanish-American War had provided that opportunity. In fact, the war and its aftermath had proved to be even more satisfying to the expansionists than expected. Those who had been advocating the expansion of American trade and political influence for so many years suddenly found their most optimistic ambitions fulfilled. With its new colonies in the Pacific and the Caribbean, the United States had undeniably begun to behave like a great world power in every respect.

5

Adjusting to Great Power Responsibilities

Because the Ansley Wilcox home in Buffalo, New York, had been closed for the summer, dustcovers draped the chairs and tables in the library. The ghostly furniture provided a somber backdrop for the melancholy cluster of men who stood about in their dark, rumpled suits. Many of them were still stunned, not yet fully accepting the harsh reality that William McKinley had died the day before, the victim of an anarchist's bullet. Equally difficult to accept was that Theodore Roosevelt, hastily summoned from a mountain climbing expedition in the Adirondacks, was, in fact, now president of the United States of America. The assembled cabinet members watched as Secretary of War Elihu Root indicated that the new president must take the oath of office. Before he did so, Roosevelt took a moment to reassure his heartbroken and wary listeners. After promising to keep the government from faltering, he concluded, "I wish to say that it shall be my aim to continue, absolutely unbroken, the policy of President McKinley for the peace, the prosperity, and the honor of our beloved country."[1]

Some historians and many contemporaries ridiculed this statement as hypocritical. An examination of the behavior of this dynamic, young president in office, however, will show that, at least in foreign affairs, Roosevelt spoke the truth. His style may have been bumptious and melodramatic at times, but the goals he pursued certainly fell well within the bounds his martyred predecessor had mapped out. As historian Tyler Dennett asserted, "by September, 1901, the major

[1]Henry F. Pringle, *Theodore Roosevelt: A Biography* (New York: Harcourt, Brace, 1931), pp. 232–33.

foreign policies were all well defined. It remained for the Roosevelt administration only to apply the accepted principles."[2] The McKinley administration had already decided to take colonies, to intrude in the Far East with its Open Door policy, and to build the isthmian canal. Dennett's remark could be taken to imply that Roosevelt had little to do. On the contrary, the new president and his colleagues frequently found the application and implementation of the principles already laid down both difficult and exciting. This chapter will provide a brief pause, so that we may determine where the United States was at the end of the war with Spain and where it was likely to go under its new leadership.

Obviously, the United States' drive for economic, political, and ideological expansion had advanced dramatically in the last two years of the nineteenth century. The war had definitely accelerated the achievement of several American foreign policy goals. One should hardly be surprised that imperialistic sentiments seemed less urgent after the Spanish-American War; almost everything the expansionists had been calling for had already been obtained—and with disconcerting suddenness. The immediate postwar years saw American foreign policymakers fully engaged simply in sorting out, rationalizing, and establishing procedures for dealing with all of the changes the wartime frenzy had left in its wake. In doing so, however, they fell back and relied upon the traditional themes which had characterized policy during the previous two decades.

Looking outward, Americans found others now treating the United States with respect. For some time the nation had possessed great physical power—and the United States' performance in the war showed an ability and willingness to use this power. The decision to collect the remnants of the Spanish Empire in the Caribbean and the Pacific further added to the United States' prestige. The contemporary "civilized" world considered the creation of a colonial empire a praiseworthy diplomatic goal at the turn of the century. American imperialism did not necessarily violate the democratic mission spirit as long as the United States made sure its colonies were closer to being free, self-governing entities than any other nation's dependencies.[3]

In addition to recognition as a great power, the nation's growing economic and political influence threatened to entangle the United

[2] Tyler Dennett, *John Hay: From Poetry to Politics* (New York: Dodd, Mead, 1933), p. 212.

[3] Foster Rhea Dulles, *Prelude to World Power* (New York: Macmillan, 1965), p. 220; Ernest R. May, *Imperial Democracy: The Emergence of America as a Great Power* (New York: Harcourt, Brace, 1961), p. 267.

States in great-power diplomacy. But at least until 1917, if then, no one was sure of the exact ranking to assign to the United States. Assessing America's overall strength and importance proved difficult as long as the United States insisted upon functioning somewhat differently than did most of the other great powers. The United States' physical and traditional isolation from Europe enabled the country to continue playing a lone hand. Internal European events seldom touched American interests, and no one sought to draw the United States in. Americans thus could choose when and where they wished to expend their diplomatic energies, and they decided to concentrate on the Far East and the Western Hemisphere. As the only great power indigenous to the New World, the United States was in a position to dictate to the nations in the Caribbean and to provide a more diffuse protectorate for the entire hemisphere. In the Orient, American interests competed directly with those of Japan and the European great powers, but the United States' isolation permitted it to limit or expand its objectives at will. Consequently, even though the United States had become irrevocably involved in external affairs, it retained a great deal of freedom, allowing its internal traditions to continue to shape its behavior in international relations.[4]

During the nation's trial period as a great power, however, the traditional themes were subjected to strain and sometimes to subtle alteration. Economic considerations continued to exercise their usual influence over the nation's diplomatic behavior. The prosperity which had finally returned in McKinley's first term cut some of the urgency out of the drive for economic expansion. Nevertheless, the dedicated market expansionists argued that the nation's enhanced international status offered opportunities too great to be wasted or ignored. Economist Charles Conant insisted:

> It has been by no series of accidents, not even by the thirst for military grandeur apart from its economic results, that the great civilized states have been expanding their spheres of influence in all quarters of the world. It was an economic necessity. . . . and the occupation of Cuba and the Philippines by the United States only marks the entry of the latter into the contest for financial and commercial supremacy.[5]

Conant led the way in advocating a capital export strategy for competing with other powers. By the turn of the century, the advisability

[4]Dulles, *Prelude*, p. 226; R. G. Neale, *Great Britain and United States Expansion: 1898–1900* (East Lansing: Michigan State University Press, 1966), p. 213; Bradford Perkins, *The Great Rapprochement* (New York: Atheneum, 1968), p. 272.

[5]Charles A. Conant, "The Struggle for Commercial Empire," *Forum* 27 (June 1899): 428.

of American investment abroad was becoming apparent as other powers extended their economic and political influence in China and elsewhere by financing the building of railroads and factories. The investing nation seized the upper hand and was able to discourage others from a share of the local market. American capital export began to appear essential in order to protect American markets as well as to maintain American political influence overseas. President Taft's Dollar Diplomacy program represented the most vigorous government-sponsored attempt to implement this strategy.

The democratic mission theme also underwent redefinition after the United States became a major world power. "Our greatest victory will not be over Spain," one editorial writer commented, "but over ourselves—to show once more that even in its righteous wrath the republic has the virtue of self-restraint."[6] A sense of responsibility for the politically unsophisticated peoples suddenly under its control helped keep the United States from immediately instituting self-government in the Philippines and Cuba. What in the abstract had appeared to be a black and white choice between democracy and tyranny or autocracy, in practice turned out to involve a whole spectrum of moral and political shadings. The democratic mission's goals needed certain revisions if full independence could not immediately be granted to those deemed incapable of responsible self-government. Democratic government could be considered ideal if, and only if, it were also stable and responsible government. The clumsy, sometimes even ruthless, actions the United States took in Latin America prior to World War I represented attempts to grapple with the dilemma of how to assure a balance between responsible rule and independence.

With the exception of a few who vainly hoped to annex Canada, the expansionists had never envisioned more than the extension of American political control over the Philippines, Puerto Rico, Hawaii, and Cuba. The imperialists were sated. Consequently, the extent of the United States' political and diplomatic influence in the Orient remained proportional to its rather minor economic interests. Although Secretary of State Hay briefly toyed with the idea just after the Boxer Rebellion in 1900, few wanted to carve out an American sphere of influence in China. The United States remained contented with its Open Door policy. The chief elements of this policy resembled the rhetorical efforts American statesmen had habitually employed in Latin American affairs. The Open Door policy had two somewhat

[6]"The War With Spain, and After," *Atlantic Monthly* 81 (June 1898): 727.

contradictory goals: to keep the United States free of any commitment which might require the use of physical force and, simultaneously, to shame other nations into respecting Chinese territorial integrity and American trade rights. In addition, the United States mediated a peace settlement for the Russo-Japanese War, only to encounter serious difficulties afterward in its relationship with Japan.

Meanwhile, the United States arrogated to itself an unquestioned leadership position in its own hemisphere. Because of their idealistic commitment in favor of republican government, Americans could not seriously contemplate seizing territory from the American republics to the south. With direct imperialism ruled out, American statesmen stretched the Monroe Doctrine into a catchall rationalization for United States intrusion in the Western Hemisphere whenever peace or stability seemed threatened. President Roosevelt added his corollary to the doctrine in 1904 to justify the establishment of an American-run customs service in the Dominican Republic. No self-denying statements or invocations of the Monroe Doctrine could conceal the fact that the United States' political influence in Latin America was constantly expanding. When American engineers began digging the Panama Canal, the United States government developed defense arrangements for the entire Caribbean area. The Platt Amendment assured continuing American dominance of Cuba even after the island attained independence, and the other nations near the canal became little more than American protectorates. As vaguely defined as the Monroe Doctrine, "defense of the canal" could and did provide the United States with excuses to expand American political influence throughout its hemisphere.

The president who guided the United States in its initial steps toward great power status did not live to see the results of his handiwork. William McKinley easily won reelection in 1900, probably because many Americans believed the Republican party's contention that its policies had restored prosperity. To balance the ticket and because he had made enemies in the Republican party machine while serving as governor of New York, Theodore Roosevelt had been kicked upstairs to the vice-presidency. Consequently, when McKinley was assassinated in the fall of 1901, Roosevelt suddenly found himself president. Fortunately for the United States, Roosevelt, like the nation itself, had matured a great deal as a result of the emotional imperialist surge of the 1890s.

Theodore Roosevelt was an extraordinarily complex individual. His interests were catholic, his writings prolific, and his enthusiasms boundless. Literally hundreds of historians and biographers have attempted to tap the core of his personality. In fact, there may never have been one. Perhaps Henry Adams's description was correct: Theodore Roosevelt was "pure act." The sparks and steam Roosevelt emitted sometimes so obscured the substance of the man that one can never be absolutely certain what his views and motivations really were. Just as one has too little of McKinley to work with, one has far too much of Roosevelt.

Throughout his life, Roosevelt was dedicated to nationalism. He not only adhered to Stephen Decatur's philosophy of supporting his country right or wrong, but he almost never doubted that his country was in the right. Social Darwinism colored Roosevelt's vision of his own duty to the United States and of the nation's duty to the world. He firmly believed in the superiority of the white race over colored ones, and of the Anglo-Saxon strain of the white race over all. In Roosevelt's mind, however, this racial superiority placed a great burden upon the American people: they had a responsibility to control, defend, uplift, and civilize those less fortunate.[7] Roosevelt's attitudes thus coincided nicely with America's traditional democratic mission. He favored the acquisition of colonies in part because they would provide a direct opportunity for the spread of American culture and a benign, just rule. Willing to appear tough and aggressive if necessary, he tried to temper the spread of United States influence abroad with moral uprightness and humaneness. He was genuinely pleased that during his terms as president the United States had never fired a shot in anger.[8]

A compassionate foreign policy did not mean a weak one. Roosevelt was certainly a realist. He recognized the importance of backing the policies he formulated with force. "It is not merely unwise, it is comtemptible, for a nation, as for an individual, to use high-sounding language to proclaim its purposes, or to take positions which are ridiculous if unsupported by potential force, and then to refuse to provide this force," he proclaimed in 1904. "If there is no intention of providing and keeping the force necessary to back up a strong at-

---

[7]Howard K. Beale, *Theodore Roosevelt and the Rise of America to World Power* (New York: Collier Books, 1962), pp. 22, 39–40; John Morton Blum, *The Republican Roosevelt* (Cambridge, Mass.: Harvard University Press, 1954), pp. 30–31, 130–31; William Henry Harbaugh, *Power and Responsibility* (New York: Farrar, Strauss & Cudahy, 1961), p. 99.

[8]Harbaugh, *Power and Responsibility*, p. 183; Theodore Roosevelt, *An Autobiography* (New York: Scribners, 1913), p. 557.

titude, then it is far better not to assume such an attitude."[9] His understanding of power politics helps explain his advocacy of naval growth. He first revealed his fascination with warships when he wrote a naval history of the War of 1812 as an undergraduate at Harvard. In the 1890s he became an avid booster of Mahan's theories about seapower. His interest in the navy grew even stronger during his years at the Navy Department and in the White House. Yet peaceful motives underlay his calls for naval construction. "My object is to keep America in trim so that fighting her shall be too expensive and dangerous a task to lightly be undertaken by anybody."[10] Not incidentally, a strong navy provided a very effective means for exercising American political influence in other parts of the world.

Roosevelt claimed that as president he never bluffed: "We made no promise which we could not and did not keep. We made no threat which we did not carry out."[11] Americans and foreigners alike learned to respect Roosevelt when he took a stand. But, despite his apparent willingness to use force, he managed to avoid it through skillful diplomacy. He became the center of an informal communications network among the diplomatic representatives of various European nations. He obviously developed friends among the diplomats and favorites among the nations, but he tried hard to avoid letting these sentiments unbalance his diplomatic initiatives. The long-standing tradition of "no entangling alliances" prevented him from formalizing any relationships he developed through treaties, but he did not complain. Treaties might well hamper him in his pursuit of a "just" policy. He strongly favored the concept of collective action through international conferences, although he was disappointed when the Second Hague Conference failed to do anything to halt the worldwide arms race. More than any of his predecessors, Roosevelt made the American president an international statesman.[12]

Roosevelt chose to exercise American influence to the fullest in Latin America. So enthusiastic was he over the canal project that he trod on quite a few toes in order to get the Panama Canal begun and to impose stability on the Caribbean nations in its vicinity. He had

[9]James D. Richardson, *A Compilation of the Messages and Papers of the Presidents,* 10 vols. (Washington, D.C.: Bureau of National Literature, 1911), 9:7051.

[10]Quoted in Tyler Dennett, *Roosevelt and the Russo-Japanese War* (c. 1925; reprint ed., Gloucester, Mass.: Peter Smith, 1959), p. 89.

[11]Roosevelt, *An Autobiography,* p. 502.

[12]Beale, *Theodore Roosevelt,* pp. 291, 303–4; Julius W. Pratt, *Challenge and Rejection* (New York: Macmillan, 1967), p. 3; William Roscoe Thayer, *The Life and Letters of John Hay,* 2 vols. (Boston: Houghton Mifflin, 1915), 2:341.

little patience with Latin American diplomats and governments, seeing them as the product of inferior racial stock, and he sometimes responded too hastily to problems in the New World. Favoring an extremely broad interpretation of the Monroe Doctrine, Roosevelt could perceive threats to it in almost any context. Now and then he took pains to point out the doctrine's defense and commercial benefits for the weaker republics to the south, but he always reserved to himself full responsibility for applying and amending it. In many ways it was fortunate for everyone concerned that he generally lost interest in Latin America during his second term, leaving its troubles to the more sympathetic ministrations of Secretary of State Elihu Root.[13]

Roosevelt's views about colonies became increasingly equivocal over time. In the 1890s he had strongly advocated the acquisition of coaling stations and had subscribed to other imperialistic concepts. A deep-seated sense of responsibility for weaker peoples tempered his expansionism, and he hoped the United States would retain its colonies only as long as it was leading them toward civilization and self-government. As president, he allowed his subordinates to run the colonies as he became increasingly disillusioned with the nation's colonial experiment. "The Philippines are our heel of Achilles. They are all that makes the present situation with Japan dangerous," he wrote Secretary of War William Howard Taft in 1907. "I think that in some way and with some phraseology that you think wise you should state to them that if they handle themselves wisely in their legislative assembly we shall at the earliest possible moment give them a nearly complete independence."[14] Possession of the Philippines meant the United States had something to lose in the Pacific. Despite his troubles with the Japanese after he had mediated a conclusion to the Russo-Japanese War, Roosevelt maintained a lower profile in China than McKinley had before him and Taft would afterwards.

Whatever may be said for or against Roosevelt's handling of foreign affairs during his presidency, he did manage to make it popular. With his aggressive nationalism, his belligerent pride, and his utter faith in his own righteousness, he seemed the personification of the United States at the turn of the century. His values were those of the American people. Consequently, even his more dangerous initiatives usually won favorable treatment in the press. His policies obviously had some detrimental effects in the long run, but they definitely suited the spirit of the times.

[13]Richardson, *Messages and Papers*, 9:6662–63; Philip C. Jessup, *Elihu Root,* 2 vols. (New York: Dodd, Mead, 1938), 1:468.
[14]Roosevelt to Taft, 21 August 1907, Elihu Root Papers, LCMD.

Roosevelt managed to surround himself with extraordinarily gifted associates. His secretaries of war, Elihu Root and William Howard Taft, ably dealt with colonial and defense problems. President McKinley's last secretary of state, John Hay, lingered on at the State Department until his death in the summer of 1905, at which point Roosevelt called Root out of retirement to assume the top cabinet post. The president had gradually taken charge of American foreign policy as Hay's health and energy waned, but he willingly relinquished most of it to Root, particularly with regard to Latin America. Throughout his terms as president, however, Roosevelt's personal interest in international relations kept him constantly attuned to the work of the State Department. Hay, at least, did not always appreciate it. "When McKinley sent for me he gave me all his time till we got through; but I always find T. R. engaged with a dozen other people, and it is an hour's wait and a minute's talk—and certainty that there was no necessity of my coming at all." Having gotten that off his chest, Hay hastened to tell his wife to "destroy this mutinous and disloyal letter as soon as you have read it."[15]

Although John Hay had begun his political career as a private secretary to President Abraham Lincoln, he divided his working life between literary pursuits and Republican party politics. A gentle, almost retiring man, Hay nevertheless felt quite comfortable with the large policy, because he had cut his political teeth on William H. Seward's heady expansionism in the 1860s. It pleased him to see the United States gain its rightful place among the great powers. He won great fame for his efforts to extend American political influence in the Far East through his Open Door Notes, but he worked equally diligently to expand American authority in the Caribbean. His patience, skill, and urbanity as a diplomat furthered the nation's international prestige, but he sometimes had trouble winning domestic approval for his initiatives. His most spectacular domestic failure concerned his early negotiations with British Ambassador Julian Pauncefote aimed at altering the Clayton-Bulwer Treaty. He was particularly sensitive to criticism from those he considered less capable than himself. He would probably have favored a government run entirely by experts like himself, not one which required truckling to the coarse tastes of the uninformed public or to the whimsies of the United States Senate.

He once complained to ex-Secretary of State John W. Foster about his efforts to obtain support for a cooperative policy with Great Britain: "How can I make bricks without straw? That we should be

[15]Quoted in Dennett, *John Hay*, p. 347.

compelled to refuse the assistance of the greatest Power in the world, *in carrying out our own policy,* because all Irishmen are Democrats and some Germans are fools—is enough to drive a man mad."[16] Hay was an unashamed Anglophile. He felt that the American and British governments and people shared identical moral values and exerted similar civilizing influences throughout the world. A firm sponsor of America's democratizing mission, Hay considered Great Britain closer than any other great power to the American ideal. He thoroughly enjoyed his tour as American ambassador in London, where he was welcomed warmly. His friendships with many Englishmen coupled with his negotiating skills enabled Hay to wring from the British many compromises favorable to the United States. Hay's pro-British attitudes carried over into his Far Eastern policy as well. Because England cooperated closely with Japan, Hay ended up being more tolerant of the Japanese than he might otherwise have been.[17]

At the same time, Hay's Anglophilia no doubt helped strengthen his instinctive distrust of Germany. During the seven years Hay headed the State Department, the United States treated the German Empire with great care and trepidation. No matter how frequently the German government tried to reassure the Americans that it had no intention of interfering in Latin America, Hay remained suspicious of the motives of the authorities in Berlin. No German menace ever actually developed, but the secretary of state never overcame his doubts about German sincerity. Fortunately, Roosevelt was more tolerant and, therefore, more reasonable in his behavior toward the Teutonic great power.[18]

Hay's successor as secretary of state, Elihu Root, had been an extremely successful corporation lawyer in private life. He had already shown great prowess as an administrator during his tour as secretary of war from 1899 to 1904. Both the Philippines and Cuba remained under martial law for some time after the war with Spain had ended, so the War Department ended up with the responsibility for developing and administering the early governmental arrangements for America's wartime conquests. Conservative, yet dedicated to the idealism implicit in America's democratic mission, Root did an outstanding job of designing a humane colonial policy for the United

[16]Ibid., p. 334.

[17]Ibid., pp. 220, 278; Alfred L. P. Dennis, *Adventures in American Diplomacy 1896–1906* (New York: E. P. Dutton, 1928), p. 117.

[18]Dennett, *John Hay,* pp. 384–87; Dexter Perkins, *The Monroe Doctrine 1867–1907* (Baltimore: Johns Hopkins University Press, 1937), pp. 300–301; Thayer, *John Hay,* 2:238.

States. Working closely with Leonard Wood in Cuba and William Howard Taft in the Philippines, Root created governments based upon realistic assessments of the political capabilities of the people under American control. Root's system worked, and it worked well. His efforts greatly eased the burden the expansionists had so enthusiastically inflicted upon the United States in 1898 and 1899.[19]

When Elihu Root returned to government service as secretary of state, he described his guiding principle as follows: "to keep the country out of trouble . . . in the right way, is the main object of diplomacy."[20] This philosophy caused Root to develop diplomatic policies characterized by caution, maturity, and rationality. Although he generally favored economic expansion, during his tenure at the State Department, Root carefully avoided showing favoritism for any particular American businessman. He considered the entire nation his client and his responsibility. One might assume that Root's conservative attitudes would clash with those of the more emotional man in the White House. Roosevelt was wise enough to recognize the merits of moderation, however, so he and Root got along very well.

After he had entered the United States Senate in 1909, Elihu Root won the 1912 Nobel Peace Prize in recognition of his advocacy of arbitration, his enlightened colonial administrations, and his contributions to peace in Latin America. In the latter area Root really shone during Roosevelt's second term. He kindled the spark of the Good Neighbor Policy which Cordell Hull and Franklin Roosevelt finally breathed into flame in the 1930s. Roosevelt's earlier intrusions into Panama, Venezuela, and the Dominican Republic had alienated much of Latin America, but Secretary Root managed to win many personal friends south of the border and to cushion the impact of the United States' growing political influence in its own hemisphere.[21] Root's conservative temperament was particularly useful to the nation after its frenzy of expansionist activity. As secretary of state, he exercised a calming influence after 1905, enabling the United States to reflect and reassess its relationships with nations around the world.

On an international scale, the rapprochement between the United States and Great Britain also had a pacifying effect. These two great

[19]Jessup, *Elihu Root*, 1:299; David Healy, *US Expansionism* (Madison: University of Wisconsin Press, 1970), pp. 148–49.

[20]Quoted in Jessup, *Elihu Root*, 2:4.

[21]Howard C. Hill, *Roosevelt and the Caribbean* (Chicago: University of Chicago Press, 1927), p. 165; Richard W. Leopold, *Elihu Root and the Conservative Tradition* (Boston: Little, Brown, 1954), pp. 53, 196.

English-speaking nations rather suddenly found themselves becoming fast friends. James G. Blaine and Richard Olney had obviously disliked Great Britain, but this antagonism must be viewed within the context of the long series of disturbances which marred the United States' relations with its mother country from 1776 to 1895. Mutual needs, dependencies, and interests drew the two nations close together. The British Isles, for example, provided the largest single market for American exports. As the leading maritime and commercial nation in the world, however, Great Britain took the lead in all European involvement in the Western Hemisphere, thereby constantly trespassing in what the United States considered its own private preserve. Conflicts erupted over westward expansion, the isthmian canal, Canadian annexation, North Atlantic fisheries, Bering Sea sealing practices, and commercial rivalries. The discord had fortunately triggered war only once, in 1812, but the Americans considered the British a constant irritant.

The subjection of the long-standing fisheries and sealing disputes to rational negotiation proved that the traditional hostility was on the wane toward the end of the nineteenth century. As Americans became more worldly, they realized how fundamentally similar American and British diplomatic attitudes and goals were, particularly when compared to those of other great powers. Both the United States and Great Britain had deliberately remained isolated from any power struggles on the European continent, but those struggles began to have global ramifications when the European nations entered the imperialist race in the 1870s and 1880s. As international tensions multiplied in the 1890s, statesmen in both English-speaking nations saw how much they needed each other's friendship. England willingly recognized the United States as a great power because the British wanted to have a strong, reliable friend in the world. Competent diplomatic representatives on both sides of the Atlantic definitely helped bring the two nations together.

In the late 1890s various journals began suggesting close cooperation or even a formal union between the two nations.[22] Both countries assigned the highest social status to the so-called Anglo-Saxon race to which a majority of the British and American people belonged. The British Empire served as a model for the United States' colonial experiments precisely because Americans rated the British

[22]Carl Schurz, "The Anglo-American Friendship," *Atlantic Monthly* 182 (October 1898): 433–40; "The War With Spain, And After," *Atlantic Monthly* 183 (June 1898): 721–27; John Fiske, "Manifest Destiny," *Harper's Monthly* 70 (March 1885): 578–90.

second only to themselves as purveyors of "civilization" to the rest of the world. In 1898, Lyman Abbot claimed that

> the United States is of kin to Great Britain. The two represent the same essential political ideals: they are both democratic; they both represent the same ethical ideals; they are Christian; and they both represent the same race leadership; they are Anglo-Saxon. In so far as their conjoint influence dominates the world, it will carry with it a tendency toward liberty in the political institutions organized.[23]

The British cabinet's surrender to American pressure over the Venezuelan boundary dispute in 1896 represented a victory for those favoring greater cooperation. When the United States declared war on Spain a couple of years later, the British carefully refrained from criticism, while praising and complimenting the Americans on their victories. They were virtually alone in Europe in these sentiments. "It is a very curious fact that the only power cordially friendly to us on either side of the water is England," Ambassador Hay wrote during the war, "and England is the one power which has most to dread from our growing power and prosperity. We are her most formidable rival, and the trade balances show a portentious leaning in our favor. But not withstanding all this, the feeling here is more sympathetic and cordial than it has ever been."[24] The United States reciprocated when the British became enmeshed in a brutal conflict with the Boers in South Africa a year later. In fact, the Americans had to ignore their historic mission in refusing to support the supposedly democratic Boer republics in their fight for freedom against an imperialistic power.

The key to the growing friendship between the two nations was a series of incidents in which Great Britain caved in to American wishes. The British did so in order to stay on the good side of the major power in the Western Hemisphere while they encountered serious problems in Europe and the Far East. Fortunately, the British did not suffer any serious losses because of their decision to resolve issues in favor of the United States. American exports, particularly of agricultural commodities were crucial to England's survival, and the early years of the twentieth century proved prosperous for those on both sides of the Atlantic. Furthermore, England's cultivation of friendly relations with the United States made practical sense as well. As late as 1897, Henry Cabot Lodge was expressing confidence that Can-

---

[23]Lyman Abbot, "The Basis of an Anglo-American Understanding," *North American Review* 166 (May 1898): 520.

[24]Hay to Day, 19 July 1898, William R. Day Papers, LCMD.

ada would eventually come into the Union. Canada would clearly be an American hostage in any major conflict, so the British walked carefully.[25]

A boundary dispute between Alaska and Canada threatened the growing friendship between the two powers. The disputed area consisted of a long stretch of coastline, thirty or more miles wide which the United States claimed had been included in Alaska when Seward bought it from Russia in 1867. The Canadians suddenly became interested in this remote part of their dominion when gold was discovered in the Klondike. The United States felt certain any neutral judge would uphold its position, while Canada apparently hoped to overpower the Americans by drawing England into the dispute. Ambassador Hay reported in 1897 that British Prime Minister Salisbury had compared Canada "to a coquettish girl with two suitors, playing off one against the other. I should think a closer analogy would be to call her a married flirt, ready to betray John Bull on any occasion, but holding him responsible for all her follies."[26]

President Grover Cleveland had vainly called for a bilateral agreement between Canada and the United States on the Alaska boundary issue in the 1880s. The Americans refused to consider arbitration because they had a solid claim to all of the disputed territory; an arbitrator might simply divide it down the middle. Roosevelt forced the issue to a conclusion. He prodded Secretary of State Hay and British Ambassador Julian Paunceforte into signing a convention in 1903 which would establish a tribunal of "six impartial jurists of repute" to settle the issue. The United States Senate did approve the convention, but only after Roosevelt had deliberately let slip the names of the three "jurists" he intended to appoint: Henry Cabot Lodge, Elihu Root, and ex-Senator George Turner of Washington. Canada selected two representatives and England contributed its lord chief justice, Lord Alverstone, the only one on the tribunal who really was an impartial jurist of repute. Alverstone's vote made it four to two in favor of the American position which was, by far, the more convincing. The fact that the British representative had voted

[25]Abbot, "Anglo-American Understanding," pp. 526–27; Neale, *Great Britain*, p. 167; Perkins, *Rapprochement*, p. 130; J. A. Hobson, *Imperialism: A Study* (c. 1938; reprint ed., Ann Arbor: University of Michigan Press, 1965), p. 336; Brooks Adams, "The Spanish War and the Equilibrium of the World," *Forum* 25 (August 1898): 645; J. A. S. Grenville, *Lord Salisbury and Foreign Policy* (London: University of London Press, 1964), p. 371.
[26]Hay to Foster, 27 December 1897, John Watson Foster Papers, LCMD.

with the Americans definitely helped strengthen British-American friendship.[27]

The trend of European events—specifically Germany's decision in 1898 to build an enormous navy, convinced the British government it must concentrate its naval strength nearer home. Consequently, in 1902, the Royal Navy withdrew the bulk of its forces to the Eastern Atlantic and the Mediterranean. This evacuation incidentally removed the only serious obstacle to full exploitation of the Monroe Doctrine. Now the United States could safely expand its own political influence to the south without great-power interference.[28]

The situation in the Far East was almost exactly the reverse. The only hope for America's China policy lay in winning and maintaining British cooperation and support. Neither nation wanted China broken up into colonies or exclusive spheres of influence, however, so England supported the open door concept which formed the basis for American policy in the Orient. The same worries that had pulled the Royal Navy back across the Atlantic caused the British to reassess their position in the Far East. In 1902, they hammered out an alliance with Japan, designed to protect their interests while they concentrated their fleet. American dependence upon British power in that part of the world forced the United States to cooperate informally with Japan in its China policy. When, with tacit British support, Japan began extending its influence unilaterally after 1905, American and British Far Eastern policies began to diverge.[29]

Events in the Western Hemisphere and the Far East basically could not seriously undermine the burgeoning Anglo-American friendship, however, and the two nations' interests did not clash in Europe either. This was due largely to the fact that, even though the United States had thrown off its isolation after the war with Spain, it tried very hard to avoid involvement in Europe's internal affairs. The complex constellation of European alliances which eventually precipitated World War I had little bearing on American diplomacy except as it complicated American policies in the Far East. Only once did the United States participate in any significant way in Europe's

---

[27]U.S., Department of State, *Papers Relating to the Foreign Relations of the United States* (Washington, D.C.: Government Printing Office, 1903), p. 489; John A. Garraty, *Henry Cabot Lodge* (New York: Alfred A. Knopf, 1953), p. 245.

[28]Perkins, *Rapprochement*, pp. 157, 160; John A. Logan, Jr., *No Transfer* (New Haven, Conn.: Yale University Press, 1961), p. 271.

[29]Perkins, *Rapprochement*, p. 238; Grenville, *Lord Salisbury*, p. 389; Andrew Carnegie, "Americanism *versus* Imperialism," *North American Review* 168 (January 1899): 3.

great-power politics. The Moroccan crisis and its resolution at the Algeciras Conference also represented virtually the only time the rapprochement between the United States and Great Britain seemed threatened during Roosevelt's presidency.

To test the strength of the 1904 Entente Cordiale between Great Britain and France, Germany fomented a crisis out of the unstable situation in Morocco. With British acquiescence, Spain and France had secretly agreed to divide Morocco into spheres of influence. The German government urged the sultan of Morocco to publicize and blunt these imperialistic initiatives by calling an international conference to embarrass France and Spain. Early in 1905, Germany sought American support for the conference idea, claiming it would help insure an open door for trade in Morocco. Roosevelt's endorsement infuriated the British who realized an international conference would force it to state openly its support of French imperialism.[30]

The conference met in the early spring of 1906 at Algeciras, a city in southern Spain. The United States sent its ambassador to Rome, Henry White, and its minister to Morocco, Samuel R. Gummeré. Roosevelt and Secretary of State Root apparently hoped the conference would guarantee stability and order within Morocco so that commercial nations like the United States could safely and profitably trade in North Africa. The American statesmen, therefore, did not insist upon complete independence for Morocco; they were quite willing to permit the creation of foreign spheres of influence if those spheres would make Morocco a more valuable market area. "While it is to the advantage of the powers to secure the 'open door,'" Root told the delegates, "it is equally vital to their interests and no less to the advantage of Morocco that the door, being open, shall lead to something; that the outside world shall benefit by assured opportunities, and that the Moroccan people shall be made in measure fit and able to profit by the advantages of the proposed reform."[31] The economic expansion theme in American foreign policy seems to have overwhelmed mission in this particular case. The conferees eventually granted France control of some Moroccan ports and Spain others, leaving Casablanca as an international port. The Algeciras Conference thus reaffirmed the Anglo-French Entente position in opposition to Germany's wishes. The American delegates voted with Britain and France. Having acceded to Germany's request to attend the con-

---

[30]Dennis, *Adventures*, pp. 487–88, 496, 506–9; Dennett, *Russo-Japanese War*, pp. 87–88.

[31]*Foreign Relations* (1905), p. 629.

ference, the United States ultimately showed itself to be more favorably disposed to the British point of view.

This meddling in European politics was dangerous, however, and none too popular at home. Congressmen became engaged in a caustic debate over whether American participation in the Algeciras Conference violated the Monroe Doctrine's promise of noninvolvement in European affairs. Having signed a treaty of peace and friendship with Morocco in 1786, however, the United States did have a precedent for concerning itself in Moroccan affairs which predated the Monroe Doctrine. Furthermore, American delegates had attended another Moroccan conference in Madrid in 1880. Those who favored sending delegates to Algeciras insisted that President Roosevelt knew what he was doing and should be trusted to carry out policies in the best interests of the nation.[32] Acutely aware of the unusual circumstances surrounding the American participation, Secretary of State Root made sure his representatives did not go too far. He drafted a qualifying statement to be inserted along with the American delegates' signatures on the conference's final act. It disavowed any United States responsibility for the enforcement of the conference's decisions.[33]

The episode did prove that the United States could, if it chose, act like a great power in Europe's own backyard. Yet the Americans were not comfortable in the role. They would avoid full participation in European affairs for another decade, and then only with great reluctance in order to end World War I. American foreign policy after the Spanish-American War remained focused in those areas into which the United States had expanded its empire. Latin-American and Far-Eastern developments gave American policymakers plenty of problems to occupy their time.

[32]*Foreign Relations* (1906), pp. 1421–23, 1470, 1529.
[33]Ibid., p. 1492; Jessup, *Elihu Root*, 2:59.

6

The Great Power
in the Western Hemisphere, 1899-1909

After it had won first prize at the St. Louis Exposition of 1904, the Brazilian pavilion was carefully dismantled and shipped, piece by piece, back to Rio de Janeiro. There, in just nine months, the graceful, domed structure was reassembled. Work on the building was completed only three days before the Third Inter-American Conference was to open there. The grounds were pleasantly landscaped with pools, fountains, palms, tropical shrubbery and even blooming rose-bushes. Within the vaulted halls, deep red carpets and light green silk curtains set off the pure white pillars and walls. "The Monroe Palace" awaited the arrival of its distinguished guests.

The guest whose presence evoked the most popular curiosity arrived on board the U.S.S. *Charleston* four days after the conference had officially opened. Secretary of State Elihu Root and his family were welcomed with great pomp and ceremony. On each day of his week-long stay at the Brazilian capital, he was entertained in a style that might have embarrassed an Oriental potentate. The high point of Root's visit came on 31 July 1906. First, he was feted at a "tea" held at the island-based customshouse in Rio harbor—a feast involving some seventeen different dishes and an equally large selection of wines for approximately four hundred members of Rio society. Then the American statesman returned to the shore for his address to the conference delegates at the Monroe Palace.

"We are alike in this," he told the assembled representatives of the Latin American nations, "we are all engaged under new conditions, and free from the traditional forms and limitations of the Old World in working out the same problem of popular self-government." The secretary of state then sounded a cautionary note: "Capacity for self-government does not come to man by nature. It is an art to be learned."[1] Root scrupulously stopped short of adding that his nation felt self-government was also an art which could be taught. The United States' relationship with its southern neighbors in the first decade of the twentieth century resembled that of an impatient teacher, alternately cajoling and chastising its students as they struggled toward full self-realization. The American sense of mission faced a stern test in the Western Hemisphere; after a decade of dominance, no one could be sure whether progress toward the United States' ideal had actually occurred.

Probably no nation proved more disappointing to American idealists than Cuba. After the Spanish-American War, the United States found itself completely in charge of mapping out a future for the Cuban people. Although the Teller Amendment indicated that the United States would not make Cuba a permanent American colony, it said nothing about how quickly the impoverished and war-ravaged island would become independent. Elihu Root was serving as secretary of war when President McKinley became responsible for creating interim governing arrangements for Cuba. Root frankly admitted that many people both in the United States and abroad were convinced that the United States would never give up the island.[2] Those Americans who wished to annex Cuba relied upon traditional foreign policy themes for justification. One annexationist thus called for the incorporation of Cuba into the Union because "higher political privileges no people can possibly acquire—for our federal system combines the maximum of safeguard against foreign aggression which is compatible with the exercise of self-government in state, county and municipal affairs."[3]

No one was quite sure whether the Cuban people were really capable of responsible self-government. Reminiscent of similar attitudes about the Hawaiians and the Filipinos, some considered the Cuban people children who would require many years of guidance and training. Drawing the island directly into the American political system would make this tutelage more efficient as well as guarantee

---

[1] U.S., Department of State, *Papers Relating to the Foreign Relations of the United States* (Washington, D.C.: Government Printing Office, 1906), pp. 127–28.

[2] U.S., Congress, *Congressional Record*, 55th Cong., 3d sess., p. 1385; Philip C. Jessup, *Elihu Root*, 2 vols. (New York: Dodd, Mead, 1938), 1:286; Mark Twain, "To the Person Sitting in Darkness," *North American Review* 172 (February 1901): 175; "The Logic of Our Position in Cuba," *North American Review* 169 (July 1899): 109.

[3] Mayo W. Hazeltine, "What is to be Done with Cuba?" *North American Review* 167 (September 1898): 318–19.

Cuban stability and economic growth. Those opposed to annexation might change their minds if the Cuban people themselves decided democratically to ask for admission to the United States. The American military governor on the scene, General Leonard Wood, worked hard to bring about just such an outcome. He instituted sanitation, education, and cleanup programs on the island, hoping to show the Cuban people how much better off they would be if they chose to remain under American control.[4]

Despite the extensive public discussion of the annexation alternative, the McKinley administration evidently had always planned to prepare the island for self-government. The president personally believed in the democratic mission theme inherent in the justifications for the declaration of war by the United States against Spain. But he also intended to insure that Cuba had an orderly transition from Spanish control to independence. Although he was speaking after the key decisions had been made, President Roosevelt aptly summed up the Republican leadership's sentiments in his first annual message: "Our aim is high. We do not desire to do for the islanders merely what has elsewhere been done for tropic peoples by even the best foreign governments. We hope to do for them what has never before been done for any peoples of the tropics—to make them fit for self-government after the fashion of the really free nations."[5]

The man directly dealing with Cuban affairs, Elihu Root, felt the United States had neither a right nor any desire to annex the island. At the same time, he doubted that the Cuban people were politically sophisticated enough to create and operate their own government responsibly. Root thus faced the dilemma all mission-oriented American policymakers encountered when dealing with developing nations. A majority of the Cuban people were illiterate in 1900, most had never participated meaningfully in the island's political processes, and a good many nursed a generalized distrust of all government after living under autocratic Spanish rule. Root's awareness of these factors was evident when he wrote to a friend that the three elements essential in preparing Cuba for independence were:

1. To secure a conservative and thoughtful control of Cuba by Cubans during the formative period, and avoid the kind of control which

---

[4]Jessup, *Elihu Root*, 1:307; Thomas Jordan, "Why We Need Cuba," *Forum* 11 (July 1891): 561, 566; John T. Morgan, "What Shall We do with the Conquered Islands?" *North American Review* 166 (June 1898): 643; Herbert Pelham Williams, "The Outlook in Cuba," *Atlantic Monthly* 133 (June 1899): 827, 831.

[5]Quoted in Howard C. Hill, *Roosevelt and the Caribbean* (Chicago: University of Chicago Press, 1927), p. 206.

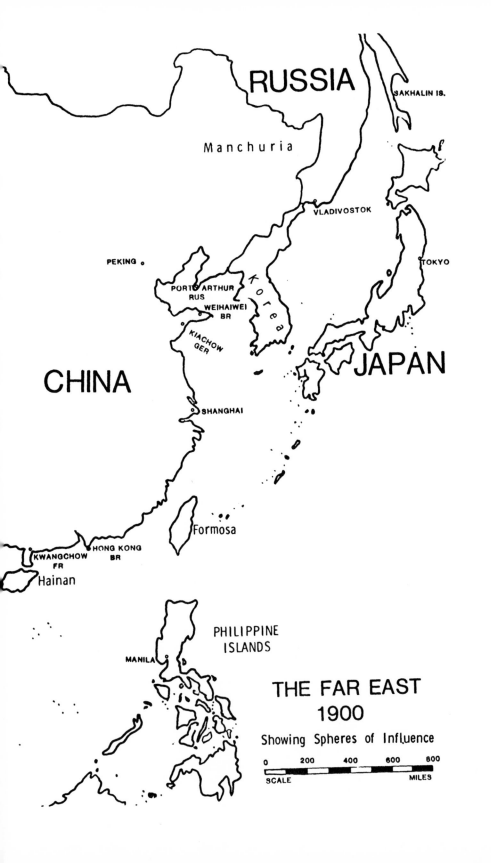

RUSSIA

SAKHALIN IS.

Manchuria

VLADIVOSTOK

PEKING

PORT ARTHUR
RUS

WEIHAIWEI
BR

KIACHOW
GER

Korea

TOKYO

CHINA

JAPAN

SHANGHAI

Formosa

KWANGCHOW
FR

HONG KONG
BR

Hainan

PHILIPPINE
ISLANDS

MANILA

THE FAR EAST
1900

Showing Spheres of Influence

| 0 | 200 | 400 | 600 | 800 |

SCALE   MILES

leads to the perpetual revolutions of Central America and the other West India Islands.

2. To make the suffrage respected so that there will be acquiescence in its results.

3. To stimulate the people to thrift and education.[6]

One mission of the United States Army's occupation program was to instill in the Cuban people respect for and understanding of democratic forms and processes. This program could have stretched on for years, but Root joined both Presidents McKinley and Roosevelt in favoring a speedy withdrawal of American forces. Yet the American leaders had no intention of leaving a power vacuum behind in the Caribbean. The United States government intended to build an interoceanic canal; an unstable or weak Cuba might encourage foreigners to intervene and, in turn, pose a threat to the American canal. In other words, the United States had vastly expanded its political influence in the Caribbean as a result of the war, and it would not throw away that influence by leaving Cuba open to external domination. Therefore, Secretary Root's task was to create an American protectorate out of Cuba while simultaneously freeing the Cubans to handle their own domestic affairs. Using ideas General James H. Wilson had developed in 1899 while serving in Cuba, Root drew up a set of proposals and turned them over to Senator Orville Platt of Connecticut. Platt added these proposals as an amendment to the Army Appropriations bill that Congress approved on 2 March 1901. The Platt Amendment's provisions were designed to be incorporated into the treaty the United States would sign with Cuba granting its independence, as well as into the constitution Cuban representatives were preparing to draft.

Two of the Platt Amendment's provisions were straightforward. One enjoined the Cubans to maintain the sanitation programs that the United States' occupation forces had begun, because these measures would hopefully reduce the incidence of tropical disease in southern American coastal cities. The other called upon Cuba to lease to the United States sufficient territory for a naval coaling station. A Cuban base was deemed essential because Puerto Rico had no harbor capable of handling the American fleet which would defend the Caribbean approaches to the proposed isthmian canal. The United States eventually settled upon Guantanamo as its naval base, and it still maintains control of that Cuban bay.

[6]Quoted in Jessup, *Elihu Root,* 1:305.

Of a more controversial nature was the Platt Amendment's article prohibiting Cuba from entering into treaties or agreements with foreign governments which would in any way impair Cuban independence. This article served as a functional equivalent to American colonization in that it prevented Cuba from exercising an independent foreign policy. It would also maintain American political influence on the island while the Cubans learned how to conduct their own affairs. Secretary Root thought the Cuban people would welcome this provision: it gave them an internationally recognized guarantee to freedom and independence from non-American interference, something they could obtain in no other way.[7] On the other hand, the Cubans could consider it an affront to their honor, because it denied them full self-government.

Even more likely to offend the Cuban sense of dignity was the statement that the United States reserved to itself the responsibility for intervening in Cuban affairs "for the preservation of Cuban independence, the maintenance of a government adequate for the protection of life, property, and individual liberty." The Cubans were most unhappy with this part of the Platt Amendment, despite Root's contention that it, too, was designed for their own protection. He hoped it would enable them to avoid "the perpetual revolutions" that troubled other Caribbean nations. As a conservative statesman, he expected the United States to intervene only in most extraordinary circumstances—disturbances on a scale similar to that of the revolution against Spain. The secretary of war tied this provision to traditional policy by insisting it was "the Monroe Doctrine, but with international force. Because of it, European nations will not dispute the intervention of the United States in defense of the independence of Cuba."[8] In effect, Root was assigning to the United States an indisputable right to exert political control over a foreign nation. The United States was thus assuming much broader responsibilities in Latin American affairs than ever before.

At first, the Cubans declined to incorporate the Platt Amendment into their constitution, but the American army refused to leave until a second constitution including the amendment had been promulgated. The occupation finally terminated on 20 May 1902, to the relief of the many Cubans who had feared that the United States

---

[7]Ibid., p. 309.
[8]Ibid., p. 319. See also Richard W. Leopold, *Elihu Root and the Conservative Tradition* (Boston: Little, Brown, 1954), p. 31; Dana G. Munro, *Intervention and Dollar Diplomacy in the Caribbean 1900–1921* (Princeton, N.J.: Princeton University Press, 1964), p. 26.

would never relinquish its control of the island. Yet the release was in line with the nation's traditional policies. American statesmen had established the framework for a democratic government, had assured continued political influence by the United States, and had reinforced American economic dominance in Cuba. Freeing the island evoked widespread congratulations, although some critics claimed that the Platt Amendment was as oppressive to Cuban liberty as the occupation had been. The restrictions seemed necessary at the time, however, given the traditional American sensitivity to the possibility of European encroachment in the Western Hemisphere. Most Americans felt no shame because of the Platt Amendment. They joined President Roosevelt in expressing pride in the island's release from direct American control, a virtually unprecedented action in an imperialistic age.

Theodore Roosevelt heartily approved of the imposition of the Platt Amendment restrictions upon Cuba in 1902, but he was not yet ready to demand exclusive American control in the Caribbean. As historian Howard K. Beale pointed out, although Roosevelt placed a premium upon "civilizing" less developed peoples, he did not feel that the United States had an exclusive right to perform this function. He was quite willing to allow other nations to do so as long as their actions did not interfere detrimentally with American interests.[9] His famous statement in 1901 that "if any South American country misbehaves toward any European country, let the European country spank it," bluntly expressed his sentiments prior to the start of work on an American-controlled isthmian canal.[10] This viewpoint explains Roosevelt's rather unconcerned attitude toward the 1902 European power-display in Venezuela.

Throughout the nineteenth century, the peoples who lived in the islands and countries ringing the Caribbean Sea remained poverty-stricken and economically backward. Economic weakness had in several cases led to governmental deterioration, thus many of the Caribbean states had fallen under the control of ruthless or corrupt dictators. Cipriano Castro had become Venezuela's strongman and had managed to run his nation's economy into very serious economic straits. European investors were willing to take substantial credit risks

[9]Howard K. Beale, *Theodore Roosevelt and the Rise of America to World Power* (New York: Collier Books, 1962), pp. 347–48.

[10]Elting E. Morison, ed., *The Letters of Theodore Roosevelt*, 8 vols. (Cambridge, Mass.: Harvard University Press, 1951–54), 3:116.

in order to obtain high interest rates and possibly to increase trade, so they continued to lend money to even the most patently untrustworthy governments. Castro was a past master at obtaining loans; unfortunately his financial talents did not include any adeptness at paying them off. An international crisis developed when the Venezuelan government forfeited on its payments to European creditors.

On 11 December 1901, the German government officially notified Secretary of State Hay that it intended soon to stage a naval demonstration off the coast of Venezuela to shock the government at Caracas into meeting its financial obligations. Recognizing the United States' traditional sensitivity over any European move in the Western Hemisphere, the German note promised that "under no circumstances do we consider in our proceedings the acquisition or the permanent occupation of Venezuelan territory."[11] As previously noted, Hay had a pathological fear of Germany which Roosevelt fortunately did not share. Consequently, the president responded quite calmly and rationally to the German announcement. He immediately instructed his secretary of state to assure the German government that the United States saw no objection to the proposed demonstration inasmuch as the Germans had specifically pledged not to seize any territory. President Roosevelt was actually quite flattered that the Germans had solicited prior American approval for their contemplated foreclosure action. He considered it a major diplomatic triumph because it definitely proved that Germany considered the United States the Western Hemisphere's leading power. It also represented an implicit recognition of the anticolonization provision of the Monroe Doctrine, America's traditional rationale for all its hemispheric policies. Roosevelt did not view the contemplated European maneuvers off the coast of Venezuela as a violation of the Monroe Doctrine; indeed, the seeking of the United States' sanction actually reinforced the doctrine's importance.[12]

Great Britain decided to join Germany's armed demonstration, and Italy put in a token appearance, so ships from three nations appeared off the Venezuelan coast in December 1902. The government at Caracas simply ignored this fleet's demands until the Europeans captured and sunk a couple of Venezuelan gunboats and, later, blockaded the nation's Caribbean ports. When Castro's government

[11]*Foreign Relations* (1901), p. 194.
[12]Ibid., p. 195; Beale, *Theodore Roosevelt*, p. 336; Munro, *Intervention*, p. 75; Dexter Perkins, *The Monroe Doctrine 1867–1907* (Baltimore: Johns Hopkins University Press, 1937), p. 333.

sought the United States' assistance, Secretary of State Hay advised arbitration of the issues, a suggestion which the Venezuelans readily accepted. Meanwhile, the British government discovered that the confrontation was injuring its reputation in other Latin American nations, so England quickly agreed to arbitrate. Germany took somewhat longer to decide, but eventually consented to arbitration as well. World reaction had generally been highly critical of the show of force, and many Europeans feared such belligerent actions might seriously damage Latin-American interest in commercial relations with the Old World.[13]

In addition, certain American moves may have helped urge Germany toward submitting to arbitration. Theodore Roosevelt claimed much later that he had privately issued a sort of ultimatum to the German diplomats in Washington. Historian Seward W. Livermore examined all of the available evidence and concluded that Roosevelt may very well have intimidated the Germans. The president had arranged for the United States Navy to conduct full fleet maneuvers in the Caribbean in the winter of 1902–1903 under the command of Admiral George Dewey. The American war vessels assembled off a small island named Culebra because no Puerto Rican port could accommodate them; then they engaged in training exercises and war games. Any suggestions the president made to Germany would obviously carry great weight as long as the United States Navy was conducting maneuvers in full fighting trim not far from Venezuela. Roosevelt recalled having warned that if Germany did not agree to arbitration he would order Dewey to sail to Venezuela and physically prevent any German seizure. If one takes this story at face value, it was a direct assertion of American power. Whatever actually transpired on the diplomatic front, the presence of the American fleet restricted Germany's options.[14]

When the kaiser's government eventually agreed to arbitration, it requested Roosevelt himself to serve as the arbitrator. Roosevelt wished to avoid any direct involvement in the emotional controversy, so he refused. Instead he urged all parties to submit their cases to the International Court of Arbitration at The Hague, which he hoped would become the accepted method for resolving all such financial

[13]*Foreign Relations* (1903), p. 420; Munro, *Intervention*, p. 71; Samuel Flagg Bemis, *The Latin American Policy of the United States* (c. 1943; reprint ed., New York: W. W. Norton, 1967), pp. 147–48; Alfred L. P. Dennis, *Adventures in American Diplomacy 1896–1906* (New York: E. P. Dutton, 1928), p. 289.

[14]Seward W. Livermore, "Theodore Roosevelt, the American Navy, and the Venezuelan Crisis of 1902–1903," *American Historical Review* 51 (April 1946): 452–71.

imbroglios rather than a resort to armed demonstrations.[15] Unfortunately, the arbitration ruling proved less than satisfactory as far as the Roosevelt administration was concerned. Having ruled, reasonably enough, that Venezuela must make provisions to pay its foreign debts, the court further decreed that creditors from those nations which had staged the naval demonstration should receive priority in any payoff arrangements. This ruling essentially placed a premium upon naval demonstrations as a way to assure debt repayment.

Argentine Foreign Minister Luis Drago strenuously objected to the whole concept of naval demonstrations: "The collection of loans by military means implies territorial occupation to make them effective, and territorial occupation signifies the suppression or subordination of the governments of the countries on which it is imposed." With a nod to his northern neighbor, the Latin American statesman continued: "Such a situation seems obviously at variance with the principles many times proclaimed by the nations of America, and particularly with the Monroe Doctrine."[16] Here the Argentine diplomat was outlining what came to be called the Drago Doctrine, which decried any use of armed force to collect debts. Despite their explicit references to American traditions, Secretary of State Hay was quite cautious in responding to Drago's initiatives. They threatened to remove the Monroe Doctrine from the exclusive possession of the United States' policymakers who had been accustomed to redefining it periodically to suit their own purposes. Furthermore, Drago was essentially calling upon the hemisphere's self-proclaimed great power to protect weaker nations from any future naval demonstrations.

Argentina found several sympathizers in its campaign to saddle the United States with the responsibility of preventing external interference in Latin American nations guilty of financial misconduct. The most important of these was the British government, which had been displeased with the unfavorable publicity its participation in the joint demonstration had aroused both at home and in South America. Consequently, it, too, urged the United States to step in and assume the functions President Roosevelt himself had mentioned just prior to the Venezuelan incident: "More and more the increasing interdependence and complexity of international political and economic relations render it incumbent on all civilized and orderly powers to insist on the proper policing of the world."[17] The president's attitudes

---

[15]*Foreign Relations* (1903), pp. 426, 428.

[16]Ibid., p. 3.

[17]James D. Richardson, *A Compilation of the Messages and Papers of the Presidents,* 10 vols. (Washington, D.C.: Bureau of National Literature, 1911), 9:6758.

about what sort of policing should be done and, more to the point, which nation should do that policing crystallized very quickly once the United States became engaged in the actual construction of the Panama Canal.

Building, fortifying, and operating an interoceanic canal absorbed much of the United States' surplus energy around the turn of the century. It helped divert and diffuse the American jingoist drive because, like a foreign war, it was a vast, costly enterprise which would bring the nation great international respect and prestige. For decades, American leaders had been discovering or inventing justifications for a canal and ticking off the benefits it was expected to bring to the nation. The successful completion of the Suez Canal intensified America's interest in carrying out a similar project in its own hemisphere. The formidable technological difficulties gradually grew less awesome as the nation and the world constructed bigger and better machines for altering the natural environment. Even the ignominious failure of de Lesseps's Panama project in the 1880s did little to discourage the committed canal advocates.

Enthusiasm for the canal tied in naturally with the expansionist themes of American foreign policy. The anticipated commercial benefits alone made the project tremendously desirable. The canal would greatly increase the United States' contacts in Central America which, in turn, would inevitably lead to more trade and investment. The western Caribbean was a stagnant backwater, tucked well away from the world's major trade routes; the construction of a canal would draw it into the mainstream of international commerce and would enormously stimulate the economic development of the whole region. If Americans dug the canal, Americans would be in the best possible position to take advantage of this development. Furthermore, the completed canal would bring the United States' east coast ports and distribution centers much closer to the west coast of South America, an area British and French traders had traditionally dominated. And, of course, it would greatly reduce the time required to reach the fabled Orient.[18]

Increased commercial contacts with Central and South America would inevitably enhance the United States' political and strategic position. As one advocate claimed, "The canal will, for the first time, make possible an enforcement of the Monroe Doctrine, hitherto a mere dogma in American policy. The communion of interests be-

[18]John Sherman, "The Nicaragua Canal," *Forum* 11 (March 1891): 5.

tween the American states will be enormously strengthened by this work."[19] The defense capabilities of the United States would be similarly affected. An American-controlled waterway would expedite the speedy assembly of all American naval vessels off either coast of the United States. During the Spanish-American War, the U.S.S. *Oregon* had stunned the world by making the arduous, time-consuming passage from San Francisco all the way around Cape Horn in time to participate in the actions off Cuba. The next war might not provide enough time for such an epic voyage, but an isthmian canal would dramatically increase the flexibility and deployable strength of the United States Navy.[20]

To assure its strategic usefulness, the canal must be under exclusive American control. The United States had become capable of building the projected canal in the latter part of the nineteenth century, possessing the requisite wealth, manpower, and technical skills. As Theodore Roosevelt claimed in 1901, the construction of the canal would be "one of those great works which only a great nation can undertake with prospects of success, and which when done are not only permanent assets in the nation's material interests, but standing monuments to its constructive ability."[21] The canal would thus serve as proof of the United States' growing international stature. Simultaneously, the export of American manpower and influence associated with the construction effort could extend, as one report put it, "a share in our own advanced civilization and in the blessings of civil and religious liberty."[22] The canal project definitely embraced all of the expansionist themes basic to foreign policy in this period.

Enthusiasm for the canal project had survived President Cleveland's killing of the Arthur administration's canal treaty with Nicaragua in 1885. Cleveland's personal opposition made it necessary for the canal advocates to rely upon a private American company to plan

[19]*Congressional Record*, 57th Cong., 1st sess., p. 6317; Tyler Dennett, *John Hay: From Poetry to Politics* (New York: Dodd, Mead, 1933), p. 217; Alfred Thayer Mahan, *The Problem of Asia* (Boston: Little, Brown, 1900), p. 183; U.S., Congress, Senate, *Compilation of Reports of the Committee on Foreign Relations, 1789–1901*, 56th Cong., 2d sess. (1901), Ex. Doc. No. 231, 8 parts (volumes), 4:464.

[20]Richardson, *Messages and Papers*, 9:6661–62.

[21]U.S., Congress, Senate, *The Maritime Canal of Suez from its Inauguration, November 17, 1869, to the Year 1884*, 48th Cong., 1st sess. (1884), Ex. Doc. No. 198, p. 153.

[22]Richardson, *Messages and Papers*, 8:5624, 5870, 6366; Senate, *Reports of Committee on Foreign Relations*, 4:471; U.S., Congress, Senate, *Nicaragua Canal Company*, 51st Cong., 1st sess., (1891) Report No. 1944, pp. 7, 20; U.S., Congress, House, 54th Cong., 1st sess., Report No. 2126; Charles Callan Tansill, *The Foreign Policy of Thomas F. Bayard 1885–1897* (New York: Fordham University Press, 1940), p. 677.

the Nicaraguan canal. The company sought governmental sanction, however, and Congress finally chartered the Maritime Canal Company of Nicaragua on 20 February 1889. Expansionist President Harrison also gave his blessing to the company, which began digging in 1890. As the de Lesseps organization had some years earlier, the American company rather quickly exhausted its capital and had to suspend its construction efforts in 1893. With solid backing from canal advocates on the Senate Foreign Relations Committee, the company repeatedly sought to obtain a government guarantee of interest on its bonds. President Cleveland publicly expressed approval of the project, but he definitely opposed any federal guarantee. Official backing by the United States was never granted, and Nicaragua announced that the American company had forfeited its contract in 1899. Essentially, the construction of a canal was such an enormous undertaking that only public funding and administration could accomplish it.[23]

Any move the United States government made, however, might raise protests from the British because of the Clayton-Bulwer Treaty. Canal advocates in Congress usually dismissed the 1850 treaty as obsolete. As the Senate Foreign Relations Committee insisted in 1891, the United States was a great power equipped with both a right and the capability to maintain uninterrupted transit through the canal: "We are the only power on this hemisphere that can secure such guarantees to the lawful commerce of all nations."[24] Such nationalistic assertions from the legislative branch embarrassed American statesmen seeking to promote good relations with the British government. Both Richard Olney and John Hay concluded that the best approach would be a straightforward renegotiation of the treaty with England.

Even though the American embassy in London had assured John Hay that the British government recognized the advisability of United States governmental involvement in the construction of the canal, Hay had a difficult time negotiating a revised treaty with British Ambassador Julian Pauncefote. This gentleman hoped to work other issues into any agreement he signed. The American secretary of state eventually got Pauncefote to agree that the only major sore point in Anglo-American relations at the time, the Alaskan boundary dispute, had no relation to the canal. The Hay-Pauncefote Treaty of 5 February 1900, therefore, dealt strictly with the canal issue, absolving the

[23]U.S., Congress, Senate, *Nicaragua Canal Company*, 52d Cong., 2d sess., (1892) Report No. 1142, p. v.

[24]Hay to Olney, 14 November 1898, John Hay Papers, LCMD; Dennett, *John Hay*, pp. 248–49; Dennis, *Adventures*, p. 156.

United States of any need to obtain British permission before beginning work on the project. Significantly, it did not revoke the Clayton-Bulwer Treaty's prohibition against American fortifications, the provision Blaine had so vehemently criticized in 1881. The Hay-Pauncefote Treaty would also guarantee the absolute neutrality of the canal in wartime. Finally, it included an invitation to other nations to join the United States and England in ratifying the document.[25]

Although Hay had become accustomed to Senate criticism of his handiwork, he failed to anticipate the storm of disapproval the treaty evoked. The self-assertive American people seldom concealed their indignation over anything they could construe as an affront to their nation's prestige, and this treaty virtually dictated what the United States could and could not do. It dissatisfied those like Lodge and Roosevelt who favored a greater international role for the United States; at the same time it angered more conservative spokesmen who wished to preserve American isolation and insulation from external influences. The prohibition against American fortification of the canal cast the United States in the role of an untrustworthy, irresponsible child. Worse still, the neutrality clause negated the canal's usefulness to the United States as a defensive weapon. Finally, the treaty's call for international ratification would essentially void the Monroe Doctrine by inviting European interference at the most strategic location in the Western Hemisphere. The American people would not permit any international agreement to weaken their recently broadened political influence in the Caribbean. As public ridicule mounted, the Senate resoundingly defeated the treaty. When Secretary Hay attempted to resign, President McKinley would not allow him to do so.[26]

The secretary of state's greatest fear was that Congress might unilaterally abrogate the Clayton-Bulwer Treaty, thereby wrecking the rapprochement with Great Britain that Hay favored. He made certain that American Ambassador Joseph Choate, in London, understood his personal views, so that the British government would be more forthcoming, before he once again began negotiating with Ambassador Pauncefote. Hay realized that nothing less than a full release

[25] Hay to Joseph Choate, 6 February 1900, John Hay Papers, LCMD; Beale, *Theodore Roosevelt*, pp. 103–4; William Roscoe Thayer, *The Life and Letters of John Hay*, 2 vols. (Boston: Houghton Mifflin, 1915), 2:273; Karl Schriftgiesser, *The Gentleman from Massachusetts: Henry Cabot Lodge* (Boston: Little, Brown, 1914), p. 191.

[26] Hay to Choate, 5 February 1901, John Hay Papers, LCMD; *Foreign Relations* (1901), p. 243; Thayer, *John Hay*, 2:229; John A. S. Grenville, *Lord Salisbury and Foreign Policy* (London: University of London Press, 1964), pp. 388–89.

from European dictation could win Senate approval. Fortunately, the British government shared Hay's desire to smooth relations between the two nations. Consequently, the second Hay-Pauncefote Treaty, signed on 18 November 1901, proved quite satisfactory to the American people because it superseded and therefore cancelled all the restrictions of the Clayton-Bulwer Treaty. It thus permitted the United States to build and fortify the canal as it chose. This treaty granted to the United States everything James G. Blaine had unsuccessfully sought from Great Britain in 1881. Britain's friendly acquiescence in 1901 illustrates how much the United States' international stature had changed in two decades.[27]

After years of discussion, the final choice of a route for the canal remained undecided in 1901, although attention had narrowed to two possibilities: a route across Panama, at that time a province of Colombia, and another along the southern border of Nicaragua. De Lesseps's Panama Canal Company had given up on the first route in the early 1880s, and the American Maritime Canal Company of Nicaragua had failed while attempting the other in the 1890s. The United States government appointed Rear Admiral John G. Walker to head a commission charged with investigating both these alternatives. The Walker Commission considered the labor, technological, and financial aspects of the project—including the exorbitant price being demanded for the assets left over from the de Lesseps attempt. This factor weighed heavily in the commission's decision favorable to the longer Nicaraguan route. Many approved this decision, most importantly, the Democratic party's leading canal enthusiast, Senator John T. Morgan.[28]

Nevertheless; the matter was hardly settled. Supporters of the Panama route contended that its engineering problems would be less awesome and its shorter route would offer faster transit times. The New Panama Canal Company, which had been formed solely to sell to the United States all of the tangible assets of the earlier French company, carried on a strident public relations campaign. The company's most active lobbyists were its French treasurer, Philippe Bunau-Varilla, and an American lawyer, William Nelson Cromwell, whose clients included both the canal company and the American-owned

[27]*Congressional Record,* 52d Cong., 1st sess., p. 4286; U.S., Congress, Senate, *Report of the Isthmian Canal Commission, 1899–1901,* 57th Cong., 1st sess. (1901), Doc. No. 54, pp. 26–63.

[28]Dennett, *John Hay,* pp. 369, 372; Dennis, *Adventures,* pp. 314–15; William Henry Harbaugh, *Power and Responsibility* (New York: Farrar Strauss & Cudahy, 1961), p. 202; Theodore Roosevelt, *An Autobiography* (New York: Scribners, 1913), p. 513.

railroads in the isthmus which stood to benefit if the canal were built in Panama. The publication of the Walker Commission's report caused the company to reduce its selling price from $109 million to only $40 million, a reduction which brought the projected costs for building a Panama canal into line with the estimated expenses of constructing one in Nicaragua. Cromwell and Bunau-Varilla lost the first round when the House of Representatives approved a bill authorizing a Nicaraguan canal. When the bill went to the upper house, however, Wisconsin Senator John C. Spooner added an amendment to it which ordered the president to try to obtain rights to the canal route in Panama. If these diplomatic negotiations should prove unfruitful, the Isthmian Canal Act of 28 June 1902 did provide for Nicaragua to be used as an alternative.

President Roosevelt had thoroughly studied all of the technical aspects of the two routes, and, at some point, became irrevocably convinced that Panama was the only feasible one. He anticipated little diplomatic trouble. The Colombian government had charged its minister to the United States, José Vicente Concha, with the duty of making certain the Americans chose the Panama route. In fact, so eager had the Colombian government been to cut Nicaragua out, that Secretary of State John Hay later insisted that Colombia, not the United States, had initiated the canal treaty negotiations. The Colombian minister lacked his superiors' enthusiasm for the project, however, so he abruptly stopped negotiating in 1902 when he became enraged at the United States government's decision to order its troops to quell a riot in Panama. Colombia then recalled Concha, leaving Secretary of State Hay to work out a canal treaty with Colombian Chargé d'Affaires Tomás Herrán. The Hay-Herrán Treaty would allow the United States to construct and fortify a Panamanian canal in return for a $10 million payment and a $250,000 annual fee. The United States could exercise exclusive control over a canal zone extending three miles on either side of the canal. The oddest provision of the Hay-Herrán Treaty forbade the Colombian government from contacting or attempting to negotiate with the Panama Canal Company to which the United States intended to pay $40 million. The United States Senate quickly approved this treaty in the spring of 1903.[29]

Colombia was much slower to respond. Having seized dictatorial power a few years earlier, Colombian Vice-President José Manuel

[29]*Foreign Relations* (1903), pp. 133–35, 142–43, 146, 168; Hill, *Roosevelt*, p. 49; Munro, *Intervention*, p. 47.

Marroquín lacked a popular mandate. He feared that if he gave up his nation's most important natural resource, he might be toppled from power. He chose to dilute his personal responsibility by calling a congress into being to approve the treaty before he would ratify it. The Colombians showed particular annoyance at the prohibition against any dealings with the Panama Canal Company. They naturally wanted to get a share of the $40 million payment. From Bogotá, American Minister Arthur M. Beaupré warned Hay of the widespread Colombian dissatisfaction and asked whether the United States might offer more money directly or allow Colombia to negotiate with the company. The secretary of state responded indignantly that Colombia had forced the treaty upon the United States. If Colombia refused to ratify it without changes, Hay threatened, the United States would simply move on to the Nicaraguan alternative. Despite this warning, the Colombian senate unanimously refused to approve the Hay-Herrán Treaty.[30]

After this rejection in the late summer of 1903, President Roosevelt took full control of the problem from Hay and considered his alternatives. He apparently never seriously considered the Nicaraguan route even though Senator Morgan and others claimed it to be superior. At the same time, others were calling for a forcible American annexation of Panama, but Roosevelt ruled that out even though he later claimed the Spooner Amendment had made it incumbent upon him to gain control of the Panama route through any possible means. He was well aware of the long history of Panamanian hostility to Colombian authority, so he chose to await political developments on the isthmus.[31]

The people who lived on the isthmus itself were keenly aware of how important its use as a transit point was to their prosperity. Furthermore, they had little respect for the distant, dictatorial government in Bogotá, and civil disorder was quite common. American statesmen had consistently claimed that the treaty of 1846 had assigned to the United States the responsibility of securing neutrality and freedom of transit across the Isthmus of Panama. Indeed, on six different occasions, the Colombian government had sought the United States' assistance to end rioting in Panama. The incident which had angered Colombian Minister Concha in 1902 differed from these earlier American interventions in two respects: Colombia had not

[30]Harbaugh, *Power and Responsibility*, pp. 210–11; Richardson, *Messages and Papers*, 9:6881; Roosevelt, *An Autobiography*, p. 521; Thayer, *John Hay*, 2:297.
[31]Hill, *Roosevelt*, pp. 44–46.

requested help and United States forces prevented the transfer by railroad of Colombian government troops across the isthmus. The Americans appeared to be interpreting their obligation under the 1846 treaty as the preservation of free transit regardless of the current Colombian regime's wishes.[32]

When the Colombian government refused to ratify the canal treaty which the people of Panama considered vital to their future development, talk of revolution spread. Later, Roosevelt insisted that "I did not lift my finger to incite the revolutionists. The right simile is totally different. I simply ceased to stamp out the different revolutionary fuses that were already burning."[33] These fuses were, of course, burning all the brighter because of the United States government's willingness to pay large sums of money for the right to build a canal. Monsieur Bunau-Varilla took personal credit for planning the revolution as well as supplying the hesitant Panamanian rebel leaders with advice, funds, and encouragement. In early November 1903, the rebels bought off several high-ranking Colombian officials, while the American-owned railroads refused to transport Colombian reinforcements to the crisis centers. The revolution was swift and almost bloodless. The newly installed leaders immediately promulgated republican governmental forms specifically designed to attract the sympathy and approval of the United States.

Those who blamed the Roosevelt administration for carrying out the revolution tried to prove their case by describing the suspicious actions of United States Navy vessels in the vicinity of Colón and Panama City. The American commanders had orders to prevent the landing of any armed forces with hostile intentions, and they liberally interpreted this to include some Colombian army units sent to quell the rebellion. Once again, the great-power practice of using naval vessels for prestige and the protection of national interests had triggered controversy. As in the case of the U.S.S. *Maine* some five years earlier, the administration had dispatched the warships to the isthmus in mid-October because it had received information that a revolution was being planned. Roosevelt claimed he had "directed the Navy Department to issue instructions to send ships to the Isthmus so as to protect American interests and the lives of American citizens if a revolutionary outbreak should occur."[34] No full-scale intervention had been authorized or even considered, Roosevelt insisted, as the

---

[32]Roosevelt, *An Autobiography*, p. 525.
[33]Quoted in Thayer, *John Hay*, 2:316–17.
[34]Dennis, *Adventures*, p. 331; *Foreign Relations* (1903), p. 271; Munro, *Intervention*, pp. 53–54.

U.S.S. *Nashville,* standing off Colón, had only forty-two marines and sailors available for landing at the same time the Colombian government was engaged in sending hundreds of troops to the isthmus. Besides, if a major interference had developed, the United States could have justified its actions with the 1846 treaty and the procedures it had used so often in the past to prevent any disruption of free passage across the isthmus.[35]

Looking back on the incident after more than a decade, Roosevelt saw nothing wrong with the American actions relating to Panama. He was proud of his quick recognition of the new government, and for the protection the American navy afforded it. He was also extraordinarily pleased with his own role in the affair: "I did not consult Hay, or Root, or any one else as to what I did, because a council of war does not fight; and I intended to do the job once for all."[36] This particular statement reveals a great deal about Roosevelt's personal views of a president's responsibility for bringing the United States greater international influence and respect. In his opinion, the nation must always be prepared and willing to act decisively. Roosevelt thus made a point of trying to escape from the restrictions upon presidential power which had shackled his predecessors since the Civil War. The United States could only exercise its worldwide political influence to the full when its leadership was free to respond instantly, forcefully, and convincingly to disturbances within its areas of interest. Roosevelt's actions relating to the Panamanian revolution helped accomplish this larger goal because, although they aroused severe criticism, they were never reversed. After Roosevelt had set a precedent for asserting presidential power, his successors, Taft and Wilson, could react quickly to crises in external affairs without waiting for the delays and digressions inherent in congressional deliberations.

The architects of the Panamanian revolution had been clever in calling for the establishment of a republican government because it gave the United States an idealistic reason for underwriting the new leadership. It allowed Roosevelt to boast: "We gave the people of Panama self-government, and freed them from subjection to alien oppressors."[37] Secretary of War Root advised the Panamanians to hold a constitutional convention quickly, possibly patterned after the one which had created the Cuban government. At that point, the Cuban republic was the United States' democratic showplace.[38] Mis-

---

[35]Quoted in Thayer, *John Hay,* 2:328.
[36]*Foreign Relations* (1903), p. 233.
[37]Roosevelt, *An Autobiography,* p. 525.
[38]Jessup, *Elihu Root,* 1:407.

sion sentiment provided a handy excuse for justifying actions which the president frankly admitted also served the American purpose of extending its political influence to the strategically vital isthmus. In his special message on Panama on 4 January 1904, he insisted that American recognition of Panama's independence was "further justified by the highest considerations of our national interests and safety. In all the range of our international relations, I do not hesitate to affirm that there is nothing of greater or more pressing importance than the construction of an interoceanic canal."[39]

Acting in accordance with the plan Bunau-Varilla had drawn up, the new Panamanian government immediately chose the Frenchman to serve as its first minister to the United States. He eagerly cooperated with Secretary of State Hay in drafting a canal treaty quite similar to the one Colombia had refused to ratify. The only major difference involved a widening of the canal zone from six to ten miles. The $10 million payment provided the Republic of Panama with instant financial solvency. The isthmus became a United States protectorate because the first article of the Hay-Bunau-Varilla Treaty promised that "the United States guarantees and will maintain the independence of the Republic of Panama." The rapid recognition and the equally speedy treaty negotiations left those who still advocated the Nicaraguan route no time to organize. Senator Morgan eventually wrote a turgid, fifteen-page letter denouncing Hay and implying that questionable connections existed between the Roosevelt administration and Bunau-Varilla's Panama Canal Company.[40] The new canal treaty easily won Senate approval, however, and the United States could finally embark upon its monumental interoceanic canal project.

The United States encountered persistent turbulence in its relations with the Republic of Panama right up to the time of the canal's official completion. As early as December 1905, internal disorders had provoked the Panamanian president into asking for United States armed forces to supervise the republic's national elections. Intermittent political instability gave ample opportunities for American interference in Panama's internal affairs. By 1913, the republic had acquiesced to the same sort of arrangements Cuba had under the Platt Amendment regarding the United States' right to intervene. The United States had thus turned Panama into a close approximation to a colony. The creation of the Panamanian protectorate shows that the

[39]Richardson, *Messages and Papers,* 9:6921.
[40]Morgan to Hay, February 1904, Papers of John T. Morgan, LCMD.

expansion of political influence theme accompanied the more obvious economic expansionism associated with the canal.[41]

Although historian Howard C. Hill readily admitted that the Spanish-American War expanded American interests in Central America, he maintained that the construction of the Panama Canal exerted a much more important influence than the war upon the United States' Latin-American policies.[42] Strategic naval planning in both the Caribbean and the Pacific now became preoccupied with defense of the isthmus. The canal stretched the American defense perimeter far to the south, and, like the annexation of Hawaii, it stimulated increased defense spending. One can clearly perceive the sort of impact the canal had upon American foreign policy in the Caribbean by contrasting President Roosevelt's rather mild reaction to Venezuela's financial insolvency in 1901 and 1902 with his much more forceful response to a similar insolvency in the Dominican Republic in 1904, after the canal treaty had been approved.

The situation the Roosevelt administration faced in 1904 resembled the one in Venezuela two years earlier in that the Dominican government had become over-indebted to foreigners. One of the Dominican Republic's creditors, a United States company, had earlier forced the island government to agree to arbitration in order to insure repayment of its loans. The resulting arbitration settlement authorized an American agent to take over one of the nation's customshouses if the government defaulted on its payments—an event that occurred on 17 October 1904. European governments protested that this arrangement discriminated against creditors in their own nations, and they appealed to the United States in order to obtain redress. Rumors circulated about a possible naval demonstration if nothing was done.[43]

Although Roosevelt personally cared little for the plight of the creditors involved, whether they were American citizens or Europeans, he did have an abiding desire to create political and financial stability in the vicinity of the Panama Canal. He also felt it would be wise to reemphasize the Monroe Doctrine's prohibition against European interference in the hemisphere, and he definitely wished to avoid another unpopular and dangerous European naval demonstration. He could, of course, have accomplished all of these goals by

[41]Sheldon B. Liss, *The Canal* (Notre Dame, Ind.: Notre Dame University Press, 1967), pp. 22, 30.
[42]Hill, *Roosevelt*, pp. 174–75.
[43]Ibid., pp. 154–55; Munro, *Intervention*, p. 87.

simply annexing the Dominican Republic, a proposal which had maintained a persistent if limited popularity in the United States ever since President Grant's failure to do so. President Roosevelt had long since tired of carrying the burden of colonial responsibility for a great many impoverished, illiterate peoples and, according to John Hay, he told a cabinet meeting he had about as much desire to annex more islands as "a gorged anaconda wants to swallow a porcupine wrong end to."[44]

The alternative the Roosevelt administration developed reinforced and extended American political influence in the Caribbean area without encumbering the United States with unwanted responsibilities. The basic elements of the policy had been successfully applied in China and Turkey for some time, and Secretary of State James G. Blaine had provided an American precedent for Roosevelt's action. In 1881, France had threatened to stage a naval demonstration off Venezuela to coerce the government at Caracas into paying its debts. The Venezuelans had responded by asking for the United States' help in establishing a competent, professionally-run customs service to collect its import duties and create a fund for the repayment of its outstanding obligations. Intrigued as Blaine was by any plan that would strengthen American commercial and political influence in South America, he began to work on the proposal, but, like so many of Blaine's policies, Frelinghuysen unceremoniously canceled it.[45] Roosevelt revived the idea, calling upon his minister to Santo Domingo, Thomas C. Dawson, to work out a protocol by which American-designated agents would take charge of all customs collections in the country. These agents would funnel 45 percent of the receipts into a fund for the payment of outstanding debts and deliver the remainder to the republic's treasury. The Roosevelt administration set up the system and then, as a sort of afterthought, decided to formalize it by seeking Senate approval.

The message Roosevelt sent to the Senate accompanying the Dominican customs protocol on 7 February 1905 promulgated a new corollary to the Monroe Doctrine. First, the president assured the world that the United States had "not the slightest desire for territorial aggrandizement at the expense of any of its southern neighbors, and will not treat the Monroe Doctrine as an excuse for such aggran-

---

[44]Quoted in Thayer, *John Hay*, 2:352.

[45]*Foreign Relations* (1881), pp. 1192, 1198; *Foreign Relations* (1905), p. 378; Perkins, *Monroe Doctrine*, pp. 116–17; Alice Felt Tyler, *The Foreign Policy of James G. Blaine* (Minneapolis: University of Minnesota Press, 1927), pp. 78–79.

dizement on its part."[46] In line with his earlier attitudes, he admitted that European nations with complaints directed at New World nations had every right to demand settlement, "provided that action does not take the shape of interference with their form of government or of the despoilment of their territory under any disguise." Recalling Olney's contention in 1895, Roosevelt indicated that Europeans who overstepped these restrictions also violated the Monroe Doctrine and, "the United States then becomes a party in interest." Having thus reemphasized the predominance of American political influence in the region and having noted America's readiness to defend it if necessary, Roosevelt rung in the commercial theme:

> The conditions in the Dominican Republic not only constitute a menace to our relations with other foreign nations, but they also concern the prosperity of the people of the island, as well as the security of American interests, and they are intimately associated with the interests of the South Atlantic and Gulf States, the normal expansion of whose commerce lies in that direction.

Finally, the president added to his justifications for American intercession in Dominican affairs the revised democratic mission theme which placed a premium upon responsible, republican government:

> The ordinary resources of diplomacy and international arbitration are absolutely impotent to deal wisely and effectively with the situation in the Dominican Republic, which can only be met by organizing its finances on a sound basis and by placing the customhouses beyond the temptation of insurgent chieftains. Either we must abandon our duty under our traditional policy toward the Dominican people, who aspire to a republican form of government while they are actually drifting into a condition of permanent anarchy, in which case we must permit some other government to adopt its own measures in order to safeguard its own interests, or else we must ourselves take seasonable and appropriate action.

Roosevelt's linking of his policy for policing the Western Hemisphere to all of the United States' traditional foreign policy themes did not save it from criticism at that time and later. Some historians have gone so far as to call it an antithesis of the Monroe Doctrine because it called for the United States to carry out precisely what Monroe's original statement had opposed: a foreign intervention into an independent Latin American nation.[47] The president's policy drew

[46]See *Foreign Relations* (1905), pp. 334–42 for Roosevelt's comments on the Dominican Customs Protocol.

[47]Perkins, *Monroe Doctrine,* pp. 397, 433; Albert K. Weinberg, *Manifest Destiny* (Baltimore: Johns Hopkins University Press, 1935), pp. 428–29.

all sorts of contemporary criticism as well. Some senators saw the protocol as a sellout of American commercial interests because it interfered with the American company's first lien on Dominican customs revenue. Others denied that the United States had any obligation to rescue other peoples from the dangers their own financial recklessness had engendered. The Democrats were particularly annoyed, claiming that the president had usurped power by setting the customs arrangement in motion without first consulting the Senate.[48]

Republican Senators Lodge and Spooner staunchly defended Roosevelt, insisting that the president had full authority to take such an action without Senate approval. They described the logic behind the protocol as follows: the United States had chosen to assume responsibility for Latin American political stability, and Dominican instability stemmed from its financial insolvency; therefore, the administration's financial arrangements were essential to restore stability. Lodge praised the customs protocol as highly preferable to the alternative of resolving the Dominican government's instability by annexing the republic to the United States. Despite his friends' best efforts and Roosevelt's own self-confidence, his policy failed to win immediate congressional approval. Secretary of State Root finally managed to cajole two-thirds of the senators into approving the Dominican customs protocol more than two years after it had gone into operation.[49]

From a financial standpoint, the American-run Dominican customs service proved to be an outstanding success in eliminating graft and incompetency. The central government actually received more operating revenue than ever before, even after the customs service had set aside 45 percent of its income to service foreign debts. The American intercession also had favorable effects upon the republic's political condition, providing welcome relief from its chronic instability. While many Dominicans resented the patronizing American intrusion, it seemed acceptable to most other Latin Americans. And, as the protocol appeared to be serving as a bulwark against political breakdown, it became the model for all subsequent United States initiatives in Latin America. Unfortunately, succeeding presidents failed to enjoy the same degree of success in applying the Roosevelt Corollary as had the policy's originator. The 1904 action was something of a moral high point in the nation's extension of its political

[48]*Congressional Record*, 58th Cong., 3d sess., pp. 1287–88; *Congressional Record*, 59th Cong., 1st sess., pp. 793, 797, 799, 1174, 1178.
[49]Ibid., pp. 1424–38; Hill, *Roosevelt*, p. 162; Jessup, *Elihu Root*, 1:470; Leopold, *Elihu Root*, p. 63.

influence in Latin America because it involved neither the colonization which had gone before nor the use of American armed forces
which characterized later interventions.[50]

The Roosevelt Corollary definitively restated what both Blaine
and Olney had previously claimed: the United States was unquestionably the greatest power in the New World, and outsiders had to
take cognizance of its desires in any dealings they had in the Western
Hemisphere. Roosevelt's strident assertion of American predominance aroused much less opposition from across the Atlantic than had
earlier declarations of United States supremacy. The British government was particularly pleased that the United States had assumed the
responsibility of guaranteeing peace and financial responsibility in
the Western Hemisphere, thereby protecting British economic and
trade interests as well. The United States' widely-recognized position
of prominence essentially turned the Caribbean into a private American lake in the first decade of the twentieth century, giving the nation
its desired strategic control of the eastern approaches to the canal.[51]
"We have become a great nation, forced by the fact of its greatness
into relations with the other nations of the earth, and we must behave
as beseems a people with such responsibilities," President Roosevelt
proudly noted in his 1905 inaugural address. "But justice and gen-
erosity in a nation, as in an individual, count most when shown not by
the weak but by the strong. While ever careful to refrain from
wronging others, we must be no less insistent that we are not wronged
ourselves."[52]

The president's call for national vigilance and responsibility
coincided with the beginning of a decline in his personal interest in
Latin America. After 1905 he generally let his capable secretary of
state, Elihu Root, handle hemispheric problems. Although he shared
Roosevelt's ambitions to protect the canal and to encourage stability,
Root tried to deal with Latin Americans on a cooperative basis rather
than with a dictatorial, great-power assertiveness. He sincerely believed in America's democratic mission, and he hoped responsive
democratic governments would eventually supplant the persistent
political instability in the southern republics. He enjoyed the company

[50]*Foreign Relations* (1905), pp. 336, 378; Hill, *Roosevelt*, p. 160; Perkins, *Monroe Doctrine*, p. 455.
[51]Bradford Perkins, *The Great Rapprochement* (New York: Atheneum, 1968), pp. 184, 194; Dexter Perkins, *The United States and the Caribbean* (rev. ed., Cambridge, Mass.: Harvard University Press, 1966), p. 107.
[52]Richardson, *Messages and Papers*, 9:7060–61.

of Latin American diplomats, and for the first time since Blaine's tours of duty, a secretary of state personally attempted to establish emotional bonds between North and South America.

To underwrite the United States' peaceful influence throughout the hemisphere, Root favored greater commercial activity by American businessmen and bankers. The economic theme thus played a part in his desire for responsible governments as well as his efforts to cultivate Latin American friendships. It should be noted, however, that expansionist pressures from American businessmen influenced the Roosevelt administration much less than the possible diplomatic advantages American commercial expansion might bring. For example, the establishment of profitable trade with the United States could improve a Latin American nation's economic health, an improvement which, in turn, might protect it from revolution. Secretary Root felt commercial expansion would sustain American political influence as well as discourage European interference in the New World. He was, of course, not opposed to the strictly economic benefits of hemispheric trade, and he apparently believed the southern republics to be on the verge of developing into a much more substantial market area. "Ninety-seven percent of the territory of South America is occupied by ten independent republics living under constitutions substantially copied or adapted from our own," he told a group of American businessmen in 1906. "With the increase of population in such a field, under free institutions, with the fruits of labor and the rewards of enterprise secure, the production of wealth and the increase of purchasing power will afford a market for the commerce of the world worthy to rank even with the markets of the Orient as the goal of business enterprise."[53]

Root's Latin American trade-expansion program was reminiscent of those his Republican predecessors had advocated in the 1880s and 1890s except in one respect: it was something of a success. For example, he used the Pan-American conference system Blaine had founded to kindle better United States relations with other Americans. Root did not magisterially summon Latin American representatives to Washington as Blaine had in 1889, nor did he send a lower-ranking delegation as Hay had to the Second Inter-American Conference at Mexico City in 1901. Instead, even though no previous secretary of state had ever left the United States while in office, Root decided to attend personally the Third Inter-American Conference in Rio de Janiero. After his visit the American delegation to the confer-

[53]*Foreign Relations* (1906), p. 1459.

ence commented: "We believe the visit of the Secretary of State to South America has resulted in greater good to our relations with Central and South America than any one thing that has heretofore taken place in our diplomatic history with them."[54]

Roots's stopover in Brazil was only the first in a series of state visits he made on a goodwill tour to several Latin American nations. The mission theme provided the common denominator for the secretary of state's speeches, each of which alluded to the similarities between the United States' political system and those of his host countries. He also emphasized the advantages Latin Americans would gain through closer commercial and political relationships with their northern neighbor instead of continued dependence upon European imports. As important as any other aspect of his tour was the opportunity it provided him to issue assurances that the United States, now clearly the dominant power in the New World, had no desire whatsoever to expand its territorial control.[55] President Roosevelt firmly restated this pledge in his annual message following Root's tour:

> We wish for no victories but those of peace; for no territory except our own; for no sovereignty except the sovereignty over ourselves. We deem the independence and equal rights of the smallest and weakest member of the family of nations entitled to as much respect as those of the greatest empire, and we deem the observance of that respect the chief guaranty of the weak against the oppression of the strong.[56]

Despite the success of Root's tour, he returned to Washington only to find the United States' Latin American policy in turmoil. Cuba, that proud example of America's democratic mission, had become immersed in a dangerously unstable political situation. The island government's failure personally disappointed President Roosevelt as well as Root, who had superintended the creation of the Cuban governmental structure while serving as McKinley's secretary of war. American officials had lavished praise on the Cuban constitutional system which, like the Dominican customs protocol, they considered impressive evidence of the beneficial effects United States intervention could have in other countries. Root had been confidently reassuring Latin Americans that he had no desire to meddle in their

[54]*Report of the Delegates of the United States to the Third International Conference of the American States held at Rio de Janeiro, Brazil, July 21 to August 26, 1906* (Washington, D.C.: Government Printing Office, 1907), p. 23.

[55]For representative examples of Root's speeches, see *Foreign Relations* (1906), pp. 27, 127, 136, 153.

[56]Richardson, *Messages and Papers*, 10:7439.

domestic affairs at the very moment when the Cuban political crisis was inexorably drawing the United States toward intervention.

The crisis developed when a group of liberals charged President Tomás Estrada Palma's moderate government with using illegal methods to retain control in the 1905 Cuban elections. When Palma disdainfully ignored these charges, the liberals staged a rebellion which, by the summer of 1906, had brought the moderates to their knees. Like the Spaniards in 1898, however, the Cuban president and his associates preferred to surrender to the United States rather than to the disorderly Cuban rebels. Secretary of War William Howard Taft and Assistant Secretary of State Robert Bacon rushed off to Cuba to investigate. Although these American officials concluded that the 1905 election had indeed been rigged, President Palma stubbornly refused to capitulate to the liberals he hated. Instead, he requested the United States government to intervene, implementing the Platt Amendment's provision for the protection of life, property, and individual liberty. When the United States balked, Palma simply resigned, throwing the island's political system into utter chaos and leaving the Americans no choice but to intervene.[57]

Those dealing with the crisis in Washington were particularly solicitous of Secretary Root's feelings. "I feel very much regret that you are not here so that you could go to Cuba instead of myself," Taft wrote, "but the truth is, that the Cuban government has proven to be nothing but a house of cards. It has almost collapsed, and we have to take action at once."[58] There seemed to be nothing else to do, Roosevelt confessed later in the year, because the United States had "assumed the sponsorship before the civilized world for Cuba's career as a nation."[59] The American officials who made the decision to intervene publicly and privately expressed great reluctance about the move. After all, the intervention represented an admission that the earlier American endeavors in the island had failed to guarantee the sort of democratic and responsible government the United States prized so highly.

The American takeover did facilitate the resolution of the political controversy. Nevertheless, Roosevelt found the whole episode distasteful. He pledged to withdraw all American forces as soon as a popular government had been reestablished, which essentially meant

[57]Ibid., p. 7436; *Foreign Relations* (1906), pp. 474, 477–79; Munro, *Intervention*, pp. 128–32.

[58]Taft to Root, 15 September 1906, Elihu Root Papers, LCMD.

[59]Richardson, *Messages and Papers*, 10:7501.

turning political control over to the liberals who had fomented the rebellion in the first place.[60] By the winter of 1907, Roosevelt proudly announced that "absolute quiet and prosperity have returned to the island because of this [American] action. We are now taking steps to provide for elections in the island and our expectation is within the coming year to be able to turn the island over again to a government chosen by the people thereof."[61] This statement suggests that the traditional democratic mission theme was directing American policy almost exclusively, but the revision of that theme, which had occurred after 1900 is clearly evident in a letter the president wrote to Secretary Root on 20 July 1908. The president was seeking a safe way of terminating American occupation of the island, and his ideas illustrate how the successful Dominican customs arrangements had become a precedent for other United States actions in the Caribbean. Roosevelt suggested that, once the Cubans had elected a democratic government, they should

> ask us to make such arrangements, probably by leaving certain assistants in the Island as will secure permanence of government. This can be secured only by providing that the finances be kept straight; that order be maintained; and that fair elections be guaranteed. We must try to make them understand that our purpose is not to interfere with the design of limiting their independence, but to interfere so as to enable them to retain their independence.[62]

America's mission had undergone a reordering of its values; self-government was still desirable, but responsible government was even more essential. The United States was offering its assistance and advice to keep Cuba's democratic government from deteriorating through irresponsible administration. Historian Allan R. Millett argues persuasively that the Cuban intervention discomforted American officials to such an extent that afterwards they tried to avoid military involvement and direct interference in governmental and political affairs in Latin America. The Dominican Customs Protocol seemed to provide a much more palatable alternative, one which was unsuccessfully emphasized under Taft.[63]

More immediately, the Cuban intervention definitely reinforced Secretary Root's efforts to project a low profile in hemispheric affairs.

[60]Hill, *Roosevelt*, pp. 103–5; Munro, *Intervention*, pp. 134, 140.

[61]Richardson, *Messages and Papers*, 10:7501.

[62]Elting E. Morison, ed., *The Letters of Theodore Roosevelt*, 8 vols. (Cambridge, Mass.: Harvard University Press, 1951–54), 6:1137–38.

[63]Allan Reed Millett, *The Politics of Intervention* (Columbus: Ohio State University Press, 1968), pp. 265–67.

He carefully avoided allowing the United States to become involved in various problems which arose from time to time, such as election squabbles in Panama and Venezuela's renewed credit problems with France. By 1907, however, Central America had become so unsettled that the secretary of state felt he must make an effort to establish and preserve responsible government there. The chief troublemaker in American eyes was Nicaraguan leader José Santos Zelaya whose ambitions to unite and rule all of Central America triggered one outbreak of international conflict after another.

Even when he decided to act, Root hoped that, by drawing Mexico into a cooperative policy, he could avoid giving the appearance that the United States was attempting to dictate to the Central American governments. Mexican President Porfirio Díaz had ruled the United States' southern neighbor virtually without interruption since the late 1870s. Although hardly enlightened or democratic, the dictatorial control Díaz exercised seemed to many Americans a reasonable way of guaranteeing political stability. Furthermore, Díaz had encouraged extensive American investment in his country. Most of the wealth this investment created flowed right back across the border to enrich American capitalists, however, and the impoverished Mexican peasants gained little if any benefit from their nation's economic exploitation. Secretary Root lacked information about their plight, and, even if it had been brought to his attention, he probably would have continued the mutually beneficial official relationship with Díaz. Root definitely perceived advantages in getting the Mexican leader to cooperate with his Central American policies. The secretary of state skillfully deemphasized the American role by urging Mexico to take the lead in calling upon the belligerents to come to terms.[64]

Ultimately, the two North American nations had to make several attempts to resolve the Central American difficulties. Their peacemaking efforts finally culminated at a conference in Washington in the fall of 1907. The five Central American republics agreed to sign a general treaty of peace and amity designed to bring to an end the current round of squabbling. A subsidiary convention created the Central American Court of Justice and made it responsible for ironing out conflicting claims and disputes among the Central American nations so that such claims and disputes would not inevitably lead to war. The five contracting parties also approved a remarkable article

---

[64]*Foreign Relations* (1906), p. 836; *Foreign Relations* (1907), p. 853; Jessup, *Elihu Root*, 1:516; Munro, *Intervention*, p. 147; Richardson, *Messages and Papers*, 10:7442.

that pledged that they would deny formal recognition to any government which came to power through revolutionary means or which did not have the support of "freely elected representatives of the people." This emphatic statement of the principles inherent in the United States' democratic mission theme established much more stringent rules for recognizing governmental changes than those the American State Department itself used.[65]

The enthusiastic praise with which Secretary Root greeted these treaty arrangements proved to be premature and unjustified. Even as President Roosevelt left office, Central America was entering a new round of revolutions and border skirmishes. Fortunately, the retiring president had no premonitions about the impending collapse of his administration's peacekeeping efforts. He felt he had done quite respectably in his dealings with Latin America. Under his guidance the United States had asserted its supremacy in the Western Hemisphere, created stability in the region, begun the canal, and managed to win a few friends in the process. Indeed, Roosevelt's Latin American policies were a good deal more successful than his efforts to defend American prestige and increase American influence in the Far East. Because the United States lacked the uncontested predominance in the Pacific it had commandeered for itself in the Caribbean, the effectiveness and scope of American initiatives in the Orient remained correspondingly limited. The story of America's increasing involvement in the Far East is one of a nation fighting to establish itself as a great power, a status it had already clearly achieved in its own hemisphere.

[65]Jessup, *Elihu Root*, 1:514; Munro, *Intervention*, p. 153.

7

The Great Power
in the Far East, 1880-1909

At first glance, the grounds of the American Legation in Peking might seem the most peaceful place on earth. Low-hanging trees shaded the large pots containing leafy plants and small bushes which had been set out in neat rows on the trampled, compressed earth of the legation grounds. A high wall ran all around the compound, secluding the cluster of low, one-story buildings with peaked, tile roofs from the gaze of passersby. The top half of this wall consisted of wooden latticework, and the three-foot high masonry foundations contained decorative, cross-shaped interstices. Nevertheless, the American minister to China, Edwin H. Conger, derived little comfort from the pleasant aspect his residence afforded in early June 1900. He fully realized that the walls had never been meant for protection against armed attack.

Outside the flimsy walls, beyond the limits of the legation quarter, the Chinese people seethed with an inchoate unrest. The Boxers, a group of nationalistic fanatics, had brought their anti-foreign violence into the Imperial City itself. Now they threatened to engulf the legation quarter as well. Minister Conger had some very serious decisions to make. On 31 May, a contingent of fifty United States Marines had arrived along with some three hundred troops from other nations, and the danger of an immediate confrontation had momentarily passed. But the future looked bleak. Conger had received singularly unhelpful advice from Secretary of State John Hay in Washington. On 8 June he had ordered Conger to "act independently, in protection of American interests where practicable, and concurrently with representatives of other powers if necessity arise." Had necessity arisen? Should Conger cooperate with the other foreign representatives also threatened by the violence sweeping the city? The last advice he got from Hay came on 10 June, and it concluded with the firm injunction that "there must be no alliances."[1]

Conger ultimately chose to move his family, his staff, his marine guard, and the American missionaries and businessmen under his protection into the fortified British Legation. There the Americans and all the other foreign nationals survived a siege which lasted into August. The advice Conger had received from Washington had proved to be inappropriate to the life or death situation the Americans faced in China in 1900. Yet Hay's messages at this point simply reflected the traditional American attitudes about China and the great powers. The United States prided itself on its independence from the other foreigners who seemed bent on plundering China. At the same time, Conger's decision to cooperate with the other representatives in what turned out to be a successful common self defense illustrates an interesting paradox in America's Far Eastern policy: the United States achieved the most when it cooperated with or copied the other great powers; its initiatives bore little fruit when it acted alone. Yet that seemed the more desirable course to American statesmen.

An early success of the United States' independent policy in the Far East occurred in 1854 when Navy Commodore Matthew Calbraith Perry "opened" Japan to outsiders. Four years later, American Consul Townsend Harris negotiated the world's first modern trade treaty with Japan. The European powers followed the American lead in establishing commercial relations with the Japanese Empire. Meanwhile, Japan began adopting and adapting Western industrial and commercial techniques in an extraordinarily successful modernization program. By the 1890s, Japan had become a significant competitor for a share of the China market that many Americans saw as so essential to their own nation's prosperity.

Although Americans had begun trading with China even before the end of the Revolutionary War, the United States government did not become formally involved until it negotiated trade treaties with China in 1844 and 1858. Through their most-favored-nation clauses, these treaties only gave American merchants and officials the same rights China had already granted the other powers. American interest in China lagged during the years after the Civil War, and, when it began to revive in the late 1870s, Americans encountered stiff European competition. In addition, China remained extremely reluctant

---

[1]U.S., Department of State, *Papers Relating to the Foreign Relations of the United States* (Washington, D.C.: Government Printing Office, 1900), p. 143.

to expand its contacts with westerners. The Chinese Imperial government had tried to keep foreigners at a distance by restricting their activities and trade as much as possible. Fortunately, the United States government exhibited no desire whatsoever to establish a colony or a sphere of influence on Chinese territory, and it attached few political strings to its commercial relations with China. In fact, it often seemed totally disinterested in the plight of American merchants in China.

Meanwhile, the Chinese government became exceedingly irritated at the American government's immigration policy during the 1880s. Laboring men despised Oriental workers who would accept very low wages, and, when hard times hit, severe race riots broke out. A chorus of protest arose, forcing American diplomats to consider restricting the immigration of Chinese workers or even excluding them entirely. Both Blaine and Bayard had criticized Chinese immigration during their congressional careers; they naturally pressed forward on exclusion once they took charge at the State Department. The first major Chinese exclusion law went on the books in 1882, and additional, more stringent laws followed. These laws understandably found little favor in China, however, and American immigration restrictions continued to vex those hoping to improve relations between the United States and both China and Japan well into the twentieth century.

Although most Republican diplomatic initiatives under Garfield and Arthur involved Latin America, a major change in the nation's Far Eastern policy appeared likely after the United States established relations with Korea in 1882. In fact, the United States had blundered into a very complex and ticklish situation in Korea, the full implications of which Americans failed to comprehend at the time. The weak, timid Chinese government had caved in to Japanese pressures in 1876 and permitted Japan to work out a trade agreement directly with the Koreans, rather than forcing them to deal indirectly through Peking. Even so, the Chinese Imperial government continued to claim it held suzerainty over Korea. An American naval officer, Commodore Robert W. Shufeldt, convinced Secretary of State Blaine that Japan's treaty proved that Korea had become independent of China, and that it could now work out its own commercial policies with other nations. He urged the State Department to let him follow Perry's example and "open" Korea to American trade. He would thus be implementing the American mission to support self-government, expanding trade opportunities for American merchants, and asserting an independent American political influence in the Far East.

Unfortunately, Shufeldt failed to realize how delicately Korea was balanced between Japan and China.[2]

The stubborn naval officer finally badgered the Arthur administration into allowing him to take a naval squadron to Korea. Shufeldt's grand gesture miscarried when the Chinese government forced him to negotiate his Korean trade treaty in the Chinese port city of Tientsin. Although China maintained a tenuous claim to control over the Korean peninsula, the United States was permitted to establish a legation in Seoul. One of American Minister Lucius H. Foote's first official functions was to arrange for a Korean delegation to visit the United States. "The opportunity afforded them to examine not only the practical workings of our system of Government but to see our industries and to learn our sources of wealth and prosperity," the diplomat enthused in a frenzy of mission sentiment, "as well as to come directly in contact with our citizens and to experience so many acts of personal kindness, cannot but produce a marked and beneficial result upon this strange and interesting people."[3] The enthusiasm a few American officials generated over the opening of relations with Korea never translated itself into significant American action. The government in Washington had neither the desire nor, at that time, the naval hardware essential to save Korea from being overrun by external forces. Several European nations followed the American lead and, through most-favored-nation clauses, obtained exactly the same trading privileges Korea had extended to the United States. By 1885 America's flush of excitement over Korea had faded, and it received no transfusion of new vitality from President Cleveland.[4]

The United States government's restrained interest in Korean affairs resembled all American relationships in the Far East during this period. In 1885 the United States appointed Charles Denby minister to Peking, where he was to reside for thirteen years. Fortunately, the authorities in Washington studiously ignored much of what Denby suggested—including his 1894 proposal that the United States Navy batter down some of China's coastal cities if the Imperial government did not immediately put an end to antiforeign riots. On a

[2]Tyler Dennett, *Americans in Eastern Asia* (c. 1922; reprint ed., New York: Barnes & Noble, 1941), pp. 451–61; Alice Felt Tyler, *The Foreign Policy of James G. Blaine* (Minneapolis: University of Minnesota Press, 1927), pp. 268–69; Marilyn Blatt Young, *The Rhetoric of Empire* (Cambridge, Mass.: Harvard University Press, 1968), p. 17.

[3]*Foreign Relations* (1884), p. 125.

[4]Young, *Rhetoric of Empire*, pp. 14–15; David M. Pletcher, *The Awkward Years* (Columbia: University of Missouri Press, 1962), p. 213.

more rational plane, Denby suggested a number of ways in which the United States could increase its trade relations with the Chinese Empire, and he enthusiastically praised various American businessmen's initiatives in China. Secretary of State Bayard decided he could best avoid entanglements by issuing a standing order in 1887 which forbade the American minister from using his official position to back any one American company attempting to gain concessions or privileges in China. Denby indignantly protested that the Chinese government would only agree to meet the desires and requests of foreigners if threatened or coerced by a major power's official representative. Secretary of State Olney temporarily modified the order in 1895, but it was quickly reimposed.[5] Denby was, of course, quite correct in his contention that, without the sort of strident governmental support the other powers marshaled behind their businessmen, American trade in the Far East was bound to remain restricted. Such arguments carried little weight with President Cleveland, an advocate of international free trade, who felt the government should confine itself to insisting upon free access to overseas markets and then allow American merchants to compete with those of other countries. His attitudes were thus remarkably similar to the philosophy underlying the "open door" concept Secretary of State John Hay sponsored a few years later.[6]

Japan's ambitions to seize full control over Korea led to a major disturbance of all foreign trade in the Far East. Frustrated by China's stubborn refusal to abandon its claim of sovereignty over Korea, Japan declared war in the summer of 1894. Secretary of State Gresham wisely pursued a policy of strict neutrality in the conflict. He rejected China's request for backing, and he refused to participate when Great Britain suggested a multinational intervention. The resounding victory Japan won boosted its international prestige substantially. Because the United States had maintained its independence from the other powers, the Chinese government requested American assistance in bringing Japan to the peace table. Having restricted the United States' action to an offer of good offices, Gresham was able to convince Japan to end the hostilities. Then the United States prudently withdrew completely, and thereby avoided any responsibility for the harsh peace terms Japan demanded: freedom for Korea, a

---

[5]Adee to Olney, 1 August 1895, Richard Olney Papers, LCMD; *Foreign Relations* (1897), pp. 56–59; Young, *Rhetoric of Empire*, pp. 21, 56–58; Warren I. Cohen, *America's Response to China* (New York: John Wiley, 1971), p. 44; David Healy, *US Expansionism* (Madison: University of Wisconsin Press, 1970), p. 183.

[6]Thomas J. McCormick, *China Market* (Chicago: Quadrangle, 1967), p. 63.

sizable indemnity, and the transfer to Japan of political control over Formosa and China's Liaotung Peninsula. Russia, France, and Germany subsequently coerced Japan to relinquish the Chinese territories in return for a larger indemnity.[7]

The conclusion of the Sino-Japanese War in early 1895 coincided with a great revival in American enthusiasm for Oriental trade. The upsurge in interest in the China market was, of course, part of the overall response to renewed depression in the United States. The federal government did not necessarily view Far Eastern markets as the panacea for domestic economic troubles, but a good many business and commercial spokesmen fervently called for expanded Oriental trade. Actually, the China market did not exist in the form its enthusiastic publicists claimed. The empire was poverty-stricken, Chinese peasants could barely supply themselves with the necessities of life, and they had little desire and less money to expend on foreign imports. Furthermore, the doors to free trade in China were gradually swinging shut. Government-backed European and Japanese companies were locked in struggles to obtain concessions and special privileges which in turn would limit or even cancel the sort of free competition the United States advocated. Although the American drive to capture a share of the Oriental trade had begun just a little too late, the myth that China would be a great market area in the future continued to exert a strong influence despite the absence of economic or social foundations.[8]

The widespread belief in the potential China market can be traced in part to those Americans who acted as links between the two cultures. While spreading the Gospel in China, Christian missionaries from the United States had been transmitting secular messages both ways. In China they lauded their home nation's culture, government, and value system, thus personally fulfilling the American democratic mission in conjunction with their religious efforts. When the missionaries returned to the United States, they told fascinating stories about Chinese life, and they spread the impression that China's enormous population would eagerly buy the cheap, mass-produced

---

[7]*Foreign Relations* (1894), Appendix I, pp. 70, 74, 79, 82; Young, *Rhetoric of Empire*, pp. 30–31.

[8]Dennett, *Eastern Asia*, p. 603; McCormick, *China Market*, pp. 60–62; Brooks Adams, "The Spanish War and the Equilibrium of the World," *Forum* 25 (August 1898): 649; Worthington C. Ford, "New Opportunities for American Commerce," *Atlantic Monthly* 82 (September 1898): 321–29; Richard W. Van Alstyne, *The Rising American Empire* (Chicago: Quadrangle, 1965), p. 192; Paul A. Varg, *The Making of a Myth* (East Lansing: Michigan State University Press, 1968), pp. 41, 58.

goods the American economy was now capable of turning out. The missionaries were well aware of how expanded American commercial and political influence would strengthen their endeavors overseas, so they deliberately reinforced the myth of the China market at the same time they solicited funds for continued missionary enterprises.[9]

Ironically, just when American interest in the commercial potentialities of China had been stimulated by Japan's victory, that triumph was setting in motion political realignments and policy alterations that would hamper any future American expansion in the Far East. The most obvious change was Japan's removal of Korea from any vestige of Chinese control. Japan's primary motive in going to war had been to end any restrictions on its extensive commercial and political influence on the peninsula. From time to time, American diplomats in Seoul tried to arouse American interest in Korea, but the government in Washington seemed content to allow Japan a relatively free hand.

The Sino-Japanese War had other, much more ominous political consequences. The European powers which had forced Japan to relinquish its territorial conquests in China expected the grateful Chinese government to offer them some sort of compensation. Germany made the first demand. When two German missionaries in China were murdered in the fall of 1897, the kaiser's government exacted from the Chinese government a lease to Kiaochow Bay, on the Shantung Peninsula. The German action set off an avalanche of similar moves through the following year as each major European power sought and won control of a Chinese port and its surrounding hinterland. This sort of political arrangement was called a sphere of influence, and it represented an extension of foreign control which fell just short of colonization. "If Germany, France and Russia proposed simply to open new ports to the trade of the world nobody would object; but they have not done so," American Minister Denby complained from Peking. "They claim, or will claim, jurisdiction exactly as if they owned the ceded territory. They will monopolize the exploitation of the adjacent country. They will construct all the railroads, and work all the mines."[10]

The British government offered the United States an opportunity to criticize the formation of these spheres of influence without

---

[9]Cohen, *America's Response*, pp. 53–54; Dexter Perkins, *The Evolution of American Foreign Policy* (New York: Oxford University Press, 1966), p. 57; William Appleman Williams, *The Tragedy of American Diplomacy* (New York: Dell, 1962), p. 56.

[10]Quoted in Alfred L. P. Dennis, *Adventures in American Diplomacy 1896–1906* (New York: E. P. Dutton, 1928), p. 181.

necessarily involving it in a show of force. Early in 1898, British Colonial Secretary Joseph Chamberlain suggested that Arthur Balfour
at the Foreign Office approach the Americans in order to obtain their
backing for a public defense of the open door concept. The British
naturally expected a positive response, because the United States had
consistently spoken in favor of keeping all of the Chinese ports open
to traders from any nation. The McKinley administration was too
distracted by the steps leading to the war against Spain, however, to
take up Balfour's suggestion. Great Britain therefore abandoned its
own open door initiative and joined the power grab, capturing additional territory in the vicinity of its Hong Kong colony and establishing its own sphere of influence at Weihaiwei. President McKinley
later excused his failure to act by claiming that none of the European
powers had closed the ports under their control to foreign commerce,
so, essentially, American access to Chinese markets had remained
unimpeded.[11]

Secretary of State Day did admit to Ambassador Hay in London,
in July 1898, that "the outcome of our struggle with Spain may develop the need of extending and strengthening our interests in the
Asiatic Continent."[12] What form such an extension of American
political influence should take became the subject of considerable debate in the next few months. Edwin H. Conger had replaced Charles
Denby at the legation in Peking, and the new American minister
strongly favored having the United States establish its own sphere of
influence in China. The McKinley administration considered such a
step too extreme, however, even when viewed in the light of the
upsurge in imperialist emotionalism in the fall of 1898. But, because
American leaders recognized how useful a Far Eastern springboard
would be in exercising United States influence in the Far East, they
were much more inclined to retain the Philippines. The islands were
already in American hands, they lay close to but not directly within
the area of the Far Eastern power struggles, and the United States'
retention of them could not be construed as granting American sanction to the European powers' establishment of spheres of influence
in China itself.[13]

[11]Hay to President, 13 January 1898, William R. Day Papers, LCMD; James D.
Richardson, *A Compilation of the Messages and Papers of the Presidents,* 10 vols. (Washing-
ton, D.C.: Bureau of National Literature, 1911), 8:6327–28; A. Whitney Griswold, *The
Far Eastern Policy of the United States* (New York: Harcourt, Brace, 1938), pp. 45, 50.

[12]Quoted in Young, *Rhetoric of Empire,* p. 93.

[13]Ibid., p. 99; John Holladay Latané, *From Isolation to Leadership* (Garden City,
N.Y.: Doubleday, 1918), p. 84; Gilbert Reid, "The Powers and the Partition of China,"
North American Review 170 (May 1900): 640.

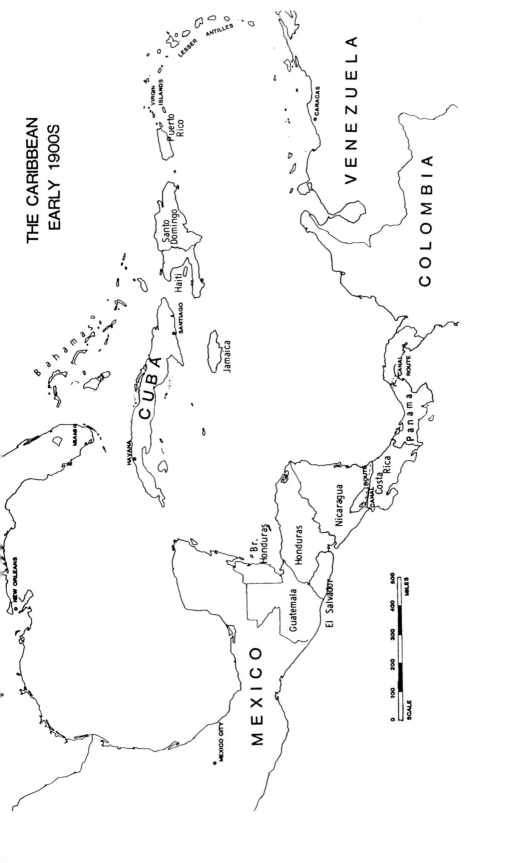

THE CARIBBEAN
EARLY 1900S

LESSER ANTILLES

VIRGIN ISLANDS

Puerto Rico

CARACAS

VENEZUELA

COLOMBIA

Santo Domingo

Haiti

Bahamas

SANTIAGO

CANAL ROUTE

Panama

CUBA

Jamaica

HAVANA

Costa Rica

MIAMI

Nicaragua

CANAL ROUTE

NEW ORLEANS

Br. Honduras

Honduras

Guatemala

El Salvador

MEXICO

MEXICO CITY

0   100   200   300   400   500
MILES
SCALE

Here, then, is a key factor underlying McKinley's decision to retain control over the Philippine archipelago. The colony would enable the United States to extend its political influence into the Far East by placing it on a par with those of the other great powers. Furthermore, the Philippines could serve as a Far Eastern showplace of America's benevolent rule, a factor which helps explain the series of self-congratulatory comments American leaders made about the islands in the next few years. Both Presidents McKinley and Roosevelt repeatedly pointed out how well off the Filipinos were under American tutelage. After all, McKinley boasted in 1899: "Our flag has never waved over any community but in blessing."[14]

Unfortunately, as we have noted, that flag was also waving over a number of American outposts being besieged by ungrateful Filipinos who did not perceive the purported blessings of the United States' colonial policies. Despite all this contrary evidence from the field, American leaders continued to relate their efforts to the democratic mission. Second only to ending the insurrection, American occupation officials considered their chief task to be that of placing local governmental operations as quickly as possible in the hands of the Filipinos themselves. To underline this resolve, Secretary of War Elihu Root speedily abolished the military occupation government and replaced it with a civil administration.[15] The civil government naturally became much stronger after the rebellion's leader, Emilio Aguinaldo, was captured in the spring of 1901. By the winter of the following year, President Roosevelt was able, without hypocrisy, to articulate the American intention to use the Philippine government as a model for others:

> Civil government has now been introduced. Not only does each Filipino enjoy such rights to life, liberty, and the pursuit of happiness as he has never before known during the recorded history of the islands, but the people taken as a whole now enjoy a measure of self-government greater than that granted to any other Orientals by any foreign power and greater than that enjoyed by any other Orientals under their own government, save the Japanese alone.[16]

While trying to decide how best to deal with the Chinese ambitions of the European powers, the United States was finally acting rationally in concert with them over another trouble spot in the Pacific. The acquisition of Hawaii, Guam, and the Philippines had

---

[14]Richardson, *Messages and Papers,* 9:6399.

[15]Root to Lodge, 1 July 1901, Elihu Root Papers, LCMD; Philip C. Jessup, *Elihu Root,* 2 vols. (New York: Dodd, Mead, 1938), 1:360.

[16]Richardson, *Messages and Papers,* 9:6760.

shown that Pacific colonialism was acceptable to the American people, so American statesmen could consider extending it to Samoa as well. President Cleveland had disliked the tripartite condominium the Berlin Conference had established in 1889, but his own dedication to anti-colonialism prevented him from considering a partition of the group into separate colonies. The only other viable alternative to the condominium, surrendering the whole archipelago to Germany, would have sent the large policy advocates in the United States onto the warpath.[17]

Although Cleveland's Republican successor had fewer anticolonial scruples, President McKinley's concentration upon Cuba diverted his attention from Samoa until 1899. Then the three nations involved in the condominium sent a commission to the islands to investigate the situation. The commissioners unanimously concluded that the archipelago should be split up, with a single great power assigned unilateral control over each division. The British and German governments readily agreed to this partitioning scheme as they had favored a similar one a decade earlier. Consequently, the United States acquired a new colony consisting of the eastern part of the group, including the large island of Tutuila with its superb harbor at Pago Pago. Germany took control of the western part, and Great Britain obtained territorial compensation from Germany elsewhere in the Pacific. Partition had been the logical solution to the great power antagonisms all along, but in 1889 the United States had not been ready to expand its political influence through colonization. A decade later, conditions and attitudes had substantially changed in both the United States and the Far East generally.[18]

The recently acquired colonies in the Pacific equipped the United States with a firm basis from which to expand its political influence in the Far East. American economic interest in China continued to grow after 1899. Furthermore, the Far East had become a major arena for great-power confrontations, causing aggressive Americans to maintain that the United States' prestige demanded definitive action on its part. "The United States, being one of the greatest Powers of the world, must hold relations wherever relations are held by other

[17]Henry Cabot Lodge, "Our Blundering Foreign Policy," *Forum* 191 (March 1895): 10; George Herbert Ryden, *The Foreign Policy of the United States in Relation to Samoa* (New Haven, Conn.: Yale University Press, 1933), p. 556.

[18]*Foreign Relations* (1899), pp. 631, 638, 663–64; Ryden, *Foreign Policy*, p. 558; Tyler Dennett, *John Hay: From Poetry to Politics* (New York: Dodd, Mead, 1933), p. 281.

Powers," one writer insisted. "If European Powers regard the Far-Eastern Question as of supreme importance, the United States must do the same."[19] This statement clearly illustrates that the American drive for increased political stature abroad had an imitative aspect—a dangerous aspect indeed, given the aggressive, contentious attitudes of the great-power models the United States felt an urge to copy. European moves and maneuvers in China bore a close relationship to the power struggles upon the European continent itself, and American interference in Far Eastern affairs might well bring unwanted American entanglements in European politics.

The McKinley administration carefully sought a method for asserting American influence in the Far East which would simultaneously protect the United States from being sucked into the European political morass. When John Hay returned to Washington after his stint at the American Embassy in London, he brought along some very definite opinions about British attitudes. The new secretary of state's views coincided comfortably with those of Lord Charles Beresford, an Englishman who toured the United States speaking upon the subject of his book, "The Break-up of China." Beresford made a grim prediction: the great powers would ultimately divide the entire Chinese Empire into spheres of influence, thereby wiping out all international free trade and competition. Beresford's disturbing prognostications worried both Hay and William W. Rockhill, the diplomat he relied upon to devise an American policy for dealing with China.[20]

An old China hand, Rockhill had served for some time in the Far East prior to his appointment as minister at Athens. Hay brought Rockhill home in order to have on hand in Washington a diplomat with a background in Chinese affairs. Unfortunately, Rockhill's experience was dated; he had left China before the European spheres of influence had been created. To bring himself up to date, he consulted an English friend, Alfred L. Hippisley, who worked for the Imperial Chinese Customs Service. Hippisley sided with Beresford in lamenting the development of the spheres of influence and in sounding the alarm over the possible breakup of the empire. His opinions formed an integral part of the information Rockhill prepared for the secretary of state. Missing was any significant consultation with the Chinese government itself. Like most American statesmen, Hay

---

[19]Gilbert Reid, "American Opportunities in China," *Forum* 27 (April 1899): 237.

[20]Dennis, *Adventures*, p. 186; Griswold, *Far Eastern Policy*, p. 48; Young, *Rhetoric of Empire*, p. 123; "The Break-up of China, and Our Interest in It," *Atlantic Monthly* 84 (August 1899): 277.

treated China as an object of policy, not as a partner worthy of consultation. The Chinese were, therefore, naturally skeptical of Hay's initiatives even though he ostensibly designed them to prevent further foreign exploitation.[21]

The policy John Hay eventually adopted had firm foundations in traditional American precepts. From their first official contacts with China, American diplomats had fought to win for the United States absolute equality with other foreign nations. Whenever the Chinese government had granted concessions or privileges to other powers on trade issues, the Americans had insisted upon most-favored-nation treatment. President Cleveland had even insisted upon an open door for American traders during the Sino-Japanese War. Furthermore, United States policymakers had always felt that the surest guarantee of equal treatment for American merchants lay in preserving the Chinese Empire as a single unit rather than letting it become fragmented or divided into colonies and spheres of influence. Secretary of State Hay thus did not require much encouragement to become convinced of the wisdom of a forthright stance in favor of an open door. He did scrupulously refrain from overtly criticizing the spheres of influence, confining his attention strictly to obtaining an assurance of equal treatment for all traders in any Chinese ports which the European powers held. This carefully circumscribed approach reassured those Americans who wanted their government to avoid over-commitments in the Far East. "We are, of course, opposed to the dismemberment of that Empire, and we do not think that the public opinion of the United States would justify this Government in taking part in the great game of spoliation now going on," Hay admitted in 1899. "For the present we think our best policy is one of vigilant protection of our commercial interests, without formal alliance with other Powers interested."[22] Hay did hope his commercial policies would deflate the economic importance of the existing spheres of influence and, consequently, their political significance in Chinese affairs as well.

On 6 September 1899, Hay dispatched his famous Open Door Note: a circular letter calling upon several great powers to observe and enforce within the spheres of influence the commercial treaty rights all nations had traditionally enjoyed in trading with China. Hay had informed Rockhill in August that he had already received substantial assurances from the major powers that they did not intend to

[21]Cohen, *America's Response*, pp. 50–51; McCormick, *China Market*, p. 155.
[22]Quoted in William Roscoe Thayer, *The Life and Letters of John Hay*, 2 vols. (Boston: Houghton Mifflin, 1915), 2:241.

exclude anyone from trading in their spheres of influence, so the favorable replies the secretary of state received did not particularly surprise him. Most of the great powers answered to the effect that they would abide by the standard treaty provisions within their spheres—but only if all of the other powers promised to do the same. Although the Russian reply was actually quite negative in tone, Hay chose to view it as fundamentally responsive. On 20 March 1900, therefore, he publicly proclaimed that all the powers had agreed to his request.[23] Statesman and historian George Kennan describes Hay's notes as nothing more than dangerously inexact and confusing clichés "which made it difficult for other governments, when summoned by us to stand up and be counted in their feelings about them, to do anything but reply: 'Why, yes, if you put it that way, we agree, of course.'" Kennan concludes that "it was easier to agree than to try to explain."[24]

The apparent confidence with which Hay promulgated his Open Door policy concealed the awkward problem he had encountered with respect to Great Britain. Hay had expected unqualified British acquiescence to his plan; after all, he had served as the go-between when the joint Anglo-American open door proposal had been made while he was serving as ambassador in London in early 1898. Once the United States refused to go along, however, the British had joined the imperialist race, first by extending their Hong Kong colony with a lease to Kowloon on the Chinese mainland, and, second, by establishing a sphere of influence at Weihaiwei, opposite Russian-leased Port Arthur. So eager was Hay to win British acceptance of his Open Door policy that he told Ambassador Joseph Choate in London that the United States would consider Kowloon an integral part of the Hong Kong colony, thereby absolving England of the need to alter its exclusive control over trade through that port. Consequently, the British government's official response ignored Kowloon but did promise to treat Weihaiwei like all other Chinese treaty ports. The incident shows Hay's willingness to bend his own rules to retain Britain's friendship. He recognized the crucial nature of British support; after all, England, not the United States, had the only naval force capable of imposing its will in the Far East![25]

[23]*Foreign Relations* (1899), pp. 128–42.

[24]George F. Kennan, *American Diplomacy: 1900–1950* (Chicago: University of Chicago Press, 1951), p. 45.

[25]Ibid., p. 136; Hay to Choate, 13 November 1899, John Hay Papers, LCMD; Young, *Rhetoric of Empire*, p. 132; Mark B. Dunnell, "Our Policy in China," *North American Review* 167 (October 1898): 405.

The European powers acquiesced to the Open Door policy not for altruistic reasons but because it allowed them to retain the advantages of their spheres while simultaneously reassuring them of unrestricted access to all of the ports open in China. Once all had agreed to preserve free access for traders, no further encroachments seemed necessary, as long as each power possessed a Chinese port as a base for its naval and political activities in the Far East. In other words, Hay's initiative essentially worked, providing a welcome cooling off period in the imperialistic contest over Far Eastern trade and dominance. More to the point, the Open Door policy rescued Hay from the necessity of capturing a sphere of influence for his own country. The United States had simply fallen back on the unilateral declaration approach it had used in Latin American affairs prior to 1898, hoping to maintain or advance its relatively limited political influence in China at little cost or risk.

It is hardly surprising, then, that Hay's Open Door policy proved remarkably popular at home. It precisely matched the American people's concept of the ideal foreign policy: executed through the writing of a few letters which in no way involved a commitment of American armed forces and designed to achieve moralistic goals as well as concrete commercial advantages. It satisfied those who longed to see the United States behaving as an equal of the other great powers. At the same time, it pleased those who wished the United States to avoid becoming involved in international squabbles.[26]

Historian Paul Varg comments that the Open Door policy created a myth about John Hay and about American responsibilities toward China which influenced policymakers for years afterward. "The Hay myth, like other myths, was not necessarily wholly lacking in reality but it conformed more to the apparent need of his generation for assurance that the United States counted for something in world affairs, and the 'something' was morality and justice."[27] Varg thus emphasizes the mission sentiment and the striving for greater political influence theme as elements which helped the Open Door policy win popular approval. Revisionist Thomas J. McCormick has examined the Open Door policy in detail and finds the political influence theme combined in it with the economic expansion one. He insists that the policy was designed to preserve existing American trading rights until such time as the United States generated the power and interest

[26]Cohen, *America's Response*, p. 49; Young, *Rhetoric of Empire*, p. 136; Alfred Thayer Mahan, *The Problem of Asia* (Boston: Little, Brown, 1900), pp. 155–56.
[27]Varg, *Making of a Myth*, p. 121.

sufficient to dominate the entire China market.[28] This interpretation essentially answers those who see the Open Door Notes as the desperate gesture of a weak nation hoping to avoid any responsibility for protecting China.

Further light may be shed on the true meaning of the Open Door policy by an examination of the American response to the Boxer Rebellion in the summer of 1900, when circumstances forced Secretary of State Hay to issue a second set of notes aimed at staving off a very obvious threat to China's political integrity. This threat clearly dismayed those Americans who believed in the United States' responsibility to preserve self-government. On the other hand, one can view Hay's second effort from McCormick's perspective, in which it becomes a restatement of the American intention to preserve all of the China market intact for later domination by the United States. Then again, it may simply have been an unavoidable consequence of the inherent weakness of Hay's 1899 initiative.

There can be no doubt, however, that several American officials were unimpressed by the actions of the Imperial government. Like Charles Denby, his predecessor in Peking, American Minister Edwin H. Conger frequently betrayed an exasperation with the Chinese government's weakness and with his own government's limitations upon his activities. Even before the Boxers had moved their violent, antiforeign activities into Peking, Conger was pleading with the government in Washington to order American war vessels to join with those of other nations in demonstrating "along the Chinese coast in order to emphasize our demands and to frighten the Chinese into a compliance with them. . . . The Chinese Government really care little for anything but power, and an earnest exhibition of it always promptly moves them."[29] As he did throughout the affair, Secretary Hay showed great reluctance to authorize any sort of joint action, and, in March 1900, he even criticized Conger for cooperating with other foreign diplomats in presenting a protest note to the Chinese government.

As already noted, Hay's advice to Conger continued along the same lines right up until the moment the Boxers cut off all outside communication with the foreign legations. Symptomatic of the antiforeign sentiments which had festered for years in China, the "Righteous and Harmonious Fists" had originally directed their killing and destruction against Catholic converts and foreign missionary instal-

[28]McCormick, *China Market*, p. 129.
[29]*Foreign Relations* (1900), p. 94.

lations. When the Boxers rampaged into Peking, murdered the German minister, and besieged the diplomatic quarter, Chinese diplomats stationed abroad responded with great solicitation to external criticisms and protests. The insincerity of these gestures became increasingly apparent as the outside world learned that the crusty, aging "Dowager Empress" and her government were clandestinely supporting the Boxers. In fact, they had been egging them on from the very beginning.

Nevertheless, the United States persisted in acting as though no connection existed between the rioters and the Chinese government. Rear Admiral Louis Kempff had laid out the pattern the United States would follow with respect to the rebellion when he had declined to join the other powers' fleets in bombarding the government-manned coastal forts at Tientsin. His refusal underlined the United States' contention that its quarrel lay strictly with the rebels, not with the Chinese government. The great powers followed the American lead at least to the extent of never declaring war on China, although they did decide to assemble an international relief expedition to fight its way from the coast into Peking's beleaguered diplomatic quarter. The United States contributed 2,500 men. When the relief expedition arrived after fifty-five days without contact, Conger was able to report that American casualties consisted of seven marines killed and seventeen wounded.[30]

Up to that point American policy had succeeded only because the United States had cooperated with the other powers. Secretary Hay had fallen ill, leaving America's Far Eastern policy during the summer of 1900 in charge of Rockhill, who recognized that force alone could break the back of the rebellion. Furthermore, the fact that all the great powers had combined their efforts made it much more effective than separate actions would have been. American cooperation had an additional benefit in that it guaranteed that the other powers would pay attention when the United States attempted to add an important supplement to its Open Door policy at the height of the siege.[31]

On 3 July 1900, a circular note was sent off to the major powers, stating the United States' desire to "bring about permanent safety and peace to China, preserve Chinese territorial and administrative entity . . . and safeguard to the world the principle of equal and impartial trade with all parts of the Chinese Empire."[32] Like the two

[30]Ibid., pp. 161, 276, 280; Dennett, *John Hay*, p. 300.
[31]*Foreign Relations* (1901), Appendix, pp. 6–7; Dennett, *Eastern Asia*, p. 667; Dennett, *John Hay*, p. 308.
[32]*Foreign Relations* (1900), p. 299.

messages quoted at the beginning of this chapter ordering Conger to stay clear of any alliances, the 3 July note was clearly designed to win popular approval for the McKinley administration at home. Beyond its domestic political impact, however, Hay and Rockhill hoped this note would have a braking influence on those powers which might view the rebellion as an opportunity to expand their own influence in China. Unlike the first Open Door note in 1899, the 1900 circular did not call for replies, a wise move in view of the equivocal responses it did generate.

The second note had raised the American ante. Whereas, in 1899, Hay had uncritically noted the existence of the great powers' spheres of influence and requested the preservation of free trade within them, the second note sought to protect China from any further external political encroachment. Although the United States relied exclusively upon moral persuasion to enforce its China policy, to a degree, it succeeded. None of those nations participating in the Boxer relief expedition wanted to see China totally disintegrate; each feared its rivals might get a bigger or better share. The July 1900 note reinforced the stubborn American contention that the Chinese Imperial government was not at fault in the Boxer uprising despite the encouragement it had given the rioters. This deliberate American misrepresentation of what was actually going on in China nevertheless acted as a restraint on the external pressures the empire encountered at the height of the disturbances. As a momentary expedient, the American circular was a masterful stroke, but its long-range effectiveness was less certain.

Once the legations in Peking had been rescued, the United States discovered that it had undergone a definite change in its relationship to China and the other powers. For the first time, it had physically exerted itself as a major power in the Orient, and the July note had more or less unilaterally committed the United States to the future preservation of China as a unit. President McKinley, however, nearly wiped out the influence the United States had just won by suggesting that all American forces withdraw immediately from China in the early fall of 1900. Along with the predictable domestic criticisms of the American military action, the president was influenced by a Russian announcement that it would pull its troops back into Manchuria and out of Peking. Secretary Hay advised against McKinley's plan because it would cancel the restraining influence the American presence had upon the ambitions of the other powers. A too-hasty retreat could easily have neutralized the success of the second circular note.

Actually, the fate of the Open Door policy hinged upon the preservation of an international balance of power far more than it did upon anything the United States alone could do. The United States' position remained stalemated until 16 October 1900, when Great Britain and Germany announced that they had come to an understanding. To the relief of the American State Department, the Anglo-German Agreement did restate the open door concept of free access for traders in the bulk of China. But, it deliberately left the situation in Manchuria unclear. Because they knew both Russia and Japan had designs upon this northernmost province of the Chinese Empire, the British and German governments wisely decided to exclude the province from their pledges to support Chinese territorial integrity elsewhere. Although Secretary Hay carefully hedged in his comments on the agreement, he did express pleasure that the two powers had seen fit to include in it both the open door and the integrity of China concepts.[33]

While the other great powers continued their acrimonious discussion over what punishment China should suffer because of the rebellion, Hay permitted the advancement of an initiative which seems totally inconsistent with his whole China policy. American naval officers had been openly calling for the acquisition of an American coaling station on the Chinese coast since July. In November, after the Anglo-German Agreement had been announced, Hay instructed Minister Conger in Peking to see if China would acquiesce to the establishment of an American naval station at Samsah Inlet. A desire to establish naval bases around the world fit right in with the United States' expansionist mood in 1900, and, as President McKinley had just won reelection, no domestic political considerations need stand in the way of such a venture. Despite his generally well-received diplomatic efforts, Secretary Hay was clearly worried about the possible disintegration of China, and he was apparently willing to consider the coaling station as a means of maintaining American influence in China. When Conger discovered that Japan had already decided to incorporate the region into its sphere of influence, however, the United States dropped the idea.[34]

Fortunately, the Anglo-German Agreement shored up the Far Eastern balance of power—the keystone to preserving China's territorial integrity. Consequently, the United States could devote its

---

[33]Hay to McKinley, 26 October 1900, John Hay Papers, LCMD; Cohen, *America's Response*, p. 59; Dennett, *John Hay*, p. 321.
[34]Griswold, *Far Eastern Policy*, p. 83; Young, *Rhetoric of Empire*, pp. 204–6.

attention to the negotiations over the so-called Boxer Indemnity. All of the powers felt China should compensate them financially for the losses and insults suffered during the rebellion. The injured parties agreed to discuss the size and disposition of the indemnities on a cooperative basis, although the Americans feared that some powers, particularly Russia, would demand a territorial cession in addition to monetary compensation. Because such a cession would definitely go counter to the intent of the 3 July note, Hay dispatched his most talented Far Eastern troubleshooter, W. W. Rockhill, to Peking to represent the United States during the great-power negotiations which dragged on well into 1901. Rockhill's efforts do appear to have limited the final indemnity figure to one that would strap but not bankrupt the Chinese government.[35]

The end of the Boxer negotiations coincided with a fundamental change in the United States' Far Eastern policy. When Theodore Roosevelt became president in the fall of 1901, he deemphasized high moral principles and paid correspondingly more attention to the practical aspects of great-power diplomacy in the Orient. This policy resulted in greater interplay between the United States and the emerging great power in the area, Japan. The president greatly respected the Japanese people for their modernization program, their civilization, and their fighting spirit. Under Roosevelt's leadership, the United States cooperated informally with Japan and Great Britain in order to counter French, German, and Russian ambitions. The Far Eastern balance of power that Roosevelt saw as the key to peace might well have been better preserved if the United States had entered into a closer, formal association, but the traditional American fear of such "entanglements" prevented this. Besides, an alliance with the British might not have served the United States' best interests. Although Roosevelt apparently believed that England and the United States shared identical goals in the Far East, the British had much more at stake, with their extensive trade on the Chinese mainland and their colony in India. Furthermore, Britain's Far Eastern policy was always tempered by European power politics closer to home.[36]

In part because United States reticence ruled out any official relationship with Great Britain, the British initiated secret negotia-

---

[35]*Foreign Relations* (1901), Appendix, pp. 5, 70, 142, 359, 366–67.

[36]Cohen, *America's Response*, p. 76; Griswold, *Far Eastern Policy*, pp. 89, 102; Howard K. Beale, *Theodore Roosevelt and the Rise of America to World Power* (New York: Collier Books, 1962), p. 233; Raymond A. Esthus, *Theodore Roosevelt and Japan* (Seattle: University of Washington Press, 1966), p. 38.

tions with Japan. The resulting Anglo-Japanese Alliance of 30 January 1902 apparently came as a surprise to Secretary of State Hay, but he heartily approved of the arrangement which he interpreted as embodying the very principles the United States favored. If the United States had forthrightly joined the alliance rather than simply riding its coattails, American influence upon Far Eastern affairs would have been greatly enhanced. As it was, the United States' policy suffered from a crippling lack of willpower and from a disinclination to use the threat of its military force. The Open Door Notes had been bluffs which, for a time, no one called. The insipid character of American policy was starkly revealed when the United States chose to engage in rhetorical fencing with the Russians rather than join the Anglo-Japanese Alliance—the only substantial counter to Russian advances in Manchuria.[37]

The Russians had succeeded in annoying all of the other great powers by refusing to withdraw from northern China after the Boxer Rebellion. The Russians planned to use their military presence to coerce the Chinese government into granting Russia exclusive rights to operate mines, construct railroads, and build factories in Manchuria. American policymakers feared that if China gave in, other powers would feel free to make similar demands, which would end in destroying China's territorial integrity. Predictably, Secretary of State Hay's major response was to send out yet another circular memorandum on 1 February 1902, this time objecting that any exclusivity agreement was a violation of the open door spirit. The unrepentent Russian government replied that it was merely seeking the same sort of rights Germany already exercised within its sphere of influence. Meanwhile, the State Department had also been trying to get Russia to open certain Manchurian ports to free trade. Because the American efforts resembled similar efforts backed by the Anglo-Japanese Alliance, the Russians eventually caved in. In line with the open door concept, they agreed to open two Manchurian cities to international trade in conjunction with the signing of a Sino-Russian treaty on 8 October 1903.[38]

Russia's tardy and hardly magnanimous capitulation did not impress the Japanese who feared that Russia intended to use Man-

---

[37]*Foreign Relations* (1902), pp. 929–31; Latané, *From Isolation to Leadership,* pp. 93–94; Charles Vevier, *The United States and China 1906–1913* (New Brunswick, N.J.: Rutgers University Press, 1955), p. 12.

[38]*Foreign Relations* (1902), pp. 26, 274, 276; *Foreign Relations* (1903), pp. 17, 619; Varg, *Making of a Myth,* pp. 82–83; Tyler Dennett, *Roosevelt and the Russo-Japanese War* (c. 1925; reprint ed., Gloucester, Mass.: Peter Smith, 1959), pp. 118, 134.

churia as a springboard from which it could dominate Korea. In 1903 Japan opened discussions with Russia, hoping to find a diplomatic formula that would protect its Korean interests. The Russians were not forthcoming. The Japanese government even complained to the United States in December 1903 that Russia was clearly violating the open door principle. President Roosevelt naturally sympathized with the Japanese position; after all, the United States certainly considered the Russian presence in northern China ominous. Then again, the United States would never have considered going as far as the Japanese did. While still going through the motions of diplomatic negotiations with Russia, the Japanese government secretly ordered its armed forces to stage a preemptive attack upon Russian-held Port Arthur in February 1904. The Russo-Japanese War had begun.

"Wasn't the Japanese attack bully!" Roosevelt enthused, as much impressed with Japan's grit and decisiveness as he was with the cause for which it fought. Even there, however, the American president found reason to be satisfied with the conflict. He was profoundly interested in preserving a Far Eastern balance of power that would obviate the need of committing United States armed forces in the defense of American colonies or for the protection of American trade. Because Russia's growing preponderance in northern China had threatened that balance, Roosevelt hoped Japan could effectively limit Russian power. The Japanese were no doubt appreciative of American moral support for their war efforts, but the essential element was British backing. The 1902 Anglo-Japanese treaty had promised Japan that England would forcefully prevent any other power from militarily aiding Russia. Furthermore, in 1904, Russia's major European ally, France, was engaged in hammering out an entente with England, thus effectively neutralizing the possibility of anything but moral support from France.

Playing a lone hand in the Far East, Germany's primary goal was to prevent any other power from taking advantage of the war. The kaiser therefore requested President Roosevelt to seek assurances that China would remain neutral in the conflict, a request with which American policymakers were happy to comply. Secretary Hay duly called upon Russia and Japan to respect Chinese integrity during the war, and the warring parties responded affirmatively. The State Department then issued yet another circular note on 20 February 1904, announcing that China should be preserved and insulated as much as possible from the war.[39] The United States had once again

[39]Roosevelt to Root, 16 February 1904, Elihu Root Papers, LCMD; Esthus, *Roosevelt*, pp. 24–25; *Foreign Relations* (1904), p. 2.

assumed its accustomed position in Far Eastern affairs as the moral referee among contending great powers, protecting China and the existing status quo. "What we want to do," Hay explained, "is to *poser le principe* of the neutrality of China and of the utmost limitation of the area of hostilities compatible with the military interests of the belligerents."[40] And, of course, the support of Chinese self-government conformed nicely with America's mission sentiments.

Perhaps inadvertently, however, Hay's February 1904 circular extended the geographical scope of the Open Door policy, an extension which would greatly trouble American statesmen in the future. The degree of control China exercised over its northern province of Manchuria had fluctuated for many years. Hay's note seemed to imply that China's territorial integrity included this northern region at the very moment both Russia and Japan were fighting a bloody, costly war to defend and extend their interests there.[41] The Americans were once again bluffing. The American consul at Shanghai had been warned "not to commit himself to any theory that the United States could be called upon by China or by the foreign consuls to guarantee Chinese neutrality," Alvey Adee informed Minister Conger, "and that he is to safeguard only as far as possible American neutral interests if threatened, and to avoid all indications of general policy. Utmost circumspection required."[42]

Although President Roosevelt wanted the Russo-Japanese War ended as quickly as possible to prevent any great power from chipping away at Chinese integrity, he refused to consider a unilateral American peace effort. The French turned out to be even more anxious than Roosevelt to stop the war, because Russia provided their major defense against German power in Europe, and Russia had stumbled into serious domestic political and economic troubles after suffering several costly defeats on the battlefield. At the same time, Japan's victories had severely strained Japan's resources, so the Tokyo government also considered peace desirable. Consequently, because Roosevelt represented the one great power least committed in the Far East, the Japanese sought his assistance in getting the Russians to agree to a termination of hostilities. As a prior condition, the president demanded a promise from Japan that it would maintain an open door in Manchuria and help restore it to China's political control. Roosevelt could then mediate between the belligerents, secure in the

---

[40] Hay to White, 12 February 1904, John Hay Papers, LCMD.
[41] Esthus, *Roosevelt*, pp. 31–32; Griswold, *Far Eastern Policy*, pp. 94–96.
[42] *Foreign Relations* (1904), p. 137.

knowledge that he had obtained Japanese acquiescence to the basic American aim. Furthermore, the Japanese victory effectively reestablished the balance of power in the Orient which Roosevelt considered essential to the protection of American interests.[43]

In the spring of 1905, Roosevelt took over complete charge of American diplomacy from the ailing John Hay, and he continued to do so after the secretary of state died on 1 July 1905. It was Roosevelt personally, then, who secretly contacted the Russian government in order to obtain its promise to respond to a public call for peace negotiations. With that assured, he issued the call and publicized the affirmative replies from Japan and Russia. Finally, the president arranged for Japanese and Russian diplomats to meet at Portsmouth, New Hampshire, in August 1905, to negotiate a peace treaty.[44]

After the conclusion of the Portsmouth Peace Conference, Roosevelt claimed that, "I would have been powerless to speak for peace if there had not been in the minds of other nations the belief, in the first place that I would speak with absolute sincerity and good faith, and in the second place that I did not wish peace because the nation I represented was either unable or unwilling to fight if the need arose."[45] One might well question whether America's strength—or, for that matter, its weakness—had been a factor in the belligerents' decision to allow the United States to arrange negotiations. Both nations wanted an end to the fighting, so they naturally sought a neutral go-between to help expedite an armistice. The president did offer advice to Japan as to what it could reasonably expect to obtain from Russia. The Japanese government subsequently publicized Roosevelt's suggestions as an excuse to its own people for the relatively mild concessions it won at Portsmouth. The ensuing outbreak of anti-American sentiment in Japan did not particularly bother the president. Peace had been his chief goal, and he was quite pleased that the two powers had written into the treaty itself a pledge to restore Manchuria to Chinese political sovereignty.

The Portsmouth Peace Conference established for the American president a reputation commensurate with his country's growing stature in the Far East. Roosevelt's endeavors won him a Nobel Peace Prize, but more important, they earned for the United States interna-

[43]Dennett, *Russo-Japanese War*, pp. 174, 179; Dennis, *Adventures*, p. 402; Esthus, *Roosevelt*, p. 63; Griswold, *Far Eastern Policy*, p. 103.
[44]Beale, *Theodore Roosevelt*, p. 272; Dennett, *Russo-Japanese War*, pp. 6-7; Esthus, *Roosevelt*, p. 76.
[45]Quoted in Dennett, *Russo-Japanese War*, p. 333.

tional recognition as a major element in the great-power maneuverings in the Orient. This recognition helped the nation to pursue its limited objective of preserving international adherence to the Open Door policy. Simultaneously, its victory over Russia had greatly enhanced Japan's prestige, and this newly elevated rival in the Far East ended up causing Roosevelt and the United States more trouble in the future than any other great power.

Roosevelt's past triumphs in dealing with Far Eastern complexities encouraged him to retain a greater degree of control over American foreign policy in that area than in Latin America after Elihu Root became secretary of state. The president seemed to enjoy grappling with the problem of how to maintain and strengthen the American presence as a great power in the Far East without overreaching the United States' restricted military influence there. Thus, he turned down a German suggestion for a German-Chinese-American arrangement to offset the Anglo-Japanese Alliance because he preferred to continue his informal cooperation with England and Japan. These two dissimilar great powers had renewed their alliance in 1905, and it guaranteed peace in the region far more effectively than anything Roosevelt did.[46] The president definitely had mixed feelings about the Japanese. He admired their militarism and modernization, but he expressed some concern as to how they would behave in the future. Both he and Root hoped Japan would serve as a "civilizing" influence in the Far East. To improve American relations, Roosevelt was willing to allow the Japanese government some leeway in its dealings with China as well as to concede that, particularly after it had run the Russians out, Japan held undisputed control over Korea. Korea had been deliberately omitted from the Open Door policy, and Roosevelt hoped his indifference toward Korea would correspondingly reduce any potential Japanese threat to the American colonies in the Pacific. When Secretary of War William Howard Taft visited him on a trip to the Far East, Japanese Prime Minister Count Katsura suggested the issuance of a formal statement embodying these principles. On 29 July 1905, Katsura promised that Japan would not interfere with the American colonies, and Taft admitted that the United States recognized Japan's suzerainty over Korea. The Taft-Katsura Agreement was very carefully worded to avoid giving the impression it repre-

---

[46]Esthus, *Roosevelt*, pp. 95, 257–59; Jessup, *Elihu Root*, 2:3; Charles E. Neu, *An Uncertain Friendship* (Cambridge, Mass.: Harvard University Press, 1967), p. 12.

sented an alliance or formal association between the United States and Japan.[47]

The decision of school officials on the American West Coast to segregate Japanese students from white ones in 1906 rekindled the generally unfriendly attitude the Japanese people had exhibited toward Roosevelt after the Portsmouth Treaty. Indeed, racist actions in the United States triggered substantial resentment in Japan. Having modernized their nation more rapidly than had any European country, the Japanese naturally felt themselves equal or superior to members of the white race. Americans, on the other hand, tended to consider all Oriental peoples inferior. Perceiving little difference between Japanese immigrants and the Chinese laborers already excluded from admittance to the United States, Americans, particularly in California, demanded restrictions on Japanese immigration. Delicate and quite rational diplomatic dealings enabled the United States and Japan to devise an expedient for calming the anger and indignation in both countries. The so-called Gentlemen's Agreement of 1907 and 1908 rested upon a pledge by the Tokyo government to deny passports to Japanese laborers, thus limiting their ability to emigrate. In return, the Roosevelt administration successfully fought off domestic political pressures favoring immigration restriction laws which would have had the effect of giving official sanction to the anti-Japanese racism.

The details of the complex fencing over the immigration issue are tangential to this study, but some of the more critical events in Japanese-American relations associated with it should be noted. The most worrisome period ran through the spring and summer of 1907 when anti-American riots and political demonstrations shook Japan. Roosevelt realized that militant Japanese nationalists were using the American racial issue to embarrass their less chauvinistic rivals, so he showed more equanimity over these disturbances than less-informed Americans. He did send Secretary of War Taft to Japan and China in the summer of 1907 to take a closer look as well as to carry the president's personal assurances of friendship to the Japanese government. Taft concluded that Japan had become badly overextended in China and could not possibly consider war with the United States. These reassurances failed to stop Roosevelt from exploiting the supposed Japanese threat as a justification for planning and executing

[47]Beale, *Theodore Roosevelt*, p. 279; Dennett, *Russo-Japanese War*, p. 161; Esthus, *Roosevelt*, p. 41; Richard W. Leopold, *Elihu Root and the Conservative Tradition* (Boston: Little, Brown, 1954), p. 60.

an impressive naval demonstration. Although Roosevelt later claimed his primary purpose had been to force Japan to reconsider its anti-American policies, the United States Navy's world tour in 1907 and 1908 served a number of other functions.[48]

The cruise capped the impressive development the United States Navy underwent after the war with Spain. The proud nation inundated its naval heroes with medals and promotions; congressional appropriations committees showered them with new ships and equipment. By 1905, however, even the nation's most famous naval enthusiast admitted from the White House that the United States would soon rank second only to Great Britain in naval strength, a ranking which negated the need for additional ships. Unfortunately, other great powers, notably Germany and France, were involved in an accelerating armaments race which threatened to leave the United States in their wake; so the president decided, in 1907, that his nation needed more battleships. He hoped a well-publicized world cruise would revive the earlier enthusiasm for naval growth as well as to reconfirm the nation's commitment to press ahead on the Panama Canal. Besides, the navy could also use some practice. Once the cruise was under way, Roosevelt asked Congress to authorize the construction of four additional battleships, two of which were eventually funded.[49]

In his autobiography, Roosevelt claimed that the Germans and the British considered the circumnavigation of the globe by an entire war fleet an impossible feat. If the United States Navy could pull it off, the nation's international prestige would be greatly enhanced. The arrival of sixteen trim, modern American battleships in Japan definitely wiped out whatever minor threat had existed of the Japanese opening hostilities against the United States. On the other hand, the cruise convinced Japan's militarists and navalists of the need to improve their own war fleet, and it added further stimulus to Germany's crash naval construction program. Roosevelt ignored these somewhat negative consequences and lauded the cruise as proving beyond any doubt that the United States could back its words with force if necessary. In short, it demonstrated, without the necessity of actually going to war, that the nation was fully capable of exercising an increased political influence worldwide.[50]

[48]Esthus, *Roosevelt,* pp. 181, 192; Neu, *Uncertain Friendship,* p. 116; Vevier, *U.S. and China,* p. 58.

[49]Beale, *Theodore Roosevelt,* p. 285; Neu, *Uncertain Friendship,* pp. 90–111, 211–12, 253.

[50]Beale, *Theodore Roosevelt,* p. 288; Esthus, *Roosevelt,* pp. 185, 264; Theodore Roosevelt, *An Autobiography* (New York: Scribners, 1913), p. 548.

When anti-Americanism once again flared up in Japan early in 1908 after the American fleet's visit, the Roosevelt administration resorted to its accustomed technique for dealing with Far Eastern affairs—the announcement of a paper policy designed to smooth relations with Japan. The government in Tokyo had suggested an official exchange of notes or, better still, a treaty even before the American battleships had arrived. Roosevelt ruled out any treaty or alliance, preferring the nonentangling mechanism of a joint statement. Secretary of State Root and Japanese Minister Kogoro Takahira opened discussions in Washington in the spring of 1908, seeking a method for defusing the major diplomatic issues impeding friendly relations between the two nations.[51]

When the two statesmen finally issued the Root-Takahira Agreement on 30 November 1908, it proved to be extraordinarily vague. Naturally it contained obligatory comments on the preservation of China's territorial integrity and the open door. The agreement also entailed a commitment to maintain the existing status quo in the Pacific, in order to reassure the United States about the Philippines and Japan about Korea. All other issues were either deliberately left out or treated ambiguously, because the statesmen wished to suppress rather than emphasize the jagged points of difference between the two nations. The agreement's major purpose was to reassure the public in both countries that neither had anything to fear. The Root-Takahira Agreement also provided proof of Roosevelt's willingness to permit Japan much leeway in the Far East, as the only effective protection for the basically defenseless Philippines, and his basic disinterest in China per se.[52]

The American government's virtual abandonment of China had begun almost as soon as Roosevelt became president. Although the United States would have preferred to see the Chinese Imperial government remain strong enough to stand on its own feet, Roosevelt recognized that the United States could not do much to help the rickety empire. Furthermore, interest in the China market declined after 1900 as the United States economy entered a period of sustained prosperity. Businessmen serious enough to investigate Chinese conditions realized how unlikely impoverished peasants were to become important customers for American products. Substantial economic

[51]Esthus, *Roosevelt*, pp. 266, 273.

[52]Ibid., pp. 284–85; *Foreign Relations* (1908), pp. 510–11; Leopold, *Elihu Root*, p. 62; Neu, *Uncertain Friendship*, pp. 278, 280.

opportunities within the empire existed, but only if other nations were willing to sponsor large-scale investment programs. Such investment tended to assure favored trading positions to particular companies or merchants, so Americans seeking stronger economic ties with China began to emphasize the importance of investments and concessions. Such endeavors fell outside the scope of the Open Door policy, however, and the United States government had traditionally withheld official backing for American capitalization proposals in China.[53]

The collapse of a major American investment scheme in 1905 hardly encouraged capitalists in the United States to push into China. In 1898, after lengthy negotiations, the American China Development Company had won from the Chinese government a concession to build a railroad from Hankow to Peking. The badly-run company managed to lay only a small amount of track, and disgusted American stockholders sold so many of their shares that a group of Belgian investors eventually captured majority control of the company. At that point, the Chinese government threatened to cancel the American China Development Company's concession. Because he feared the cancellation might injure the United States' prestige, President Roosevelt personally encouraged J. P. Morgan to get the stock out of Belgian hands and back under American ownership. In August 1905, however, Morgan and his associates accepted a Chinese government offer to buy out the company and its concession. The whole affair graphically illustrated a major reason for the absence of large-scale American economic involvement in China: American capitalists and businessmen simply had no interest in moving in that direction. As shall be shown, disinterest generally characterized and weakened the government-sponsored American investment program known as Dollar Diplomacy after 1909.[54]

Normal trade began to suffer as well when the Chinese Boycott of 1905 began. Chinese consumers suddenly stopped buying American products, primarily those sold by American oil companies, as a protest against American restrictions upon Chinese immigration. Propagandists in China had stirred the people's resentment against laws which treated the Chinese as members of a second-class race. American diplomats strenuously protested the boycott, and the Chinese government reluctantly assumed responsibility for trying to end the

[53]Charles A. Conant, "The Economic Basis of 'Imperialism,'" *North American Review* 167 (September 1898): 338–39.
[54]*Foreign Relations* (1905), pp. 125–35.

interruption of Chinese-American trade. The Imperial government's slow, clumsy, and only marginally successful efforts to clamp down on the boycott strengthened Roosevelt's determination to cut American policy loose from any loyalty to the enfeebled Chinese Empire.[55]

Actually, the boycott represented nationalistic stirrings within the empire which should have attracted sympathy and support from the mission-oriented American people. Unfortunately, indications of revolutionary or democratic sentiments in China only seemed to convince the great powers that the empire was deteriorating; therefore, they could more easily increase their own influence. At the same time, the United States showed little sympathy with the Chinese people's political ambitions, and American interest in China continued to decline after the Russo-Japanese War. The Open Door policy did not require active support from the American people, and the United States government did not feel it needed to intercede for the few businessmen who ventured out to this market area.[56]

Manchuria represented something of an exception to the American government's disinterest in Chinese economic development after 1905. The Portsmouth Treaty had promised the restoration of Manchuria to Chinese political control, but both Japan and Russia continued to dominate the economic life of the province. These two nations were deeply involved in the construction, operation, and defense of railroads in Manchuria, and their economic influence carried over into the political sphere as well. Because Americans carried on a reasonable amount of trade in southern Manchuria, Secretary of State Root personally took an interest in seeing to it that the Open Door policy was enforced in that area. Responding to British as well as American protests, the Japanese government agreed to permit merchants from other countries to conduct business in certain Manchurian trading centers. Meanwhile, W. W. Rockhill, now American minister in Peking, had received assurances that the Russian government would open some of the cities in its area of influence to trade and international residence.[57]

When these areas opened, the State Department stationed a most interesting and controversial character at Mukden. Consul-General Willard D. Straight's experiences as a correspondent during the Russo-Japanese War had convinced him that Japan had aggressive

[55]Ibid., pp. 208, 212, 218, 232.

[56]Beale, *Theodore Roosevelt*, p. 223; Varg, *Making of a Myth*, pp. 124–28.

[57]Esthus, *Roosevelt*, pp. 117, 120; *Foreign Relations* (1906), p. 227; Raymond A. Esthus, "The Changing Concept of the Open Door, 1899–1910," *Mississippi Valley Historical Review* 46 (December 1959): 445.

desires on the Chinese mainland, desires that he felt must be contained. Unfortunately, Straight's opinions clashed with the two fundamental precepts of Roosevelt's Far Eastern policy: friendship for Japan and a limited American responsibility for enforcing the Open Door policy. Straight concluded that Americans could succeed in thwarting Japanese designs on Chinese territories only if they obtained concessions for railroad lines and other industrial development projects. Consequently, he sought to broaden the scope of the Open Door policy to include a guarantee of free access for American investors throughout China. Hardly the first American diplomat in China who had favored increased American investment, Straight had found, however, in the person of railroad builder Edward H. Harriman, a capitalist eager to give substance to the consul-general's grandiose schemes.[58]

Although Straight would play a leading role in outlining and executing the Taft administration's Dollar Diplomacy program in the Far East, his essentially subversive activities apparently went unnoticed in Rooseveltian Washington. Because he tended to ignore investment in order to concentrate his attention on maintaining free trade, Secretary of State Root did not consider Japan's large interests in Manchuria a violation of the Open Door policy. The gulf between the secretary's policy and that of his consul-general in Mukden became apparent in 1908. Straight and Tang Shao-yi, a high-ranking Imperial official, had developed a plan to establish a jointly-controlled Chinese-American development bank for Manchuria. To nail it down, the American diplomat helped arrange for Tang to visit Washington. The unfortunate Chinese official arrived on the very eve of the signing of the Root-Takahira Agreement which definitely favored Japanese over Chinese interests. In Tang's brief meetings with American leaders, he discovered how badly misinformed he had been about the emphasis of America's Far Eastern policy. Straight dismissed the failure of Tang's mission as a temporary setback in his drive to establish large-scale American investment in Manchuria, an endeavor he pursued even more vigorously in the next few years.[59]

Straight won a great deal of support from those who took over after Roosevelt left the White House. The succeeding administration abandoned the strict construction of the Open Door policy which had been at the heart of Roosevelt's judicious Far Eastern program.

[58]Esthus, "Open Door," p. 440; Vevier, *U.S. and China*, pp. 30, 41, 71.

[59]Esthus, "Open Door," p. 451; Esthus, *Roosevelt*, pp. 244–45; Vevier, *U.S. and China*, pp. 48–49, 61, 76, 84; Akira Iriye, *Pacific Estrangement: Japanese and American Expansion, 1897–1911* (Cambridge, Mass.: Harvard University Press, 1972), p. 206.

Roosevelt had been very careful never to extend United States influence beyond the wishes or interest of the American people. He realistically and logically assessed exactly how far he could go, given his nation's limited power in the Orient, and he went no further. Unfortunately, those who succeeded Roosevelt lacked his intelligent realism, which meant that American initiatives in both the Far East and Latin America appeared clumsier, more callous, and ultimately much less successful than those of Roosevelt, Hay, and Root.

8

Dollar Diplomacy and After, 1909–1914

In the fall of 1909, President William Howard Taft set out on a grand tour of the United States which took him through many of the western states and much of the South. While on this trip he became the first American chief executive to make an official visit to a foreign nation. It was true that Theodore Roosevelt had wandered into the Republic of Panama proper when visiting the Canal Zone a couple of years earlier, but Taft's ceremonial exchange of visits with Mexican President Porfirio Díaz symbolized the growing importance of the American president as the leader of a great world power, personally and actively involved in international affairs.

The visits took place at the sister communities of El Paso, Texas, and Ciudad Juárez, in the Mexican state of Chihuahua. Elaborate preparations preceded the actual meeting of the two leaders on 16 October 1909, including arrangements for cavalry units from each nation to escort the carriages carrying dignitaries back and forth. Taft greeted Díaz first in El Paso in the morning and later crossed the border for a formal welcome at the Juárez customhouse. To climax the day's activities, Díaz hosted a splendid banquet at the customhouse where each man toasted the other's health and neighborliness. Taft then returned to the bridge over the Rio Grande where mounted American soldiers replaced his escort of Mexican troops. Some fifteen or twenty minutes later a surprised citizen of El Paso was accosted by the officer in charge of this impressive procession and asked directions to the railroad station—it was back down the street they had just ridden up.

This portrait of Taft's entourage blundering about in the dark could stand as a symbol for his administration as a whole: whether dealing with domestic or foreign affairs Taft repeatedly failed to find proper or successful approaches to the issues and problems he confronted. He thus proved a great disappointment to the man who had handpicked him for the presidency. Theodore Roosevelt had personally liked the congenial, if straitlaced, Ohio Republican and had been impressed with his administration of the Philippines prior to his service as head of the War Department. But Taft was not a self-starter like Roosevelt; he was not slow-witted, but he lacked drive and originality. Just as he managed to disappoint a majority of Republicans and Progressives with his domestic policies, so, too, was his foreign policy generally regarded as a failure at home and abroad. Both his contemporaries and historians have tended to ridicule and criticize Dollar Diplomacy, the phrase most often associated with his international initiatives.

Taft left much of the decision-making to his inexperienced secretary of state, Philander C. Knox. A Pittsburgh corporation lawyer and former attorney general under Roosevelt, the conservative Knox resembled Richard Olney in his desire to ensure that his official duties would not interfere with his gentlemanly life-style. In pursuing that end, Knox made his greatest contribution to American statecraft by organizing a long-overdue and quite sound restructuring of the State Department into regional and topical divisions. The new structure enabled the department to function much more efficiently, thus relieving Knox of the drudgery and routine which had burdened former secretaries. Day-to-day operations were consigned to First Assistant Secretary of State Huntington Wilson who, along with Adee, dealt with most of the departmental routine.[1]

Of course, Taft and Knox set the general tone of American foreign policy during their years in office. Like so many Americans, Taft believed in the glut theory, and the Panic of 1907 had once again roused interest in a search for foreign outlets for surplus American goods. Consequently, the economic theme which had been somewhat slighted during the Roosevelt years resurfaced as a leading foreign policy determinant. Taft frequently emphasized the need for the economic expansion he had mentioned in his 1909 inaugural address: "I sincerely hope that the incoming Congress will be alive, as it should be, to the importance of our foreign trade and of encouraging it in

[1]Walter V. Scholes and Marie V. Scholes, *The Foreign Policies of the Taft Administration* (Columbia: University of Missouri Press, 1970), pp. 14, 25–26; U.S., Department of State, *Papers Relating to the Foreign Relations of the United States* (Washington, D.C.: Government Printing Office, 1912), p. vii; Charles Vevier, *The United States and China 1906–1913* (New Brunswick, N.J.: Rutgers University Press, 1955), p. 89.

every way feasible. The possibility of increasing this trade in the Orient, in the Philippines, and in South America are known to everyone who has given the matter attention."[2]

The Taft administration continued to assert American political dominance in the Western Hemisphere and to seek greater influence in the Far East. In fact, a major goal of Dollar Diplomacy was to expand American political influence. American capitalists and businessmen remained cautious when it came to extending their enterprises abroad, so the administration had to prod them to provide the economic backing essential to increasing and strengthening America's world prestige and power. Responding in part to the basic timidity in the business community, the government showed itself to be much more willing than under previous administrations to exert force to support economic and political initiatives, particularly in Latin America. Taft gave his policy its familiar name in 1912 by claiming its purpose was

> substituting dollars for bullets. It is one that appeals alike to idealistic humanitarian sentiments, to the dictates of sound policy and strategy, and to legitimate commercial aims. It is an effort frankly directed to the increase of American trade upon the axiomatic principle that the Government of the United States shall extend all proper support to every legitimate and beneficial American enterprise abroad.[3]

Familiar-sounding appeals to high moral principles accompanied virtually every one of the Taft administration's foreign policy statements. For example, when Knox requested advice for a speech outlining American policy, Latin American expert Thomas C. Dawson suggested that he say, "From the time the United States became an independent nation this Government, while preserving its obligations to European powers, has frankly and consistently encouraged the establishment and maintenance of popular, free and independent forms of government for the rest of this hemisphere."[4] The mission theme's commitment to self-government unfortunately clashed with the Taft administration's desire to stabilize its relationships, however, and the United States tended to place a higher premium on responsible, as opposed to democratic, government. Nevertheless, Taft demonstrated a strong commitment to moralism in his foreign policies through his active encouragement of international arbitration.

[2]James D. Richardson, *A Compilation of the Messages and Papers of the Presidents,* 10 vols. (Washington, D.C.: Bureau of National Literature, 1911), 10:7754.
[3]*Foreign Relations* (1912), p. x.
[4]Dawson to Knox, 28 May 1910, Philander C. Knox Papers, LCMD.

He had the State Department work out a number of bilateral treaties designed to prevent war, and he was bitterly disappointed that such respected spokesmen as Lodge, Mahan, and Roosevelt opposed them. When Lodge convinced the Senate to approve his amendments reserving to the United States ultimate control over its own affairs, Taft refused to renegotiate these emasculated treaties.[5]

Taft was naturally frustrated by the lack of support and understanding his policies received, but he became furious when Roosevelt returned from an extended world tour in 1910 and began taking potshots at his administration. The controversy actually had little to do with foreign affairs; instead, it revolved around the appropriate method for dealing with the growing split between conservative and progressive Republicans on domestic issues. Roosevelt's concerted efforts to recapture the presidency from Taft divided the Republican party's votes, permitting Democrat Woodrow Wilson to win the 1912 presidential election.

Wilson plays only a peripheral role in this story. As complex a personality as Roosevelt, and a man even more deeply immersed in guiding and rationalizing American foreign policy, Woodrow Wilson's great ordeal as a statesman and as a diplomat really began after the world's great powers had marched off to Armageddon in 1914. Some maintain that Wilson rose to the challenge fate thrust upon him in World War I; others claim he never fully comprehended the significance of the monumental events his nation participated in. For the immediate purposes of this book, these conflicting views need not be resolved. Little of what Wilson and the whole world would endure was even dreamed of when he displaced the corpulent Taft at the White House. Consequently, the policies he pursued in the world at peace bear less resemblance to those he staggered into later than they do to the traditional ones his predecessors had been following since the 1880s.

Of course President Wilson did bring his own personal emphases and idiosyncrasies into play when he took charge. For example, he seemed to stress the democratic mission theme above all others. A deeply religious man, he tried hard to discover and then follow God's will in his policies. The man he chose to head his cabinet, William Jennings Bryan, was also imbued with a religious moralism, although Bryan's had a more fundamentalist stripe than Wilson's. Having de-

[5]Roosevelt to Mahan, 8 June 1911, Mahan to Roosevelt, 2 December 1911, Mahan to Lodge, 5 January 1912, Lodge to Mahan, 9 January 1912, Alfred Thayer Mahan Papers, LCMD; *Foreign Relations* (1913), pp. ix, 8; Karl Schriftgiesser, *The Gentleman from Massachusetts: Henry Cabot Lodge* (Boston: Little, Brown, 1944), pp. 246–51.

voted his career as a historian and a professor to the study of the development of political systems in the English-speaking nations, Wilson had come to consider democratic, republican governments superior to all others. As president, he often acted as though the extension of democratic forms worldwide was the fundamental goal of American policy. His running feud with Mexico's revolutionary leaders, however, showed that his democratic missionary zeal involved a subjective judgment: democracy was the ideal only if it came in a form compatible with Wilson's own personal view of what democracy ought to be.

Wilson's zeal for the democratic mission encouraged him not only to maintain but to expand American political influence abroad. Consequently, the idealistic Wilson found himself resorting to the same sort of military and economic interference in Latin American nations that earlier presidents had authorized. In short, Wilson's commitment to moralism in no way precluded his acting upon the nation's other traditional foreign policy themes. Like Cleveland, however, Wilson favored the type of economic expansion that required little or no direct involvement or coercion on the part of the United States government. His approach could be characterized as one of seeking an open door to all world markets. The Wilson administration thus patterned its economic policy after the traditional American stance with regard to China, a policy that had been largely abandoned between 1909 and 1913.

While administering the Philippines and the War Department, William Howard Taft had frequently participated in the formulation and execution of the United States' policy in the Far East, an experience which convinced him that the Orient was the most important area in America's foreign relations. The basic thrust of Dollar Diplomacy depended upon Taft's willingness to exert the government's power to strengthen and protect American interests in China. His policy thus differed fundamentally from the customary American practice Secretary of State Bayard had outlined in 1887, prohibiting the American minister in China from giving his official support to private American enterprises. In addition to extending its blessing to existing American investment and commercial ventures, the Taft administration urged other citizens to get involved. It was an uphill struggle, because most American investors and businessmen were distinctly unimpressed with China's economic potential. Recognizing the current lack of interest, an internal State Department memorandum stated, in May 1909, that its goal should be the creation of a

firm foundation in China to insure that, when American exporters
finally did become interested, ample opportunity would be available.
The Taft administration had thus deliberately overreached the existing level of domestic interest in China, which forced Secretary of State
Knox to plead for support from businessmen for ventures the State
Department had already committed itself on. Fortunately, the Chinese government had maintained an excellent credit rating over the
years in contrast to some of the unstable Latin American republics. A
solid economic potential existed in the Far East; it remained only for
American businessmen to perceive it and seize it.[6]

Administration officials considered the prestige and political
advantages associated with greater American involvement in the Far
East just as important as the potential economic benefits. The Open
Door Notes and circulars had failed to restrain the more aggressive
powers from chipping away at China's economic and political integrity. In order to obtain its political desires, Taft's program would
substitute economic power and pressures for paper appeals.

Taft most distrusted Japan, the nation Roosevelt had cultivated
as a friend and informal ally. The Department of State came to consider Japan's encroachments in Manchuria as threats not only to
Chinese integrity but also to the peace of the entire Far East. Both
Taft and Knox thought Roosevelt had been weak-willed in truckling
to Japan and abandoning the United States' traditional support for
China. On 30 September 1909, Knox outlined his plan for reversing
the trend in a memorandum which claimed that development of
American commercial enterprise in China would "constitute a far
greater and more effective bar to any possible Japanese menace in the
Far East than would almost any other line of procedure."[7] The
Taft administration's policy of inspiring and supporting an enlarged
American commercial presence in China was thus clearly directed
against Japan. It was bound to fail. The Japanese had become well
ensconced in Korea and were much more intent upon expanding
their influence in Manchuria than the Americans. Worse still, an
anti-Japanese policy was dangerous. When Knox sought British support for his program, he was tinkering with the balance of power in
the Far East which Roosevelt had so carefully nourished and supported as the best way to preserve peace in the area.[8]

    [6]Scholes, *Taft Administration*, pp. 109–10, 124, 128, 135; Vevier, *U.S. and China*,
pp. 92, 217.

    [7]Quoted in A. Whitney Griswold, *The Far Eastern Policy of the United States* (New
York: Harcourt, Brace, 1938), pp. 144–45.

    [8]Ibid., pp. 150, 159; Warren I. Cohen, *America's Response to China*, (New York:
John Wiley, 1971), pp. 77–83.

The secretary of state allowed his new policy to develop at the State Department under the guidance of First Assistant Secretary Huntington Wilson and Willard Straight, who had returned from Manchuria to serve briefly in the Far Eastern Division. Both these men disliked Japan, and they hoped to limit Japanese expansion in Manchuria by sponsoring American investment. Dollar Diplomacy in the Far East involved several different and distinct projects, but they all shared a common characteristic: they depended upon the State Department's urging or coercing China and the great powers to open multinational capitalization schemes in the Chinese Empire to American investment. Such investment would not only give Americans an ever-larger stake in the commercial development of China, it would also hopefully dilute the influence other foreign nations would have on the Chinese government. Cooperative arrangements would also maximize the impact the limited amount of American capital available for investment would have in China, thus affording greater political leverage at less cost.[9]

Willard Straight's connections with railroad magnate Edward H. Harriman, an enthusiastic advocate of Chinese investment, had caused Straight to anticipate that sufficient funds might be available for unilateral American projects. The Panic of 1907 temporarily tied up Harriman's funds, however, which delayed for two years his concerted effort to amass the requisite capital. With the government's active encouragement, the so-called American Group, consisting of Harriman, J. P. Morgan's firm, and several other banking concerns, came into existence in June 1909. The Department of State then designated it the United States' official agent for participation in railway financing in China. The first major endeavor the American Group and the United States government cooperated in was an effort to gain a share of an international financing scheme for funding the Hukuang Railway in June and July 1909.[10]

The railway project was an enormous one involving a projected 1,500 miles of track between Hankow and Szechwan. France, Great Britain, and Germany had already hammered out a joint agreement with the Imperial Chinese government to finance, construct, and provide supplies for the project. The State Department became so insistent that American investors and engineers be admitted to the project that the authorities in Peking finally agreed, pending the ap-

[9]Raymond A. Esthus, "The Changing Concept of the Open Door, 1899–1910," *Mississippi Valley Historical Review* 46 (December 1959): 435–36; Paul A. Varg, *The Making of a Myth* (East Lansing: Michigan State University Press, 1968), p. 157.
[10]Griswold, *Far Eastern Policy*, p. 142; Vevier, *U.S. and China*, pp. 106, 126, 128.

proval of the other powers already committed. Knox immediately fired off a circular note to the three European governments, calling upon them to make room for American participation and proclaiming that financial cooperation among the four powers would reaffirm and strengthen the open door concept in China. The other governments grudgingly agreed to begin discussing the American demand. While these negotiations dragged on, Straight, who had resigned from the State Department to work for the American Group, pressed ahead with a pet project of his own. When he had been stationed at Mukden, he had hatched a plan for American financing and construction of a Manchurian railroad running from Chinchow to Aigun. This plan had greatly intrigued Harriman, but the financier died suddenly in September 1909, thus removing the most interested American capitalist from the scene. Straight was determined to drive ahead with his negotiations, and, in October, signed an agreement in which the Chinese government granted the Chinchow–Aigun railroad concession to the United States. Because the American Group wanted nothing to interfere with the ongoing Hukuang Loan negotiations, however, the implementation of Straight's project remained in limbo.[11]

On the heels of the Chinchow–Aigun agreement, Secretary of State Knox announced his most ambitious proposal: the Neutralization Scheme for Manchuria. He hoped he could reduce or eliminate the influence certain great powers had attained through their ownership of railroads in Manchuria—ownership which, incidentally, resembled just what Straight had worked out for the Chinchow–Aigun route. Knox proposed to homogenize all foreign influence in Manchuria through a mechanism he described as follows:

> . . . the most effective way to preserve the undisturbed enjoyment by China of all political rights in Manchuria and to promote the development of those Provinces under a practical application of the policy of the open door and equal commercial opportunity would be to bring the Manchurian highways, the railroads, under an economic, scientific, and impartial administration by some plan vesting in China the ownership of the railroads through funds furnished for that purpose by the interested powers willing to participate.[12]

Knox had tested the sentiment for an international loan to China to enable it to purchase control of the railroads in Manchuria, but when

[11]Scholes, *Taft Administration*, p. 137; Griswold, *Far Eastern Policy*, p. 164; Vevier, *U.S. and China*, pp. 102, 114–15.
[12]*Foreign Relations* (1910), pp. 234–35.

he had broached his proposal to the British, they had responded unenthusiastically. Recalling tactics Hay had used in 1900 when Russia had been less than forthcoming in response to the Open Door Notes, Knox publicly announced that England favored his proposal and sent it out to the other powers. They were barely polite in refusing to consider a scheme that would wipe out the very influence they had been working so hard to expand. Instead of helping China regain control in Manchuria, the Neutralization Scheme convinced Russia and Japan that they must coordinate their efforts to preserve their influence in that province. This, in turn, drastically reduced any hope of a revival of Chinese influence.[13]

Disappointed but not discouraged, Knox forged ahead on other fronts. His basic goal remained unchanged: he intended to force cooperative arrangements upon the other powers in order to weaken their individual influences and, consequently, strengthen China's integrity and autonomy. The exhaustive Hukuang Loan arrangements were finally nailed down in May 1910, granting the United States an equal share in all aspects of the railroad project. Having wormed his way into a cooperative railroad concession, Knox sought to create a similar mechanism to loan China funds for currency reform. His efforts were rewarded with the establishment in London, on 10 November 1910, of an international banking consortium whose sole purpose was to float a loan for the Chinese government so that it could revitalize and stabilize the value of its currency. At first, the consortium consisted only of the countries participating in the Hukuang Loan: the United States, France, Germany, and Great Britain. When Russia and Japan demanded a right to admission, it became the so-called Six-power Consortium. At last, the Taft administration's policy appeared to be bearing fruit, as Americans were equal partners with the other great powers in Chinese development schemes.[14]

The appearance of success quickly evaporated. Both the consortium and the Hukuang Loan added fuel to the growing nationalistic hatred for the ineffective Imperial government. President Taft had congratulated the Chinese leadership for the tentative steps it had made in the direction of more democratic local government in 1910, but such minor and long overdue gestures could not forestall the revolutionary impulses sweeping China. When the revolutionary forces led by Sun Yat-sen succeeded in overthrowing the Imperial govern-

[13]Griswold, *Far Eastern Policy*, pp. 154–57; Vevier, *U.S. and China*, pp. 147, 162–63.
[14]Vevier, *U.S. and China*, pp. 179–80.

ment late in 1911, China appeared to be moving away from autocracy and in the direction of a more broadly representative form of government. On the surface, this trend appeared to correspond with the thrust of America's democratic mission. At least Congress seemed to think so when, in February 1912, it approved a joint resolution which praised the Chinese revolution because "the American people are inherently and by tradition sympathetic with all efforts to adopt the ideals and institutions of representative government."[15] Secretary Knox had striven for nearly three years, however, to make his goal of international cooperation a reality, so he stubbornly refused even to consider giving in to public pressures for unilateral American recognition of the new Republic of China. Instead, he delayed any action by sending out notes to all of the other great powers requesting their opinions on recognition, well aware that they would oppose it. He then announced that the United States certainly could not go counter to world opinion. Furthermore, with a bow toward the revised mission theme's emphasis upon stable as well as democratic government, Knox claimed the new Chinese regime had yet to prove it could remain in power and calm the revolutionary impulses still smoldering throughout China.[16]

Late in 1912, President Taft defended his administration's policy on more practical grounds. He felt that, as long as he continued to cooperate with the other great powers, the United States could ensure than no one used China's unsettled conditions to carve out advantages for itself.[17] The steadfast American cooperation with the other hated great powers angered the new Chinese leaders and led them to distrust the United States. Worse still, the denial of international recognition coincided with an effort to force the Chinese to accept a $300 million loan from the Six-power Consortium. No one would deny that China desperately needed funds in the aftermath of the revolution. The powers felt that, by withholding recognition, they could coerce the new Chinese government into agreeing to the huge loan, even though the consortium's earlier efforts had helped bring about the downfall of the old empire. The China tangle remained unresolved when Taft surrendered the presidency to Woodrow Wilson on 4 March 1913.

Wilson sought information from a variety of sources on how he should handle the intertwined issues of Chinese recognition and the

---

[15]*Foreign Relations* (1912), p. 71.
[16]*Foreign Relations* (1913), pp. 88–91.
[17]*Foreign Relations* (1912), p. xii.

consortium's loan. Representatives of the American Group wasted no time in informing the new administration of their desire to drop out of the consortium. The president saw no reason to persuade them otherwise, so the American withdrawal from the consortium was announced on 18 March. Meanwhile, the American chargé in Peking reported that although the bulk of the Chinese people seemed to be paying little attention to the republican government, they certainly did not seem likely to topple it either. He advised recognition. The concept of recognition squared with Wilson's commitment to the democratic mission, so he decided to ignore the other powers and to open normal diplomatic relations with the new government of China on 2 April 1913. In September Secretary of State Bryan completed the reversal of Knox's China policy when he issued instructions to the American chargé in Peking which reinstated the old rules forbidding American diplomats from supporting or encouraging any particular American enterprise in China.[18]

Few in either China or the United States mourned the termination of Dollar Diplomacy. The Taft administration's Far Eastern policy had been characterized by a great-power aggressiveness which infuriated the nationalistic Chinese. Furthermore, it had consistently lacked support from the very American capitalists it was ostensibly designed to benefit. So uninterested were American capitalists in his ambitious projects that Knox had to rely upon foreign investors buying into the American companies involved in Chinese operations. Because the program alienated the Chinese, lacked financial support, and hampered American idealism, it retarded rather than advanced American prestige in the Far East.

On the other hand, if the nation's goal was to expand American economic and political influence in the Far East, Wilson's China policy turned out to be just as dismal a failure. The Japanese seized every advantage. When World War I engulfed its great-power competitors, Japan assumed a predominant position in the Far East, comparable to the one the United States enjoyed in the Western Hemisphere. Although Wilson never explicitly abandoned China to Japan, his adamant refusal to use American force to back his initiatives in favor of free competition greatly reduced their impact. In the end, Wilson hoped his League of Nations would substitute moral suasion for physical force throughout the world, but it, too, ultimately failed to protect China from Japan's expansionism.

[18]*Foreign Relations* (1913), pp. 96-97, 108, 170-71, 187; Scholes, *Taft Administration*, pp. 245-46.

Because the United States overshadowed all other powers in the New World, its initiatives were more likely to succeed there than in the Far East. Concern over defending the Panama Canal seemed to justify the United States' determination to impose and preserve political stability and American economic predominance in the Caribbean. Despite Taft's claim that he was substituting dollars for bullets, the armed forces figured prominently in his Latin American policy. When another rebellion shook Cuba in 1912, the United States responded with its second armed intervention based on the Platt Amendment. Fortunately, the troops only had to stay for a month on this occasion. Marines supported American diplomatic efforts in the Dominican Republic and began what turned out to be two decades of occupation in Nicaragua. When he took over in 1913, Wilson seemed convinced that unprincipled and immoral persons were set upon disrupting peaceful democratic government in Latin America so he, too, resorted to the use of American armed forces.

To achieve the stability and peace both Knox and Taft considered essential and desirable in the hemisphere, they continued to expand America's political influence. The Roosevelt Corollary had already arrogated to the United States a responsibility for preventing European creditors and capitalists from coercing or intervening in other New World countries. Taft's Dollar Diplomacy program had an even more ambitious goal: to exclude or limit all European influence by encouraging American investors to move in to Latin America in a big way. An expanding American economic influence would presumably limit the opportunities or excuses for external interference in the hemisphere. As it had in China, therefore, the Taft administration hoped to use economic expansion as a means for obtaining political and strategic benefits.

The Dominican customs protocol provided the philosophical basis for the policymakers in the Taft administration who became convinced that financial responsibility guaranteed by the United States would discourage instability in Latin America. Unfortunately, the Dominican political situation began to disintegrate during Taft's term. Efficient and honest collection of customs duties actually had very little to do with the popularity of the existing government. A revolution swept the nation in 1911, the president was shot, and a provisional government established. When this temporary government began to totter, the United States dispatched 750 marines to guard some special American commissioners charged with working out a more effective political arrangement. To make matters worse, by 1912 the republic had fallen into such serious financial straits that the

United States had to bail it out with a loan. The original American customs protocol had supposedly been designed to prevent the very political instability and financial catastrophe the Dominicans were now encountering. Conditions deteriorated to such a degree that the Wilson administration decided to send in American troops to enforce peace and impose stability at gunpoint.[19]

No one anticipated the eventual political and economic collapse of the Dominican Republic, however, so policymakers in the first part of Taft's term applied the principles of the Dominican agreements to governmental and economic problems in other countries. For example, when the Central American nation of Honduras ran into trouble in 1910, Secretary Knox duly arranged for it to have a customs collection agency modeled after the Dominican example. Knox's treaty with Honduras also included the other fundamental element of the Dollar Diplomacy program: a loan agreement designed to encourage American financiers to invest in the republic. The loan would displace European capital and, hopefully, create a peaceful and responsible government for Honduras that would be favorably disposed to further American investment and trade. This treaty had to be carefully harmonized with the United States' efforts to deal with the much more menacing and complex problems in Honduras' aggressive neighbor, Nicaragua.

The peace plan for Central America which Secretary of State Root had worked out in 1907 with Mexico's help had begun to disintegrate almost immediately, partly, some Americans felt, because of a lack of support from Mexican President Porfirio Díaz. Díaz was a good friend of Nicaragua's troublemaking leader José Santos Zelaya, who was spoiling for a fight with El Salvador early in 1909. When the Mexican government failed to restrain Zelaya, the United States disgustedly turned its back upon President Díaz to pursue an independent policy toward Nicaragua.[20]

Because Zelaya did not enjoy universal popularity in his own country, he encountered serious domestic opposition to his aggressive moves against the neighboring Central American republics. In an effort to solidify his position, as well as to reduce the United States' influence in his country, Zelaya borrowed heavily in Europe. By the

[19]Scholes, *Taft Administration,* p. 44; Dana G. Munro, *Intervention and Dollar Diplomacy in the Caribbean 1900–1921* (Princeton: Princeton University Press, 1964), pp. 162–63, 266; Scott Nearing and Joseph Freeman, *Dollar Diplomacy: A Study in American Imperialism* (New York: Viking, 1926), p. 127.

[20]Heriberto Baron to Knox, 13 December 1909; Philander C. Knox Papers, LCMD; Munro, *Intervention,* p. 167; Scholes, *Taft Administration,* pp. 49–51.

fall of 1909, several American companies operating in Nicaragua had become convinced that Zelaya had to go, so they secretly began to support the growing rebel movement in Nicaragua. When government troops captured a couple of American citizens the rebels had hired to lay explosives, Zelaya had the Americans summarily shot. Knox had already been considering some official response to the American business interests in Nicaragua who were protesting that the rebellion endangered their property; news of the executions caused him to adopt extreme measures. On 1 December 1909, the secretary of state announced his decision to break diplomatic relations with Nicaragua. Rather than focus solely upon the deaths of the Americans, Knox emphasized the general disapproval the United States felt toward Zelaya's government. He criticized it for failing to adhere to republican principles and praised those in rebellion as representing "the ideals and the will of the majority of the Nicaraguan people."[21] Knox clearly intended for the diplomatic break to bring about a new Nicaraguan government more compatible with America's democratic mission sentiments.

Vitalized by these expressions of the United States' moral support for their endeavors, the rebels drove ahead and managed to throw Zelaya out early in 1910. Secretary Knox then attempted to impose upon Nicaragua the sort of economic protectorate the United States had established in Honduras. In October 1910, he dispatched the head of the State Department's Latin American Division, Thomas C. Dawson, to Managua to formalize the American position. The American envoy had the Nicaraguan government pledge that it would call a constitutional convention in order to establish a truly democratic government. The so-called Dawson Agreements also included the promise of a large American loan to be backed by customs revenues. To insure repayment of the loan, the United States insisted upon imposing a Dominican-style customs collection arrangement on Nicaragua.[22]

The president under the new constitution was Adolfo Díaz, a former employee of one of the American companies which had opposed Zelaya's rule. The Díaz administration had its minister in Washington, Salvador Castrillo, work out the details of the loan with Knox. The Nicaraguan arrangements paralleled those made earlier with Honduras to replace European capital and influence in the

[21]*Foreign Relations* (1909), p. 456.
[22]*Foreign Relations* (1910), p. 762; Munro, *Intervention*, p. 188; Scholes, *Taft Administration*, pp. 59–60.

neighborhood of the canal with American financial and political support. In return for special concessions, the Knox-Castrillo Convention would establish a group of American financiers as the Nicaraguan government's primary creditors. In March 1912, while on a Latin American goodwill tour like Root's, Knox tied his whole effort into the democratic mission theme: "The full measure and extent of our policy is to assist in the maintenance of republican institutions upon this hemisphere and we are anxious that the experiment of a government of the people, for the people and by the people shall not fail in any republic on this continent," he told the National Assembly of Nicaragua. "We are equally desirous that there shall be no failure to maintain a republican form of government from forces of disintegration originating from within; and so far as we may be able we will always be found willing to lend such proper assistance as may be within our power to preserve the stabiity of our sister American republics."[23]

Shortly thereafter, a disappointed Knox found himself forced to fulfill his pledge to maintain a stable government in Nicaragua. The Republican statesman could, at least, blame it on the opposition party. The Democrats had done well in the off year elections in 1910, so the Democratic minority in the United States Senate refused to permit the implementation of the Republicans' Dollar Diplomacy program for either Honduras or Nicaragua. When the Knox-Castrillo Convention failed to win Senate approval, the secretary of state desperately pleaded with the American bankers to extend privately the loans so essential to his plans in Nicaragua. The financiers reluctantly agreed to provide financial backing for the Adolfo Díaz regime. Even so, a group of Zelaya's followers came close to overthrowing Díaz in the late summer of 1912, thus reinforcing the lesson being learned in the Dominican Republic that sound finances alone could not guarantee political stability in Latin America. In other words, the basic premise of Dollar Diplomacy was faulty. When Díaz requested assistance in September, over 2,000 United States marines were sent in. The marine contingent, eventually reduced to about a hundred men, stayed until 1925, protecting a minority government. Although this clearly violated the democratic emphasis of the mission theme, it did preserve political stability, a more important consideration for a nation so strategically located with respect to the canal.[24]

[23]*Foreign Relations* (1912), p. 1122.
[24]Munro, *Intervention*, pp. 203–4, 216; Scholes, *Taft Administration*, p. 66.

Financial difficulties continued to plague the Díaz regime, however. In 1914, Wilson's secretary of state, William Jennings Bryan, negotiated a treaty with Nicaraguan Minister Emiliano Chamorro which was designed to provide financial backing similar to that of the rejected Knox-Castrillo Convention. In return for options to the canal route in southern Nicaragua and to territory for naval bases to protect it, the United States agreed to give three million dollars to Nicaragua. The Bryan-Chamorro Treaty also included articles similar to those in the Platt Amendment pledging United States intervention in support of peace and stability, but idealists in the Senate insisted that these provisions be removed before they would allow the treaty to be ratified. Thus, even though President Wilson had publicly repudiated Dollar Diplomacy, his administration's policy in Nicaragua was virtually identical to the one Knox had pursued.[25]

The glaring contradictions between what President Wilson proclaimed and what his diplomats actually did in Latin America prior to World War I stemmed from the fundamental incompatibility between the democratic mission theme in its purest sense and the continued expansion of American political influence. The Democratic president sincerely believed in the virtue of republican self-government, but, in practice, he found it impossible to allow other nations the luxury of unrestricted political freedoms as long as the United States intended to exercise its self-assumed responsibility for preserving peace and stability in the hemisphere. Wilson may never have recognized the inapplicability of his abstract nineteenth-century moral beliefs to the twentieth-century problems he encountered. The Nicaragua case was hardly unique as an example of the divergence between his words and his actions in foreign relations. During his administration the United States also sent troops into the Dominican Republic and allowed its navy to establish dictatorial control over Haiti. But the classic example of the contradictions inherent in Wilsonian foreign policy lies in his tortured dealings with Mexico.

The American people were generally surprised, shocked, and dismayed when Mexico fell into turmoil after years of tranquility. In his meeting with Díaz in 1909, President Taft had expressed his heartfelt hope that the Mexican leader would remain in power until Taft had left office. United States investors and businessmen had pumped over a billion dollars of American capital into Mexico. When

[25]*Foreign Relations* (1914), p. 953; Samuel Flagg Bemis, *The Latin American Policy of the United States* (c. 1943; reprint ed., New York: W. W. Norton, 1967), p. 188.

the smoldering fuse of Mexican discontent finally ignited in open rebellion in 1910, the Taft administration invoked American neutrality laws designed to prevent foreign rebels from legally obtaining arms and supplies in the United States. Flaunting the official American policy, revolutionaries passed back and forth across the border with ease, causing Taft periodically to order American troops to mass along the Rio Grande. Although the president personally had no intention of choosing sides in the Mexican civil war, rumors constantly circulated that the United States would intervene. Those loyal to the existing regime may have hoped for the United States' assistance, but many of the rebels were violently anti-American, blaming the exploitation of Mexico's cheap labor and natural resources upon the wealthy American capitalists that Díaz had welcomed in.[26]

When they finally succeeded in forcing President Díaz to resign late in 1911, Francisco Madero became president of Mexico, an event which displeased American Ambassador Henry Lane Wilson. He began bombarding Washington with highly critical reports on the new Mexican leader, characterizing him as weak-willed and prone to accept poor advice. Madero also encountered serious criticism from his own countrymen; so much so, in fact, that a new rebellion broke out in 1912. To keep his enemies from obtaining weapons and supplies, Madero called upon the United States to enforce the very neutrality laws Madero himself had once evaded. Again, President Taft remained strictly neutral, but his ambassador in Mexico City became deeply involved in the efforts to oust the Mexican leader. After Madero had surrendered in early 1913, Ambassador Wilson invited the leaders of the disputing forces to meet at the American embassy, where he helped them hammer out an agreement which granted General Victoriano Huerta the position of provisional president. Without bothering to check with his superiors in Washington, Henry Lane Wilson then essentially legitimatized Huerta's regime by ordering all American consular agencies in Mexico to publicize the change in administration. The American ambassador had thus behaved very much as Minister Stevens had during the Hawaiian revolution some two decades earlier. And, like Stevens, Henry Lane Wilson quickly encountered the wrath of a newly inaugurated, moralistic Democratic president who chose to cast all of his efforts in the worst possible light.[27]

[26]*Foreign Relations* (1911), pp. 367, 431, 480–82; Scholes, *Taft Administration*, pp. 82–86.

[27]*Foreign Relations* (1911), p. 510; *Foreign Relations* (1912), p. 714; *Foreign Relations* (1913), p. 721; Scholes, *Taft Administration*, pp. 89, 101.

President Woodrow Wilson believed that the Mexican people were fully capable of establishing and operating an American-style democratic government. Free elections and a new constitution should solve all of their problems. Unfortunately, Wilson overrated the political sophistication of the Mexican peasants and grossly under-estimated the ambitions of the Mexican leaders. When Huerta's men killed Madero, claiming the ousted leader had tried to escape while being taken to prison, President Wilson became enraged, and he developed an unconcealed hatred for the Mexican general. Dramatically reversing the course Ambassador Henry Lane Wilson had pursued, President Wilson withdrew official American recognition of Huerta's government. Not incidentally, the resulting severence of relations also terminated Ambassador Wilson's services. As Knox had done when berating Zelaya in 1909, President Wilson predicated his criticism of Huerta's regime on the American mission: "We are the friends of constitutional government in America; we are more than its friends, we are its champions; because in no other way can our neighbors, to whom we would wish in every way to make proof of our friendship, work out their own development in peace and liberty." But, Wilson continued, "Mexico has no Government. The attempt to maintain one at the City of Mexico has broken down, and a mere military despotism has been set up which has hardly more than the semblance of national authority."[28] The president inserted himself much more directly in Mexican affairs than had Taft, throwing American moral support behind the Mexican Constitutionalists. Believing a constitutional system would cure all of Mexico's problems, Wilson would discover later that he fundamentally disagreed with certain provisions of the document the Constitutionalists intended to draft. He chose to ignore such finer points, however, because of his abiding hatred of Huerta, and he even went so far as to lift the American restrictions on the shipment of arms to those in rebellion. President Wilson had thus intervened in Mexican affairs more directly and forcefully than had any American president since James K. Polk declared war in 1846. Wilson self-righteously claimed he was acting because of his concern over the plight of the Mexican people who were being denied any say in their own government. The support of the United States enabled the Constitutionalists under Venustiano Carranza to mount an increasingly effective revolutionary movement.[29]

[28]*Foreign Relations* (1913), p. x.
[29]*Foreign Relations* (1914), pp. 447–48.

Following its now well-established practice for dealing with strife-torn nations, the United States stationed some of its naval vessels off several Mexican ports including Tampico on the Gulf of Mexico. A boat containing a few American sailors put into shore at one point, only to be captured and then quickly released by Huerta forces. Like President Harrison in the *Baltimore* incident more than twenty years earlier, President Wilson seized upon the episode as an affront to his nation's honor. He stoutly backed the American admiral on the scene who demanded that the Mexicans fire a twenty-one gun salute to the American flag as an apology for the incident. The Huerta government agreed to do so, but only if the United States would return the salute—an action that would violate Wilson's nonrecognition policy. The president placed the matter before Congress where he found sufficient support to justify his ordering the United States Navy to seize the Mexican port of Vera Cruz in April 1914. This port had served as the major entrepôt for European arms shipments to the Mexican government, and its capture severely crippled Huerta's defense efforts. Eventually Wilson agreed to allow Argentina, Brazil, and Chile to mediate between the United States and Mexico.[30]

An amicable resolution of the crisis became possible once Carranza's forces ousted Huerta in July 1914. Although he was a Constitutionalist, Carranza did not completely please the American president. Consequently, the United States delayed extending its official recognition of the new government until October 1915. Even then, the turmoil in Mexico had not completely ended as other rebels led by the colorful Pancho Villa continued to seek power. Lacking sufficient strength themselves to overthrow Carranza, these revolutionaries killed American citizens in Mexico and across the border in the United States in 1916, hoping the United States would send in an army. They expected that such an intervention would lead to a conflict with Carranza's forces, a conflict which might end in the Mexican leader's downfall. Fortunately, American General John J. Pershing's "punitive expedition" had little effect on internal Mexican conditions, although it did succeed in perpetuating bad feelings on both sides of the border. The immensely more menacing war in Europe compelled Wilson to withdraw Pershing in 1917 in order to send him across the Atlantic. Relieved of American pressure, Carranza and his Constitutionalists went on to create a nationalistic government which has given Mexico a high degree of stability ever since.

[30]Ibid., pp. 46–83.

Woodrow Wilson thus proved to be even more aggressive than earlier presidents in pursuing American interests abroad. Even as he repeatedly advocated self-government and democracy, he broadened the scope of American intervention in Latin American affairs. In the end, Wilson proved incapable of resolving the inherent contradiction between the altruistic democratic mission and the selfish desire for expanded American political influence and greater American economic control. Wilson's failure is hardly surprising. After all, Roosevelt's determination to control and protect the canal had interfered with his mission sentiments, and Taft had stressed economic and political expansion at the expense of independence and self-government in Latin America. Once the United States had emerged as one of the world's great powers and had, consequently, enormously expanded the scope of its international involvements, American policymakers charged with putting the traditional foreign policy themes into practice discovered that jarring and sometimes irreconcilable conflicts existed among them.

Conclusion

The United States had not always possessed the strength and prestige necessary to enable it to control its involvement in international relations. A minor, dependent nation in the late eighteenth and early nineteenth centuries, it lay at the mercy of external forces which dictated when and, to a large degree, how it made diplomatic decisions. The traditional American foreign policy themes developed as philosophical and psychological guidelines into which the United States' reactions to external events tended to fall. The United States threw off its dependency once it had attained the physical characteristics of a great power around 1880; it could then begin making its own way in the world. Its geographical isolation permitted it the freedom to allow the interplay of its internal themes and traditions to determine the extent or limits of its diplomatic activities. The nation's accelerating economic growth and its achievement of many of its expansionistic goals by 1914 transformed the United States into such an important member of the world community of nations, however, that it no longer had the freedom to ignore major international events. It was a victim of its own success. The triumphant drive to expand its economic, political, and moral influence ended in forcing the United States to accept awesome, often unwanted responsibilities as well.

The year 1914, therefore, marked the end of a unique era in the United States' foreign relations—one in which the American people's internal motivations and beliefs largely dominated their nation's decision-making process with regard to foreign affairs. The great war in Europe drew the United States into a much more active participation in world politics and international affairs than it had previously considered prudent. The internal motivations and traditions which had been shaping American foreign policy had to accommodate the intrusion of momentous external forces. Evidence of this fundamental change came when the United States found itself sucked into the European hostilities in 1917 even though the American people had no obvious direct interest in the conflict. The traditional internal themes which had been directing foreign policy since 1880 did not abruptly disappear, but they reverted to a position similar to the one they had occupied in the nation's infancy: they remained the premises upon which the United States based its reactions to compelling external events. The three themes that have been under examination also lost some of their influence to other, newer internal factors such as the defense and security worries generally ignored or deemphasized before World War I. A brief look at where each of the three major themes went after 1914 illustrates the alteration and weakening process they underwent.

External circumstances had the least effect upon the economic expansion theme. During the war years the United States prospered, enjoying an enormous export trade which President Wilson sought to insure through a variety of steps, including war itself. Having finally paid off all of its outstanding debts by 1914, the United States became the world's major creditor nation, exporting capital and lending money on a global scale. America's economic expansion continued after the fighting had ended, because war-ravaged Europe went on borrowing money from the United States. Throughout the 1920s the United States served as one of the world's chief bankers, and the whole world suffered along with the American people during the depression of the 1930s. Since World War II, the dollar has become the chief medium of international exchange and the United States has become an essential partner at all levels of international finance and trade.

The other two themes suffered rather substantial setbacks in comparison to economic expansion, however, most notably the democratic mission. One has seen how dismayed American idealists became over the behavior of peoples and governments in Latin America, the region in which the United States exerted its greatest influence before World War I. Yet, despite the disappointments in Haiti, the Dominican Republic, Nicaragua, Cuba, and Mexico, Woodrow Wilson never considered abandoning the great American mission. On 2 April 1917, he proclaimed that the United States was declaring war on Germany to make the world safe for democracy—and he meant it. His fourteen-point program for restructuring the postwar world emphasized democracy and republican forms. Unfortunately, the Russian people's adoption of communism was a step beyond what even the most liberal Americans considered reasonable and proper. This drive to what Americans considered extremism coupled with the compromises Wilson made in order to win great-power adherence to his League of Nations resulted in a widespread disillusionment on the part of the idealistic United States. After the war, democratic mission spirit died down, and the nation withdrew into isolationism in the 1920s and 1930s. World War II triggered a reactivation of the nation's mission sentiments, however, which led to a sometimes fanatical pursuit of American ideals during the Cold War. America's more recent efforts to keep the "Free World" free have been characterized by far more excessive actions than any taken in response to the mission theme around the turn of the century.

The United States' political influence unquestionably increased during World War I, perhaps reaching its zenith when President Wilson personally crossed the Atlantic to redraw the map of Europe at the close of the conflict. Although the Europeans showed some reluctance in acquiescing to Wilson's grand plan, it was a group of Americans who concluded that Wilson's plan would overcommit the United States. In a stunning reversal of the traditional American drive to expand its political influence, the United States Senate refused to approve the Versailles Treaty, cutting the nation off from any participation in the League of Nations and generally reducing substantially its political impact in Europe. The American people seemed quite content with the amount of political influence they exercised closer to home, and they continued to direct the course of events in Central America and the Caribbean. In a sense, the nation was seeking to retreat to the status it had held between 1880 and 1914, a status in which its relative freedom from external responsibilities had enabled it to predominate within its chosen spheres of interest. This vain attempt to escape great-power responsibilities was bound to fail as the world staggered into a second global conflict in the late 1930s. As it had in the case of the mission theme, American participation in World War II rejuvenated the political influence motivation. After the war, the United States commandeered control of the United Nations, financed the reconstruction of Europe, and developed the weaponry to defend more than half of the world.

Although they have obviously undergone alterations and lost some of their prominence in recent years, the themes which dominated American foreign policy around the turn of the century are still reflected today in the United States' attitudes about foreign affairs. The United States' political influence is extraordinarily widespread, its products and capital pervade markets and exchanges throughout the world, and the American people still exhibit a strong desire to make others like themselves. The diplomats and statesmen who superintended the nation's emergence as a great power from 1880 to 1914 would probably feel that the position the United States occupies in the world today represents a logical fulfillment of the very goals they had themselves pursued.

Bibliographical Essay

The abundance of materials relating to each of the subjects touched upon in this book dictates a certain amount of selectiveness in listing useful sources. One of my emphases is on the character and behavior of those relatively few individuals who fashioned the nation's aspirations and goals into day-to-day policies. Here private papers, reminiscences, and biographies are most helpful. A second emphasis is on the formal articulation of their policies which can be observed in the official correspondence, statements, and memoranda these individuals produced as they debated and publicized their decisions. Finally, there must be an investigation of what other historians have said about the motivations and consequences of these policies and decisions. Thus, the following discussion of sources is divided into three sections: personal sources, official publications, and historical works.

Personal Sources

The story opens with the Republican policymakers of the 1880s. The Frederick T. Frelinghuysen Papers at the Library of Congress Manuscript Division (LCMD) are primarily drafts of documents which later appeared in the *Foreign Relations* series. An incisive, detailed study of the policies of this period appears in David M. Pletcher, *The Awkward Years: American Foreign Relations under Garfield and Arthur* (Columbia: University of Missouri Press, 1962). Although the predominant Republican thinker in this period and into the 1890s was undoubtedly Blaine, the small LCMD collection reflects his care in destroying anything of a controversial (and therefore interesting) nature in his personal papers. Among a number of Blaine biographies, only two are objective: David Saville Muzzey, *James G. Blaine: A Political Idol of Other Days* (New York: Dodd, Mead, 1934) and Alice Felt Tyler, *The Foreign*

Policy of James G. Blaine (Minneapolis: University of Minnesota Press, 1927). Albert T. Volwiler, ed., *The Correspondence Between Benjamin Harrison and James G. Blaine 1882-1893* (Philadelphia: American Philosophical Society, 1940) provides insights into personal relationships as well as affairs of state. A minor Republican with an excellent biography is Edward Younger, *John A. Kasson: Politics and Diplomacy from Lincoln to McKinley* (Iowa City: State Historical Society of Iowa, 1955). John W. Foster's small collection at the LCMD has only a few items relating to his service at the State Department.

The activities of the Democrats who exercised executive authority in the last two decades of the nineteenth century are somewhat better documented. The president provided a statement of his views in Grover Cleveland, *Presidential Problems* (New York: Century Company, 1904), and the prolific Allan Nevins did a biography, *Grover Cleveland: A Study in Courage* (New York: Dodd, Mead, 1934), and a collection of correspondence, *Letters of Grover Cleveland: 1850-1908* (Boston: Houghton Mifflin, 1933). It is somewhat unfortunate that so few scintillating events occurred in the foreign policy arena during Cleveland's first term, because Thomas F. Bayard's LCMD collection is most comprehensive, apparently including copies of every letter he wrote as secretary of state. Charles Callan Tansill capitalized on these and other sources to write a definitive biography: *The Foreign Policy of Thomas F. Bayard 1885-1897* (New York: Fordham University Press, 1940). When Bayard went to London in 1893, his place was taken by Walter Q. Gresham whose papers at the LCMD include many bound volumes of incoming letters but few of his own responses. Fortunately the secretary's wife spent many years putting together a record of his work: Matilda Gresham, *Life of Walter Quintin Gresham 1832-1895*, 2 vols. (c. 1919; reprint ed., Freeport, N.Y.: Books for Libraries Press, 1970). The Richard Olney collection at the LCMD is on a par with Bayard's: voluminous and containing incoming, outgoing, and internal (State Department) memoranda. The fullness of the record stimulated the writing of two good biographies: Gerald G. Eggert, *Richard Olney: Evolution of a Statesman* (University Park, Pa.: Penn. State University Press, 1974) and Henry James, *Richard Olney and his Public Service* (Boston: Houghton Mifflin, 1923). Frequently at odds with his party's presidential policies, Alabama Senator John T. Morgan's collected papers at the LCMD indicate the trend of his thinking.

Republican President McKinley's first secretary of state, John Sherman, left an enormous collection of papers to the LCMD, but only one box out of 600 relates to events after 1897. William R. Day succeeded Sherman and left a large collection of primarily incoming correspondence to the LCMD. McKinley's secretary of the navy was John D. Long, whose papers at the Massachusetts Historical Society illustrate the pressures on the cabinet both for and against intervention in Cuba. Margaret Long edited *The Journal of*

John D. Long (Rindge, N.H.: Richard R. Smith, 1956) which gives revealing glimpses into behind-the-scenes activities. Long's fellow Bay Stater, Senator Henry Cabot Lodge, is the subject of two good biographies: John A. Garraty, *Henry Cabot Lodge: A Biography* (New York: Knopf, 1953) and Karl Schriftgiesser, *The Gentleman from Massachusetts: Henry Cabot Lodge* (Boston: Little, Brown, 1944). The John Hay papers at the LCMD are a thorough, fascinating collection. Hay's career is detailed in two excellent books: Tyler Dennett, *John Hay: From Poetry to Politics* (New York: Dodd, Mead, 1933) and William Roscoe Thayer, *The Life and Letters of John Hay*, 2 vols. (Boston: Houghton Mifflin, 1915).

No single individual better personified the maturing strength, adolescent openness, and youthful energy of the United States in these years than did Theodore Roosevelt, and no book better captures his moods than *An Autobiography* (New York: Scribners, 1929 [c. 1913]). Elting E. Morison, ed., *The Letters of Theodore Roosevelt*, 8 vols. (Cambridge: Harvard University Press, 1951–1954) performed heroic work in tracking down and indexing his personal papers. Howard K. Beale's intensive work *Theodore Roosevelt and the Rise of America to World Power* (New York: Collier Books, 1962) puts his actions into diplomatic context, and John Morton Blum, *The Republican Roosevelt* (Cambridge: Harvard University Press, 1954) and William Henry Harbaugh, *Power and Responsibility: The Life and Times of Theodore Roosevelt* (New York: Farrar, Straus & Cudahy, 1961) do the same on a broader scale.

Roosevelt's associates and successors reflect less vivid images. Elihu Root, a painstaking, well-organized lawyer, left literally hundreds of boxes of correspondence and scrapbooks which are available at the LCMD. Philip C. Jessup, *Elihu Root*, 2 vols. (New York: Dodd, Mead, 1938) covers his entire life, while Richard Leopold measured Root with a more selective yardstick in *Elihu Root and the Conservative Tradition* (Boston: Little, Brown, 1954). The Philander C. Knox Papers at the LCMD are well worth examining, particularly the fascinating series of dispatches and departmental memoranda on the developing revolution in China in late 1911 and 1912. The excellent Walter V. Scholes and Marie V. Scholes, *The Foreign Policies of the Taft Administration* (Columbia: University of Missouri Press, 1970), contains a most readable explanation of the various ramifications of the Dollar Diplomacy programs. Finally, because of his importance as a thinker and publicist for expansionist ideas, one should look at the Alfred Thayer Mahan collection at the LCMD, particularly his correspondence with Long and Roosevelt.

Official Publications

One must be impressed with the *Foreign Relations* series for this period. An examination of the documents in the files of the National Archives shows that those omitted from *Foreign Relations* add almost nothing to what can be derived from the published volumes. Another convenience for the latter-day researcher are the compilations of materials published at the behest of Congress on specific topics. Some of the useful ones include:

U.S. House of Representatives. *Relations with Chile.* Ex. Doc. No. 91. 52d Cong., 1st sess., 25 January 1892.

U.S. Senate. *Affairs in Chili, Peru, and Bolivia: Papers relating to the War in South America and Attempts to Bring about a Peace.* Ex. Doc. No. 79. 47th Cong., 1st sess., 26 January 1882.

U.S. Senate. *Affairs in Cuba.* Report No. 885. 55th Cong., 2d sess., 13 April 1898.

U.S. Senate. *Compilation of Reports of the Committee on Foreign Relations.* Doc. No. 231, Parts 1–8. 8 vols. 56th Cong., 2d sess., 1901.

U.S. Senate. *Correspondence respecting relations between the United States and the Hawaiian Islands from September, 1820, to January, 1893.* Ex. Doc. No. 77. 52d Cong., 2d sess., 17 February 1893.

U.S. Senate. *Independent State of the Congo.* Ex. Doc. No. 196. 49th Cong., 1st sess., 30 June 1889.

U.S. Senate. *The Maritime Canal of Suez from Its Inauguration, November 17, 1869, to the Year 1884.* Ex. Doc. No. 198. 48th Cong., 1st sess., 27 June 1884.

U.S. Senate. *Nicaragua Canal Company.* Report No. 1142. 52d Cong., 2d sess., 22 December 1892.

U.S. Senate. *Report of the Isthmian Canal Commission, 1899–1901.* Doc. No. 54. 57th Cong., 1st sess., 1901.

For certain presidential statements not included in State Department or congressional compilations, the Richardson volumes provide a convenient source. Unfortunately, a number of different editions of these volumes with differing pagination appeared over the years. The footnotes in my book refer to James D. Richardson, *A Compilation of the Messages and Papers of the Presidents* (with additions and renumbered from one through all the volumes; 10 vols., Washington, D.C.: Bureau of National Literature, 1911).

Historical Works

Although almost every diplomatic history textbook discusses the underlying philosophy and motivations behind American foreign policy, several more specialized books offer broader analyses. One of the most thought-provoking is Arthur A. Ekirch, Jr., *Ideas, Ideals, and American Diplomacy: A History of their Growth and Interaction* (New York: Appleton-Century-Crofts, 1966) which emphasizes a particular motivation behind policy formulation for each succeeding decade or two. Dexter Perkins's little book on *The Evolution of American Foreign Policy* (New York: Oxford University Press, 1966) contains a number of stimulating insights. Richard W. Van Alstyne, *The Rising American Empire* (Chicago: Quadrangle, 1965) concentrates on one of the three basic themes of the present study. Crucial to understanding expansionism and Manifest Destiny are Frederick Merk, *Manifest Destiny and Mission in American History: A Reinterpretation* (New York: Random House, 1963), Albert K. Weinberg, *Manifest Destiny: A Study of Nationalist Expansionism in American History* (Baltimore: Johns Hopkins University Press, 1935), and John A. Logan, Jr., *No Transfer: An American Security Principle* (New Haven: Yale University Press, 1961). More general commentaries on expansionism are provided by Englishman J. A. Hobson, *Imperialism: A Study* (c. 1938; reprint ed., Ann Arbor: University of Michigan Press, 1965), and two Americans, Charles A. Beard, *The Idea of National Interest: An Analytical Study in American Foreign Policy* (c. 1934; reprint ed., Chicago: Quadrangle, 1966) and Frank Tannenbaum, *The American Tradition in Foreign Policy* (Norman: University of Oklahoma Press, 1955). Two shorter pieces on the same subject are Thomas A. Bailey, "America's Emergence as a World Power: The Myth and the Verity," *Pacific Historical Review* 30 (February 1961): 1–16, and Charles Vevier, "American Continentalism: An Idea of Expansion, 1845–1910," *American Historical Review* 65 (January 1960): 323–35. The nation's economic motivation is the subject of David A. Wells, *Recent Economic Changes (And their effect on the Production and Distribution of Wealth and the Well-Being of Society)* (New York: Appleton, 1890) and Tom E.Terrill, *The Tariff, Politics, and American Foreign Policy, 1874–1901* (Westport, Conn.: Greenwood, 1973). It is also covered extensively by William Appleman Williams in his *The Roots of the Modern American Empire: A Study of the Growth and Shaping of Social Consciousness in a Marketplace Society* (New York: Random House, 1969) and his more provocative *The Tragedy of American Diplomacy*, rev. ed. (New York: Dell, 1962).

Two general histories that shed light on turn-of-the-century thinking are John Holladay Latané, *From Isolation to Leadership: A Review of American Foreign Policy* (Garden City, N.Y.: Doubleday, 1918) and Alfred L. P. Dennis, *Adventures in American Diplomacy 1896–1906* (New York: Dutton, 1928). Foster Rhea Dulles handles the period in two well-written volumes: *Prelude to World Power: American Diplomatic History, 1860–1900* (New York: Macmillan, 1965) and *The Imperial Years* (New York: Crowell, 1956). The Essays in John A. S. Grenville and George Berkeley Young, *Politics, Strategy, and American Diplomacy: Studies in Foreign Policy, 1873–1917* (New Haven: Yale University Press, 1966) are well worth reading. Walter LaFeber, *The New Empire: An Interpretation of American Expansion 1860–1898* (Ithaca, N.Y.: Cornell University Press, 1963) has become something of a modern classic, although its title is misleading as the book focuses almost exclusively on the decade of the 1890s. Milton Plesur's excellent study, *America's Outward Thrust: Approaches to Foreign Affairs, 1865–1890* (DeKalb: Northern Illinois University Press, 1971), covers the earlier years much more thoroughly. Two recently published books, Charles S. Campbell, *The Transformation of American Foreign Relations 1865–1900* (New York: Harper & Row, 1976) and Robert L. Beisner, *From the Old Diplomacy to the New, 1865–1900* (New York: Crowell, 1975), take a somewhat different tack than my own, contending that a major transformation or shift occurred in the 1890s. Julius W. Pratt, *Challenge and Rejection: The United States and World Leadership, 1900–1921* (New York: Macmillan, 1967) is the series sequel to Campbell's book although it was written several years earlier. Richard D. Challener, *Admirals, Generals, and American Foreign Policy 1898–1914* (Princeton: Princeton University Press, 1973) looks at the armed forces angle as does Peter Karsten, *The Naval Aristocracy: The Golden Age of Annapolis and the Emergence of Modern American Navalism* (New York: Free Press, 1972), which indicates that Mahan's views were hardly unique in the navy. Kenneth J. Hagan, *American Gunboat Diplomacy and the Old Navy, 1877–1889* (Westport, Conn.: Greenwood, 1973) illustrates this point with a discussion of the early naval impact on policy. Bradford Perkins, *The Great Rapprochement: England and the United States: 1895–1914* (New York: Atheneum, 1968) takes a sweeping look at Anglo-American relations throughout the period under review; Donald F. Warner, *The Idea of Continental Union* (Lexington: University of Kentucky Press, 1960) and Norman Penlington, *The Alaska Boundary Dispute: A Critical Reappraisal* (Toronto: McGraw-Hill Ryerson, 1973) cover particular aspects of that relationship.

Looking at United States–Latin American relations, Samuel Flagg Bemis, *The Latin American Policy of the United States: An Historical Interpretation* (1943; reprint ed., New York: Norton, 1967) offers a classic review, somewhat influenced by wartime events. Less biased are two works by Dexter Perkins: *The Monroe Doctrine 1867–1907* (Baltimore: Johns Hopkins University Press, 1937) and *The United States and the Caribbean*, rev. ed. (Cambridge: Harvard University Press, 1966). Herbert Millington, *American Diplomacy and the War of the Pacific* (New York: Columbia University Press, 1948) summarizes that unfortunate exercise of American interference which forms the beginning of the subject treated in Frederick B. Pike, *Chile and the United States, 1880–1962: The Emergence of Chile's Social Crisis and the Challenge to United States Diplomacy* (Notre Dame, Ind.: Notre Dame University Press, 1963). Sheldon B. Liss, *The Canal: Aspects of United States–Panamanian Relations* (Notre Dame, Ind.: Notre Dame University Press, 1967) is marginally useful for this period. Two good articles on the Olney Note are: Nelson M. Blake, "Background of Cleveland's Venezuelan Policy," *American Historical Review* 47 (January 1942): 259–77 and George B. Young, "Intervention Under the Monroe Doctrine: The Olney

Corollary," *Political Science Quarterly* 47 (June 1942): 247–80. Skipping for the moment the Spanish-American War itself and looking beyond, useful sources include: Howard C. Hill, *Roosevelt and the Caribbean* (Chicago: University of Chicago Press, 1927), Dana G. Munro, *Intervention and Dollar Diplomacy in the Caribbean 1900–1921* (Princeton: Princeton University Press, 1964), and Seward W. Livermore, "Theodore Roosevelt, the American Navy, and the Venezuelan Crisis of 1902–1903," *American Historical Review* 51 (April 1946): 452–71. Allan Reed Millett, *The Politics of Intervention: The Military Occupation of Cuba, 1906–1909* (Columbus: Ohio State University Press, 1968) draws interesting conclusions on the effects the intervention had on later policies. Scott Nearing and Joseph Freeman's scathing revisionist tract, *Dollar Diplomacy: A Study in American Imperialism* (New York: Viking, 1926) provides entertaining reading.

Expansion into the Pacific involved both Hawaii and Samoa. The two books by Merze Tate, *Hawaii: Reciprocity or Annexation* (East Lansing: Michigan State University Press, 1968) and *The United States and the Hawaiian Kingdom: A Political History* (New Haven: Yale University Press, 1965), although somewhat overlapping, are the best historical treatments. Also good are Sylvester K. Stevens, *American Expansion in Hawaii 1842–1898* (New York: Russell & Russell, 1968) and two by William Adam Russ, Jr., *The Hawaiian Republic (1894–98) and its Struggle to Win Annexation* (Selinsgrove, Pa.: Susquehanna University Press, 1961) and *The Hawaiian Revolution (1893–94)* (Selinsgrove, Pa.: Susquehanna University Press, 1959). Paul M. Kennedy, *The Samoan Tangle: A Study in Anglo-German-American Relations, 1878–1900* (New York: Barnes & Noble, 1974) dissects the international aspects, while George Herbert Ryden, *The Foreign Policy of the United States in Relation to Samoa* (New Haven: Yale University Press, 1933) is more concerned with American attitudes and policies.

Among the number of sources on the war in Cuba, French Ensor Chadwick, *The Relations of the United States and Spain: Diplomacy* (New York: Scribners, 1909) provides a good starting point. In addition to the more general works already cited are those by Ernest R. May: *American Imperialism: A Speculative Essay* (New York: Atheneum, 1968) and *Imperial Democracy: The Emergence of America as a Great Power* (New York: Harcourt, Brace, 1961). The latter takes the position that the United States was essentially tricked into participating in the affair, a victim of European power diplomacy. A standard account is H. Wayne Morgan, *America's Road to Empire: The War with Spain and Overseas Expansion* (New York: Wiley, 1965). The specific topic of expansionism is discussed in Julius W. Pratt, *Expansionists of 1898: The Acquisition of Hawaii and the Spanish Islands* (c. 1936; reprint ed., Chicago: Quadrangle, 1964), an intensive study of the debate over colonial annexation; David Healy, *US Expansionism: The Imperialist Urge in the 1890s* (Madison: University of

Wisconsin Press, 1970), which looks at several prominent individuals and their attitudes; and R. G. Neale, *Great Britain and United States Expansion: 1898–1900* (East Lansing: Michigan State University Press, 1966), which views the subject from abroad. Elmer Ellis, *Henry Moore Teller: Defender of the West* (Caldwell, Idaho: Caxton Printers, 1941) is useful on the politics of the war declaration. William Graham Sumner, *The Conquest of the United States by Spain and Other Essays* (Chicago: Henry Regnery, 1965) vehemently outlines his antiimperialist views, which are also discussed along with those of others in Robert L. Beisner, *Twelve Against Empire: The Anti-Imperialists, 1898–1900* (New York: McGraw-Hill, 1968). E. Berkeley Tompkins, *Anti-Imperialism in the United States: The Great Debate, 1890–1920* (Philadelphia: University of Pennsylvania Press, 1970) looks at the subject over a longer run. John Morgan Gates, *Schoolbooks and Krags: The United States Army in the Philippines, 1898– 1902* (Westport, Conn.: Greenwood, 1973) has the interesting view that Americans saw themselves bringing Progressive-style reforms to their new colony. The contemporary journals are replete with articles on Cuba, expansionism, and America's destiny as a great power, and representative examples appear in the footnotes of the body of my text.

The war and its consequent expansion of America's physical presence to the Philippines greatly increased the level of interest in the Far East. The classic source for this period is A. Whitney Griswold, *The Far Eastern Policy of the United States* (New York: Harcourt, Brace, 1938), but Warren I. Cohen, *America's Response to China: An Interpretive History of Sino-American Relations* (New York: Wiley, 1971) is a concise account perhaps more appealing to modern readers. Tyler Dennett, *Americans in Eastern Asia: A Critical Study of the Policy of the United States with Reference to China, Japan and Korea in the 19th Century* (c. 1922; reprint ed., New York: Barnes & Noble, 1941) covers American activities before 1900. American motivations and actions in China have been subjected to intensive analysis by Marilyn Blatt Young, *The Rhetoric of Empire: American China Policy 1895–1901* (Cambridge: Harvard University Press, 1968), Paul A. Varg, *The Making of a Myth: The United States and China 1897–1912* (East Lansing: Michigan State University Press, 1968), Michael H. Hunt, *Frontier Defense and the Open Door: Manchuria in Chinese-American Relations, 1895–1911* (New Haven: Yale University Press, 1973), and Raymond A. Esthus, "The Changing Concept of the Open Door, 1899– 1910," *Mississippi Valley Historical Review* 64 (December 1959): 435–54. Two revisionist interpretations are Thomas J. McCormick, *China Market: America's Quest for Informal Empire 1893–1901* (Chicago: Quadrangle, 1967) and Charles Vevier, *The United States and China 1906–1913: A Study of Finance and Diplomacy* (New Brunswick, N.J.: Rutgers University Press, 1955). Sometimes it is pleasant to ignore the historiographical controversy and retreat to a book like Alfred Thayer Mahan, *The Problem of Asia (and its Effect upon Interna-*

tional Policies) (Boston: Little, Brown, 1900), in which everything seems so straightforward.

American advances in the Far East were naturally of great interest to the other newly-ordained great power, Japan. Akira Iriye, *Pacific Estrangement: Japanese and American Expansion, 1897–1911* (Cambridge: Harvard University Press, 1972) delves into the cultural, philosophical, and economic sources of the two nations' expansionism. The relationship between them was dramatically emphasized by Roosevelt's mediation of the Russo-Japanese War, the subject of two good books: Tyler Dennett, *Roosevelt and the Russo-Japanese War: A critical study of American policy in Eastern Asia in 1902–5, based primarily upon the private papers of Theodore Roosevelt* (c. 1925; reprint ed., Gloucester, Mass.: Peter Smith, 1959) and, more recently, Eugene P. Trani, *The Treaty of Portsmouth: An Adventure in American Diplomacy* (Lexington: University of Kentucky Press, 1969). The wary behavior of the two nations after the war is thoughtfully treated in Charles E. Neu, *An Uncertain Friendship: Theodore Roosevelt and Japan, 1906–1909* (Cambridge: Harvard University Press, 1967) and Raymond A. Esthus, *Theodore Roosevelt and Japan* (Seattle: University of Washington Press, 1966).

Bibliography

SOURCES CITED

Unpublished Primary Materials

Papers of Thomas F. Bayard, Library of Congress
William R. Day Papers, Library of Congress
Papers of John Watson Foster, Library of Congress
Drafts; Diplomatic of Frederick Theodore Frelinghuysen, Library of Congress
Papers of Walter Quintin Gresham, Library of Congress
John Hay Papers, Library of Congress
Papers of Philander C. Knox, Library of Congress
John D. Long Papers, Massachusetts Historical Society
Papers of Alfred Thayer Mahan, Library of Congress
Papers of John T. Morgan, Library of Congress
Papers of Richard Olney, Library of Congress
Elihu Root Papers, Library of Congress

Published Primary Materials

Cleveland, Grover. *Presidential Problems.* New York: Century, 1904.
Gresham, Matilda. *Life of Walter Quintin Gresham 1832–1895.* 2 vols. 1919; reprint edition: Freeport, N.Y.: Books for Libraries Press, 1970.
Long, Margaret, ed. *The Journal of John D. Long.* Rindge, N.H.: Richard R. Smith, 1956.

Mahan, Alfred Thayer. *The Problem of Asia (and its Effect upon International Policies)*. Boston: Little, Brown, 1900.

Morison, Elting E., ed. *The Letters of Theodore Roosevelt*. 8 vols. Cambridge, Mass.: Harvard University Press, 1951–54.

Nevins, Allan, ed. *Letters of Grover Cleveland: 1850–1908*. Boston: Houghton Mifflin, 1933.

Richardson, James D. *A Compilation of the Messages and Papers of the Presidents*. 10 vols. Washington D.C.: Bureau of National Literature, 1911.

Roosevelt, Theodore. *An Autobiography*. New York: Scribners, 1913.

Sumner, William Graham. *The Conquest of the United States by Spain and Other Essays*. Chicago: Henry Regnery, 1965.

Volwiler, Albert T., ed. *The Correspondence Between Benjamin Harrison and James G. Blaine 1882–1893*. Philadelphia: American Philosophical Society, 1940.

Wells, David A. *Recent Economic Changes (And Their Effect on the Production and Distribution of Wealth and the Well-Being of Society)*. New York: Appleton, 1890.

Government Documents

U.S. Congress. *Congressional Record*. 52d Congress through 62d Congress.

U.S. House of Representatives. *Relations with Chile*. Ex. Doc. No. 91. 52d Cong., 1st sess., 25 January 1892.

U.S. Senate. *Affairs in Chili. Peru, and Bolivia: Papers Relating to the War in South America and Attempts to Bring About a Peace*. Ex. Doc. No. 79. 47th Cong., 1st sess., 26 January 1882.

U.S. Senate. *Affairs in Cuba*. Report No. 885. 55th Cong., 2d sess., 13 April 1898.

U.S. Senate. *Compilation of Reports of the Committee on Foreign Relations*. Doc. No. 231, Parts 1–8. 8 vols. 56th Cong., 2d sess., 1901.

U.S. Senate. *Correspondence Respecting Relations Between the United States and the Hawaiian Islands from September, 1820, to January, 1893*. Ex. Doc. No. 77. 52d Cong., 2d sess., 17 February 1893.

U.S. Senate. *Independent State of the Congo*. Ex. Doc. No. 196. 49th Cong., 1st sess., 30 June 1886.

U.S. Senate. *The Maritime Canal of Suez from Its Inauguration, November 17, 1869, to the Year 1884*. Ex. Doc. No. 198. 48th Cong., 1st sess., 27 June 1884.

U.S. Senate. *Nicaragua Canal Company*. Report No. 1142. 52d Cong., 2d sess., 22 December 1892.

U.S. Senate. *Report of the Isthmian Canal Commission, 1899–1901.* Doc. No. 54. 57th Cong., 1901.

Report of the Delegates of the United States to the Third International Conference of the American States Held at Rio de Janeiro, Brazil July 21, to August 26, 1906. Washington, D.C.: Government Printing Office, 1907.

U.S. State Department. *Papers Relating to the Foreign Relations of the United States.* Washington, D.C.: Government Printing Office, 1881–1914.

Articles

Abbot, Lyman. "The Basis of an Anglo-American Understanding." *North American Review* 166 (May 1898): 513–21.

Adams, Brooks. "The Spanish War and the Equilibrium of the World." *Forum* 25 (August 1898): 641–51.

Atkinson, Edward. "Eastern Commerce: What Is it Worth?" *North American Review* 170 (February 1900): 295–304.

Bailey, Thomas A. "America's Emergence as a World Power: The Myth and the Verity." *Pacific Historical Review* 30 (February 1961): 1–16.

Barrett, John. "The Paramount Power of the Pacific." *North American Review* 169 (August 1899): 165–79.

Blake, Nelson M. "Background of Cleveland's Venezuelan Policy." *American Historical Review* 47 (January 1942): 259–77.

Bradford, R. B. "Coaling-Stations for the Navy." *Forum* 26 (February 1899): 732–47.

"Break-up of China, and Our Interest in It, The." *Atlantic Monthly* 84 (August 1899): 276–80.

Carnegie, Andrew. "Americanism *versus* Imperialism." *North American Review* 168 (January 1899): 1–13.

Conant, Charles A. "The Economic Basis of 'Imperialism'." *North American Review* 167 (September 1898): 326–40.

———. "The Struggle for Commercial Empire." *Forum* 27 (June 1899): 427–40.

Denby, Charles. "Shall We Keep the Philippines?" *Forum* 26 (November 1898): 279–81.

Dunnell, Mark B. "Our Policy in China." *North American Review* 167 (October 1898): 393–409.

"End of the War, and After, The." *Atlantic Monthly* 82 (September 1898): 430–32.

Esthus, Raymond A. "The Changing Concept of the Open Door, 1899–1910." *Mississippi Valley Historical Review* 46 (December 1959): 435–54.

Fisher, Horace N. "The Development of Our Foreign Policy." *Atlantic Monthly* 82 (October 1898): 552–59.

Fiske, John. "Manifest Destiny." *Harper's Monthly* 70 (March 1885): 578–90.

Foraker, Joseph B. "Our War with Spain: Its Justice and Necessity." *Forum* 25 (June 1898): 385–95.

Ford, Worthington C. "New Opportunities for American Commerce." *Atlantic Monthly* 82 (September 1898): 321–29.

Halstead, Murat. "American Annexation and Armament." *Forum* 26 (September 1897): 56–66.

Hazeltine, Mayo W. "What Is to be Done with Cuba?" *North American Review* 167 (September 1898): 318–25.

Hilder, Frank F. "The Philippine Islands." *Forum* 25 (July 1898): 534–45.

Jordan, Thomas. "Why We Need Cuba." *Forum* 11 (July 1891): 559–67.

Livermore, Seward W. "Theodore Roosevelt, the American Navy, and the Venezuelan Crisis of 1902–1903." *American Historical Review* 51 (April 1946): 452–71.

Lodge, Henry Cabot. "England, Venezuela, and the Monroe Doctrine." *North American Review* 160 (June 1895): 651–58.

———. "Our Blundering Foreign Policy." *Forum* 19 (March 1895): 8–17.

"Logic of Our Position in Cuba, The." *North American Review* 169 (July 1899): 109–15.

Lowell, A. Lawrence. "The Colonial Expansion of the United States." *Atlantic Monthly* 83 (February 1899): 145–54.

Luce, Stephen B. "The Benefits of War." *North American Review* 153 (December 1891): 672–83.

MacDonald, William. "The Dangers of Imperialism." *Forum* 26 (October 1898): 177–87.

Mahan, Alfred Thayer. "Hawaii and Our Future Sea-Power." *Forum* 15 (March 1893): 1–11.

Money, H. D. "Our Duty to Cuba." *Forum* 25 (March 1898): 17–24.

Moore, John Bassett. "The Monroe Doctrine." *Political Science Quarterly* 11 (March 1896): 1–29.

———. "The Question of Cuban Belligerency." *Forum* 21 (May 1896): 288–300.

Morgan, John T. "The Duty of Annexing Hawaii." *Forum* 25 (March 1898): 11–16.

———. "What Shall We Do with the Conquered Islands?" *North American Review* 166 (June 1898): 641–49.

Olney, Richard. "International Isolation of the United States." *Atlantic Monthly* 81 (May 1898): 577–88.

Powers, H. H. "The War as a Suggestion of Manifest Destiny." *Annals of the American Academy of Political and Social Science* 12 (September 1898): 1–20.

Procter, John R. "Hawaii and the Changing Front of the World." *Forum* 24 (September 1897): 34–45.

———. "Isolation or Imperialism?" *Forum* 26 (September 1898): 14–26.

Reid, Gilbert. "American Opportunities in China." *Forum* 27 (April 1899): 237–42.

———. "The Powers and the Partition of China." *North American Review* 170 (May 1900): 634–41.

Schurz, Carl. "The Anglo-American Friendship." *Atlantic Monthly* 82 (October 1898): 433–40.

———. "Manifest Destiny." *Harper's Monthly* 87 (October 1893): 737–46.

Sherman, John. "The Nicaragua Canal." *Forum* 11 (March 1891): 1–9.

Sumner, William Graham. "The Fallacy of Territorial Extension." *Forum* 21 (June 1896): 414–19.

Twain, Mark. "To the Person Sitting in Darkness." *North American Review* 172 (February 1901): 161–76.

Vevier, Charles. "American Continentalism: An Idea of Expansion, 1845–1910." *American Historical Review* 65 (January 1960): 323–35.

"War with Spain, And After, The." *Atlantic Monthly* 81 (June 1898): 721–27.

White, Stephen M. "The Proposed Annexation of Hawaii." *Forum* 23 (August 1897): 723–36.

Williams, Herbert Pelham. "The Outlook in Cuba." *Atlantic Monthly* 83 (June 1899): 827–36.

Young, George B. "Intervention Under the Monroe Doctrine: The Olney Corollary." *Political Science Quarterly* 57 (June 1942): 247–80.

Books

Beale, Howard K. *Theodore Roosevelt and the Rise of America to World Power.* New York: Collier Books, 1962.

Beard, Charles A. *The Idea of National Interest: An Analytical Study in American Foreign Policy.* 1934; reprint ed.: Chicago: Quadrangle, 1966.

Beisner, Robert L. *Twelve Against Empire: The Anti-Imperialists, 1898–1900.* New York: McGraw-Hill, 1968.

Bemis, Samuel Flagg. *The Latin American Policy of the United States: An Historical Interpretation.* 1943; reprint ed.: New York: Norton, 1967.

Bishop, Joseph Bucklin. *Theodore Roosevelt and His Time.* New York: Scribners, 1920.

Blum, John Morton. *The Republican Roosevelt.* Cambridge, Mass.: Harvard University Press, 1954.

Chadwick, French Ensor. *The Relations of the United States and Spain: Diplomacy.* New York: Scribners, 1909.

Challener, Richard D. *Admirals, Generals, and American Foreign Policy 1898–1914.* Princeton, N.J.: Princeton University Press, 1973.

Cohen, Warren I. *America's Response to China: An Interpretive History of Sino-American Relations.* New York: Wiley, 1971.

Dennett, Tyler. *Americans in Eastern Asia: A Critical Study of the Policy of the United States with Reference to China, Japan and Korea in the 19th Century.* 1922; reprint ed.: New York: Barnes & Noble, 1941.

――――. *John Hay: From Poetry to Politics.* New York: Dodd, Mead, 1933.

――――. *Roosevelt and the Russo-Japanese War: A Critical Study of American Policy in Eastern Asia in 1902–5.* 1925; reprint ed.: Gloucester, Mass.: Peter Smith, 1959.

Dennis, Alfred L. P. *Adventures in American Diplomacy 1896–1906.* New York: Dutton, 1928.

Dulles, Foster Rhea. *Prelude to World Power: American Diplomatic History, 1860–1900.* New York: Macmillan, 1965.

Eggert, Gerald G. *Richard Olney: Evolution of A Statesman.* University Park, Pa.: Pennsylvania State University Press, 1974.

Ekirch, Arthur A., Jr. *Ideas, Ideals, and American Diplomacy: A History of Their Growth and Interaction.* New York: Appleton-Century-Crofts, 1966.

Ellis, Elmer. *Henry Moore Teller: Defender of the West.* Caldwell, Idaho: Caxton Printers, 1941.

Esthus, Raymond A. *Theodore Roosevelt and Japan.* Seattle: University of Washington Press, 1966.

Garraty, John A. *Henry Cabot Lodge: A Biography.* New York: Alfred A. Knopf, 1953.

Grenville, J. A. S. *Lord Salisbury and Foreign Policy: The Close of the Nineteenth Century.* London: University of London Press, 1964.

――――, and George Berkeley Young. *Politics, Strategy, and American Diplomacy: Studies in Foreign Policy, 1873–1917.* New Haven, Conn.: Yale University Press, 1966.

Griswold, A. Whitney. *The Far Eastern Policy of the United States.* New York: Harcourt, Brace, 1938.

Harbaugh, William Henry. *Power and Responsibility: The Life and Times of Theodore Roosevelt.* New York: Farrar, Strauss and Cudahy, 1961.

Healy, David. *US Expansionism: The Imperialist Urge in the 1890's.* Madison: University of Wisconsin Press, 1970.

Hill, Howard C. *Roosevelt and the Caribbean.* Chicago: University of Chicago Press, 1927.

Hobson, J. A. *Imperialism: A Study.* 1938; reprint ed.: Ann Arbor: University of Michigan Press, 1965.

Iriye, Akira. *Pacific Estrangement: Japanese and American Expansion, 1897–1911.* Cambridge, Mass.: Harvard University Press, 1972.

James, Henry. *Richard Olney and his Public Service.* Boston: Houghton Mifflin, 1923.

Jessup, Philip C. *Elihu Root.* 2 vols. New York: Dodd, Mead, 1938.

Kennan, George F. *American Diplomacy: 1900–1950.* Chicago: University of Chicago Press, 1951.

Kennedy, Paul M. *The Samoan Tangle: A Study in Anglo-German-American Relations 1878–1900.* Dublin: Irish University Press, 1974.

LaFeber, Walter. *The New Empire: An Interpretation of American Expansion 1860–1898.* Ithaca, N.Y.: Cornell University Press, 1963.

Latané, John Holladay. *From Isolation to Leadership: A Review of American Foreign Policy.* Garden City, N.Y.: Doubleday, 1918.

Leech, Margaret. *Reveille in Washington.* New York: Harper & Row, 1941.

Leopold, Richard W. *Elihu Root and the Conservative Tradition.* Boston: Little, Brown, 1954.

Liss, Sheldon B. *The Canal: Aspects of United States Panamanian Relations.* Notre Dame, Ind.: University of Notre Dame Press, 1967.

Logan, John A., Jr. *No Transfer: An American Security Principle.* New Haven, Conn.: Yale University Press, 1961.

May, Ernest R. *American Imperialism: A Speculative Essay.* New York: Atheneum, 1968.

———. *Imperial Democracy: The Emergence of America as a Great Power.* New York: Harcourt, Brace, 1961.

McCormick, Thomas J. *China Market: America's Quest for Informal Empire 1893–1901.* Chicago: Quadrangle, 1967.

Merk, Frederick. *Manifest Destiny and Mission in American History: A Reinterpretation.* New York: Random House, 1963.

Millett, Alan Reed. *The Politics of Intervention.* Columbus: Ohio State University Press, 1968.

Millington, Herbert. *American Diplomacy and the War of the Pacific.* New York: Columbia University Press, 1948.

Morgan, H. Wayne. *America's Road to Empire: The War with Spain and Overseas Expansion.* New York: Wiley, 1965.

Munro, Dana G. *Intervention and Dollar Diplomacy in the Caribbean 1900–1921.* Princeton, N.J.: Princeton University Press, 1964.

Muzzey, David Saville. *James G. Blaine: A Political Idol of Other Days.* New York: Dodd, Mead, 1934.

Neale, R. G. *Great Britain and United States Expansion: 1898–1900.* East Lansing: Michigan State University Press, 1966.

Nearing, Scott, and Freeman, Joseph. *Dollar Diplomacy: A Study in American Imperialism.* New York: Viking Press, 1926.

Neu, Charles E. *An Uncertain Friendship: Theodore Roosevelt and Japan, 1906–1909.* Cambridge, Mass.: Harvard University Press, 1967.

Perkins, Bradford. *The Great Rapprochement: England and the United States, 1895–1914.* New York: Atheneum, 1968.

Perkins, Dexter. *The Evolution of American Foreign Policy.* New York: Oxford University Press, 1966.

———. *The Monroe Doctrine 1867–1907.* Baltimore: Johns Hopkins University Press, 1937.

———. *The United States and the Caribbean.* Rev. ed. Cambridge, Mass.: Harvard University Press, 1966.

Pike, Frederick B. *Chile and the United States, 1880–1962.* Notre Dame, Ind.: University of Notre Dame Press, 1963.

Pletcher, David M. *The Awkward Years: American Foreign Relations under Garfield and Arthur.* Columbia: University of Missouri Press, 1962.

Pratt, Julius W. *Challenge and Rejection: The United States and World Leadership, 1900–1921.* New York: Macmillan, 1967.

———. *Expansionists of 1898: The Acquisition of Hawaii and the Spanish Islands.* 1936, reprint ed.: Chicago: Quadrangle, 1964.

Pringle, Henry F. *Theodore Roosevelt: A Biography.* New York: Harcourt, Brace, 1931.

Russ, William Adam, Jr. *The Hawaiian Republic (1894–98) and Its Struggle to Win Annexation.* Selinsgrove, Pa.: Susquehanna University Press, 1961.

———. *The Hawaiian Revolution (1893–94).* Selinsgrove, Pa.: Susquehanna University Press, 1959.

Ryden, George Herbert. *The Foreign Policy of the United States in Relation to Samoa.* New Haven, Conn.: Yale University Press, 1933.

Scholes, Walter V., and Scholes, Marie V. *The Foreign Policies of the Taft Administration.* Columbia: University of Missouri Press, 1970.

Schriftgiesser, Karl. *The Gentleman from Massachusetts: Henry Cabot Lodge.* Boston: Little, Brown, 1944.

Stevens, Sylvester K. *American Expansion in Hawaii 1842–1898.* New York: Russell & Russell, 1968.

Tannenbaum, Frank. *The American Tradition in Foreign Policy.* Norman: University of Oklahoma Press, 1955.

Tansill, Charles Callan. *The Foreign Policy of Thomas F. Bayard 1885–1897.* New York: Fordham University Press, 1940.

Tate, Merze. *Hawaii: Reciprocity or Annexation.* East Lansing: Michigan State University Press, 1968.

———. *The United States and the Hawaiian Kingdom: A Political History.* New Haven, Conn.: Yale University Press, 1965.

Thayer, William Roscoe. *The Life and Letters of John Hay.* 2 vols. Boston: Houghton Mifflin, 1915.

Tompkins, E. Berkeley. *Anti-Imperialism in the United States: The Great Debate, 1890–1920.* Philadelphia: University of Pennsylvania Press, 1970.

Tyler, Alice Felt. *The Foreign Policy of James G. Blaine.* Minneapolis: University of Minnesota Press, 1927.

Van Alstyne, Richard W. *The Rising American Empire.* Chicago: Quadrangle, 1965.

Varg, Paul A. *The Making of a Myth: The United States and China 1897–1912.* East Lansing: Michigan State University Press, 1968.

Vevier, Charles. *The United States and China 1906–1913: A Study of Finance and Diplomacy.* New Brunswick, N.J.: Rutgers University Press, 1955.

Weinberg, Albert K. *Manifest Destiny: A Study of Nationalist Expansionism in American History.* Baltimore: Johns Hopkins University Press, 1935.

Westcott, Allen. *American Seapower Since 1775.* Philadelphia: Lippincott, 1941.

Williams, William Appleman. *The Roots of the Modern American Empire: A Study of the Growth and Shaping of Social Consciousness in a Marketplace Society.* New York: Random House, 1969.

————. *The Tragedy of American Diplomacy.* Rev. ed. New York: Dell, 1962.

Young, Marilyn Blatt. *The Rhetoric of Empire: American China Policy 1895–1901.* Cambridge, Mass.: Harvard University Press, 1968.

Younger, Edward. *John A. Kasson: Politics and Diplomacy from Lincoln to McKinley.* Iowa City: State Historical Society of Iowa, 1955.

Index

Breinigsville, PA USA
23 February 2011
256227BV00001B/16/P